STAND YOUR GROUND

STAND
YOUR
GROUND

A HISTORY OF AMERICA'S LOVE AFFAIR
WITH LETHAL SELF-DEFENSE

Caroline E. Light

BEACON PRESS

BOSTON

For Sandy Light,
Armed with common sense and compassion

———

BEACON PRESS
Boston, Massachusetts
www.beacon.org

Beacon Press books
are published under the auspices of
the Unitarian Universalist Association of Congregations.

20 19 18 17   8 7 6 5 4 3 2 1

This book is printed on acid-free paper that meets the uncoated paper
ANSI/NISO specifications for permanence as revised in 1992.

Composition by Wilsted & Taylor Publishing Services

Library of Congress Cataloging-in-Publication Data

Names: Light, Caroline E., author.
Title: Stand your ground : A history of America's love affair with lethal self-defense /
Caroline Light.
Description: Boston : Beacon Press, 2017. | Includes bibliographical
references and index.
Identifiers: LCCN 2016023101 (print) | LCCN 2016023420 (ebook) | ISBN
9780807064665 (hardcover : alk. paper) | ISBN 9780807064689 (e-book)
Subjects: LCSH: Self-defense (Law)—Social aspects—United States. |
Firearms—Law and legislation—Social aspects—United States. | African
Americans—Civil rights.
Classification: LCC KF9246 .L54 2017 (print) | LCC KF9246 (ebook) | DDC
345.73/04—dc23
LC record available at https://lccn.loc.gov/2016023101

Contents

AUTHOR'S NOTE

Mom the Sharpshooter

vii

INTRODUCTION

When Good Citizenship Is Armed Citizenship

1

CHAPTER ONE

"That Great Law of Nature"

*The Origins of a Selective
Self-Defense Culture*

18

CHAPTER TWO

Defensive Violence
and the "True Man"

*The End of Reconstruction
and the Duty to Retreat*

39

CHAPTER THREE

"A Mighty Power in
the Hands of the Citizen"

*Justice and True Manhood
in the Western Borderlands*

63

CHAPTER FOUR

"Queer Justice" and the
Sexual Politics of Lynching

86

CHAPTER FIVE

"An American Tradition"

The Black Paramilitary Response to White
Supremacist Terror and Unequal Protection

108

CHAPTER SIX

"The Stuff of Pulp Fiction"

Unreasonable Women, Vigilante Heroes,
and the Rise of the Armed Citizen

133

CHAPTER SEVEN

Avoiding a "Fate Worse Than Death"

How We Learned to Stand Our Ground

155

CONCLUSION

Kill or Be Killed—
An American Mantra

176

ACKNOWLEDGMENTS

189

NOTES

192

INDEX

222

MOM THE SHARPSHOOTER

I have vivid memories of accompanying my parents on trips to a shooting range in southwestern Virginia. They shot skeet, in which a small, saucer-shaped clay pigeon was launched from a machine across the sky, in front of the shooter, and the more challenging trap, where the target flew up and away from the shooter. I'd interrupt my play in the field behind the range when I heard my mother shout "Pull!" and would look up. The clay pigeon would soar across the sky, then shatter into tiny bits as the pellets from Mom's gun tore through it. She was an excellent shot, particularly for someone with scant time to spend on target practice. She had three children, me and two younger siblings, and back in the early 1980s, shooting facilities and gun clubs didn't provide childcare, as some do now.[1]

Both of my parents shot for recreation. My dad, who had become familiar with guns through his service in the navy, occasionally went on hunting expeditions with friends from work, bringing back an assortment of small dead animals. At dinner after one such excursion, I recall chewing on a less-than-delectable piece of roasted quail, trying not to think about the lovely and harmless creature it had come from and pausing to spit out pieces of birdshot. Despite the occasional family dinner featuring the kill of the day, guns and hunting constituted a peripheral part of my life.

I grew up white and middle-class in the suburban South, which is to say that I grew up with a measure of security in both my social position and my sense of distance from physical danger. As a historian who studies the ways in which collectively shared memories—the histories that take shape as truth in the public imagination—influence national belonging, I look back on memories like these for a sense of what I *don't* remember. Specifically, I seek out gaps in my recollection that highlight crucial departures from today's sense of urgency around home and personal security. My early trips to the shooting range felt mundane, even boring, comparable to watching my parents play tennis. But unlike tennis rackets, guns weren't kept in our home. My parents weren't interested in armed self-defense.

In contrast to my memories of my parents' trips to the gun range, today's widespread reverence for what I call "do-it-yourself (DIY)-security citizenship" brings to mind a different world. DIY-security citizenship is based on a set of ideologies, rooted in heroic histories, that see lethal self-defense as a core responsibility of the ideal citizen who stands his ground in the face of perceived threat rather than retreating from a fight. This contemporary ideal emerged in response to a growing sense of insecurity, a belief that we must be prepared to kill or be killed, to shoot first and ask questions later. It rests on an urgent need to defend oneself from a litany of threatening figures, including (but not limited to) terrorists, undocumented immigrants, and criminal strangers. In fact, the DIY security citizen has appeared primarily in opposition to these perceived threats, and leaves no room for ambiguity between heroic good guys and dangerous bad guys.

In spite of the invocation of heroism and independence, the DIY-security ethos has a destructive downside. For one, it rests on the fallacy of urgent insecurity. In spite of falling crime rates, more people are acquiring guns for personal and home protection than ever before. When I was growing up, most gun owners were hunters; now, most own guns for personal protection.[2] Americans account for less than 5 percent of the world's population but possess 40 to 50 percent of its guns.[3] Recent studies have estimated that there are now more guns than people in the United States, far more weaponry than in any other comparably developed nation.[4] The political scientist Robert Spitzer recently characterized the nation's "contemporary gun culture, and prevailing gun narrative" as having "run amok."[5]

Our nation boasts the highest per capita rate of gun deaths and deaths by mass shooting, defined as an episode in which four or more people are killed or wounded. In 2015 alone there were 372 mass shootings, resulting in 475 deaths.[6] White men are disproportionately the shooters in these and other episodes of mass gun violence.[7] The proliferation of shootings, particularly in our schools, amplifies a national sense of vulnerability, so that citizens who see themselves as law-abiding nevertheless feel the need to take matters into their own hands.

But DIY-security citizenship is not just about gun ownership. Guns and their proliferation in the United States are only the tip of the iceberg of a much larger and more widespread belief system that frames lethal self-defense as a core ideal of good citizenship. This principle places idealized, "law-abiding citizens"—not all citizens—in the service of lethal self-defense and equates good citizenship with the capacity to stand one's ground against criminal strangers. According to the National Rifle Association, a good citizen is an armed citizen. In fact, the NRA has gone so far as to register the phrase "armed citizen" and build a political advertising campaign around it.[8] For the NRA, an Armed Citizen is the quintessential emblem of patriotism. This ideal suggests that we must *all* be prepared to defend ourselves; however, our contemporary call to arms is based on unspoken but powerful assumptions that exclude many from the protective and exonerating rhetoric of "law-abiding" citizenship.

Appeals to individual DIY security as the solution to our nation's most urgent anxieties criminalizes many who do not fit the terms of idealized citizenship, particularly people of color, gender-nonconforming people, and the poor. Moreover, women of all races, classes, and ethnicities often find themselves criminalized if they try to stand their ground against violent male partners. When contemporary advocates of lethal self-defense entreat law-abiding citizens to take up arms against criminal strangers, they participate in a prolonged tradition of excluding and criminalizing the real victims of violence, the groups historically most in need of protection.

This appeal to DIY-security citizenship is in many ways nothing new. The heroic figure of the Armed Citizen has its roots in a long history in which the privilege of violence, often justified as self-defense, has rested in the hands of the powerful few. While our legal terrain has shifted to extend the rights, privileges, and protections of citizenship to women and to people of color, the advantage of self-defensive violence continues to empower propertied white men. Ultimately, today's vocal call to arms rests on historic fallacies of reverse victimization, where those excluded from the full benefits of citizenship became the criminalized strangers against whom the Armed Citizen takes defensive action. In spite of its democratic appeals to all law-abiding citizens, DIY-security citizenship only welcomes some, to the exclusion—and endangerment—of the many.

The material traces of these histories are all around us, but we often don't notice them unless we are subject to their exclusions. Growing up white and middle-class in the South meant that I inherited a complicated but widely celebrated heritage, one concretized in memorials that dotted the Southern landscape. A certain comforting worldview was reflected in the built environment. I grew up blithely unthreatened by historical symbols of domination, like the Confederate flag emblazoned on the backs of pick-up trucks and in store windows. To a white girl born in Virginia, these everyday sights appeared like natural, common-sense reminders of a glorious past. Almost through osmosis, I learned to see the flag's presence as a benign symbol of a proud legacy, a politically neutral reminder of a true history. Given its reliable and almost ubiquitous presence, I failed, until adulthood and advanced education intervened, to develop a critical awareness of the larger significance of this and other emblems of white supremacy, ones that have shaped the way we understand history itself.

The collective memories conjured by the Confederate flag and other historical symbols never circulate in an ideological vacuum. Historian Roxanne Dunbar-Ortiz contends that our nation and its laws were built upon a regime of white supremacist settler colonialism "require[ing] violence or the threat of violence to obtain its goals."[9] The violence was necessary to maintain structures of racial and gender inequality, yet the histories we tell ourselves again and again often downplay or outright conceal our undemocratic past. Widely recognized national symbols— monuments, flags, and even our currency—perpetuate the histories that most comfortably serve existing power structures, and they help mark the boundaries between those entitled to and those excluded from the rights, privileges, and protections of full citizenship.

Although the Confederate flag resonates differently depending on one's location, the sentimental visions of Southern honor, hospitality, and tragic heroism that it evokes travel far and wide. It communicates a narrative of Southern white persecution while masking the violence of white supremacy, celebrating heroic rebels as armed protectors of Southern culture and as chivalrous defenders of white women's honor. Appeals to the tragic "Lost Cause," and a post–Civil War South subjugated by federal Reconstruction obstruct our view of the nation's ongoing assaults on Black citizenship. The Confederate flag ultimately taps into and reinforces a selectively shared memory of reverse victimization, where armed white men stood up against "negro rule" and corrupt federal intrusions on their rights.[10] These memories celebrate white, male armed citizens as heroes while blinding us to the violence of slavery and its modern progeny.

The symbolic realm has powerful material implications. For those excluded from the safety and privilege of whiteness, the Confederate flag serves as a sinister reminder of the limits of belonging. Its visual shorthand speaks what the literary scholar María Carla Sánchez calls an "unspoken language," offering the opposite of a hospitable Southern welcome mat to those excluded from our nation's democratic promises.[11]

The flag's political and racial implications remain hidden for those not immediately subject to their prohibitions, until someone commits an act of extreme violence in its name. On June 17, 2015, a white man declaring his allegiance to the Confederacy went on a shooting rampage at Charleston's historic Emanuel African Methodist Episcopal Church, killing nine people. Ten days after the massacre, thirty-year-old Brittany "Bree" Newsome, an African American filmmaker and activist, climbed up the flagpole in front of the capitol in Columbia and took down the Confederate flag. Newsome was arrested for defacing state property and taken to jail and the flag was promptly put back up. Following her bold action, and her insistence that "that flag represents fear. . . . It's a sign of intimidation," leaders from across the political spectrum rallied in recognition that the symbol's presence in official spaces threatened the inclusion and safety of people of color.[12] The flag was removed officially on July 10, and the charges against Ms. Newsome, hailed by many as a "Black superhero," were dismissed.

While we celebrate this victory of popular protest, we must bear in mind that removing this symbol of white supremacy from state buildings is just that: symbolic. The flag may disappear, at least from the state house, but the stubborn prohibitions and historical silences that give it power remain stubbornly in place.

Much has changed in the thirty-plus years since I accompanied my parents to the shooting range. Years ago, finally unfettered by small children, my mother took advantage of an expanding array of resources available to female gun enthusiasts. In 2001 she enrolled in an NRA-sponsored "Women in the Outdoors" program and took several day-long gun safety courses taught by NRA-certified instructors. She learned how to shoot various types of firearms, including .22s, .44s, rifles, and shotguns, while participating in shooting competitions. Although she enjoyed perfecting her skills through target practice, my mother found the NRA-trained instructors' emphasis on lethal self-defense alienating and wrong-headed. She could not picture herself as the NRA-trademarked Armed Citizen—prepared to take a life in order to save her own—nor was she motivated by the fear and anxiety that compelled many to carry weapons for self-protection.

Today my mother actively opposes the contemporary proliferation of DIY-security citizenship, writing letters to elected officials and to local newspapers urging the vigorous enforcement of gun regulations.[13] In our hometown, hers is a minority voice in a sea of growing opposition to even the most modest gun control efforts. With each mass shooting, the rallying cries for lethal weaponry and an armed citizenry seem to grow louder.[14] They crowd out voices like my mother's and mask the evidence that more guns correlate to more gun deaths, and that an armed citizenship amounts to safety for the few at the expense of the many.

As the culture of DIY-security citizenship spreads, mobilizing the past in a contemporary call to arms, it becomes an accepted, established viewpoint and becomes increasingly difficult to challenge. Like the Confederate flag in official public spaces, it signals welcome and confirms belonging for dominant social actors, while reaffirming exclusion and justifying violence toward the dominated. Even though the flag no longer flies near the capitol building in Columbia, we still face a long journey toward recognizing the persistent connection between historical amnesia and contemporary inequality. This book represents one white Southerner's effort to excavate an uncomfortable past in the name of justice for our future.

WHEN GOOD CITIZENSHIP IS ARMED CITIZENSHIP

There is a word for the unfounded, pre-emptive,
due-process-free (but tacitly sanctioned) form of killing
perpetrated against black people in this country in
an effort to safeguard white property: lynching.

—SABRINA STRINGS, 2014

The logic [of stand-your-ground laws] incentivizes an armed
citizenry where the beneficiary of justice is simply the last man
standing. Your side of the story is irrelevant if you are dead.

—TA-NEHISI COATES, 2012

Standing one's ground against a perceived threat has long been a white, masculine prerogative in the United States. When European settlers arrived on American soil, they justified violence as necessary to their basic survival, seizing land that was already inhabited while imprisoning or exterminating its occupants. Settler colonialism and, later, the idea of Manifest Destiny—spreading civilized Christianity across the continent—together demanded the subjugation of nonwhites. And the rights, privileges, and protections of citizenship were inaccessible to all but white, property-owning men. The legacies of this under-recognized history of repression and exclusion in the name of national survival still haunt us today.

Our textbooks and memorials celebrate armed defiance in the face of overwhelming odds, of resisting the urge to flee in the face of fear. From the American Revolution to the Alamo to Iwo Jima, our nation's favorite stories of the past venerate militaristic heroism and bold defiance over appeasement and retreat. Recently, however, roughly coincident with the turn of the millennium, our admiration for defensive militarism has transformed into a pressing call for individual, do-it-yourself (DIY)-security citizenship. The defensively armed citizen has become, in some quarters, the paragon of patriotism.

Today, a compulsion to seek individual solutions to urgent home, and homeland, security anxieties permeates our culture. A Wyoming bumper sticker welcomes visitors while warning potential criminals to "consider everyone armed." Thirty-three states have adopted laws allowing for lethal self-defense outside of one's home, and approximately thirteen million civilians are licensed to carry concealed firearms. Colorado's self-defense law is named after Clint Eastwood's much-quoted provocation, "Make my day," and homeowners across the nation post "We Don't Call 911" signs in their yards, warning would-be burglars that a home intrusion will be met with immediate lethal violence. Celebratory depictions of armed citizens populate our news media and entertainment, where fantasies of righteous vengeance and DIY security frame familiar redemption stories. Popular television shows and movies depict ordinary citizens fending off criminal strangers—often depicted as zombies, extraterrestrial "aliens," or other fictional threats to humanity—when the apparatus of the state has failed to protect them. Ordinary citizens-turned-defensive-warriors are today's ultimate action heroes.

Our popular narratives of heroism disparage the state's incapacity to protect citizens from a growing list of urgent threats. Foremost among them is terrorism in the wake of the September 11, 2001, attacks, which shook the nation's collective sense of security. Stephen Kinzer argues that insecurity about terrorism has fed the growth of an aggressively militaristic "United States of Fear and Panic," in which anxiety about terrorism far exceeds the actual threat.[1] In *The Terror Dream*, Susan Faludi explores the nation's centuries-long obsession with home(land) security, in which women kept the proverbial home fires burning while white men fought off wild animals, Native Americans, and foreign threats to the young nation. A longing for these comforting gender ideals in the service of safety and self-sufficiency reawakened with a vengeance in response to 9/11 under the new rubric, homeland security.[2] Since then, self-defense has been invoked as a civic obligation as much as a right.

Even as we channel tax dollars into national security, fighting terrorism abroad, reinforcing our borders at home, and furnishing some local police forces with military grade equipment, we seek out the latest technologies of home security and armed self-defense.[3] A growing throng of what sociologist Jennifer Carlson calls "citizen protectors" claims to fill in where the government is perceived to be inept or inadequate.[4] In 2004 Dave Grossman, a retired lieutenant colonel in the US Army and a former West Point instructor, coauthored an article called "On Sheep, Sheepdogs, and Wolves," which became a manifesto for DIY-security citizens in the new millennium. According to Grossman, the only thing protecting unarmed, peace-loving "sheep" from criminal "wolves" are the heroic "sheepdogs" who selflessly stand at the ready to defend themselves and others.[5] In Grossman's narrative, there is a tidy delineation between good and bad—each transparently recognizable to the other—and "heroes" resort to deadly violence only to defend themselves and the weak. His message is an empowering one, promising that those who take their safety into their own hands will triumph in the end.

Answering widespread insecurity and fear with individualized might, the DIY-security message resonates with those distrustful of the American government and suspicious of the nation's first Black president.[6] Journalist Lindsay Cook traces the record growth in gun sales following Hillary Clinton's concession speech in July 2008 to what some are calling the Obama effect. Just after President Obama's election, gun sales saw a 60 percent spike over average sale volumes.[7] Advocates of armed citizenship argue that a liberal federal government intrudes into citizens' private affairs, infringing on personal gun rights, while failing to protect people from a litany of encroaching threats. Although these fears are not supported by facts, conservative news media and gun rights activists insist that progressive government constitutes a direct threat to private citizens' right to own and bear arms.

These suspicions have at least as much to do with the president's race as they do with his liberal governance. The Colombian economist and sociologist Emilio Depetris-Chauvin collected and compared regional data on the number of background checks made in the course of gun purchases during the election years 2000, 2004, and 2008, and revealed a radical spike in gun sales in the wake of Barack Obama's election.[8] If these changes reflected ideology alone, we would expect to see a spike in gun sales whenever liberals were elected. Indeed, fears of the president's Black "rage" and rumors of his covert Muslim identity populate conservative media, fanning the flames of white reactionary security panic.[9] Given widespread "fear of a Black president," the need to take up arms in self-defense intensified into a national imperative.[10]

But the turn to DIY security is not limited to self-identified "conservatives," or to those who perceive liberal governance as a threat to their personal liberty. Today the spread of perceived insecurity, as well as a lack of faith in the protective powers of the government and local police, transcends ideological boundaries, with members of targeted minority groups also arming themselves against criminal threats. A recent example is the National African American Gun Association (NAAGA), established in 2015 to "expose, educate, and motivate as many African American men and women to go out and purchase a Firearm for Self-Defense and to take training on proper gun use."[11] Described on the website as a "civil rights organization," the NAAGA emphasizes the need for Black self-protection in a nation that—in spite of popular appeals to color blindness—disproportionately subjects people of color to sustained violence and exclusion. The organization sees itself as part of a long legacy of Black armed self-defense whose antecedents include the Buffalo Soldiers, the Tuskegee Airmen, the Deacons of Defense, and the Black Panther Party (BPP). Jews for the Preservation of Firearms Ownership (JPFO) similarly appeals to historic discrimination and violence in its effort to expose the "racist roots of 'gun control,'" which the JPFO characterizes as "victim-disarmament."[12] The JPFO website features a "genocide chart," which contains statistics on all "victims of disarmament," from the Armenian genocide and Nazi Holocaust to the mass murder of Tutsi in Rwanda in the 1990s. For the JPFO and NAAGA, historic racism and antisemitism—which have featured government and police complicity—justify the present accumulation of firearms for minority communities.

The voices promoting self-defense as an urgent individual need grow louder with each mass shooting, characterized as an episode of gun violence in which four or more people are killed. After a young, white gunman killed twenty-six people at Sandy Hook Elementary School in Newtown, Connecticut, in December 2012, gun sales spiked.[13] Public figures, including Senator Rand Paul of Kentucky and Representative Louie Gohmert of Texas, lamented that, had the classrooms and teachers been outfitted with firearms, the tragedy would never have happened.[14] Shortly thereafter, the National Rifle Association sponsored a report, *National School Shield*, calling for armed guards in all American schools.[15]

Although they make up less than 2 percent of the nation's total gun-related deaths, mass shootings grab media attention and generate panic. In 2015 alone, the US experienced 372 mass shootings that killed 475—out of a total 12,942 gun-related deaths that year—and wounded 1,870.[16] After a white gunman killed nine worshippers at Charleston's historic Emanuel African Methodist Episcopal Church on June 17, 2015, renewed cries for commonsense restrictions on civilian gun ownership were accompanied by another increase in gun sales.[17] Philip Smith, founder of NAAGA, opined, "I generally like to say no to guns in church, but I can't help but think that if someone had a gun, they might have had a chance to defend themselves; just maybe a chance to survive or kill the shooter."[18]

On June 12, 2016, a US-born Muslim man in possession of a legally purchased semiautomatic handgun and a military-grade assault rifle opened fire on the patrons at an LGBT nightclub in Orlando, Florida. As the nation mourned the tragic death of forty-nine mostly young, mostly Latino/a and African American, LGBT-identified people, many across the political spectrum held up this event and others as evidence of a pressing need for expanded civilian access to firearms. Republican presidential nominee Donald Trump asserted his support for a widely armed citizenry, insisting, "If you had some guns in that club . . .

you wouldn't have had the tragedy that you had."[19] Nicki Stallard, spokeswoman for the Pink Pistols gun club, echoed this sentiment, urging LGBT-identified people to arm themselves against transphobic and homophobic violence. Citing the inadequacy of law enforcement, she warned, "If you don't defend yourself, no one else will."[20] The Pink Pistols were founded in 2000 in response to police and civilian violence against gay, lesbian, and gender nonconforming individuals to empower members to channel their "ammosexuality" by learning how to defend themselves with lethal weapons. Like NAAGA and JPFO, the group's mission is preventative as well as reactive. According to founding member Gwendolyn S. Patton, "We teach queers to shoot, then teach the world that we have done it."[21]

Our nation's growing sense of vulnerability in the wake of mass shootings and the threat of terrorism has shaped a new set of rights and responsibilities, where citizens must be prepared to stand up to danger instead of relying for protection on local police and the government. Perception is everything: if we live in a world full of terrorists, violent criminals, and "illegal" immigrants, with a government unwilling or unable to protect us, we law-abiding citizens must take matters into our own hands. More and more we look to the heroic armed citizen who refuses to depend on others for protection as the ethical core of this powerful, ostensibly democratic and democratizing impulse. DIY-security citizenship holds each of us responsible for our own self-defense and celebrates self-reliance and independence in the face of danger. In the oft-repeated words of the NRA's executive vice president, Wayne LaPierre, "The only thing that stops a bad guy with a gun is a good guy with a gun."[22]

Increasingly many of us are taking this message to heart, and more people than ever seek to carry their firearms beyond the confines of their homes. Since 1990, the number of people with concealed-carry permits has risen from one million to approximately thirteen million; as of 2014, every state has provisions allowing qualified civilians to apply for concealed-carry licenses. The rapid normalization of gun-carrying DIY-security citizenship owes much to the 2008 Supreme Court ruling in *District of Columbia v. Heller*, which affirmed an individual's "right to keep and carry weapons in case of confrontation." Delivering the majority opinion, Justice Antonin Scalia interpreted the Second Amendment as "surely elevat[ing] above all other interests the right of law-abiding, responsible citizens to use arms in defense of hearth and home."[23]

The *Heller* decision rested on Justice Scalia's "originalist" interpretation of the Second Amendment, in which he considered its intended meaning at the time of its adoption in 1791. At that time, a "law-abiding citizen" openly carrying a firearm was perceived as earnestly invested in an effort to protect himself, his wife and children, and his property.[24] Open carry in the eighteenth and nineteenth centuries was based on the logic that a visibly displayed weapon would discourage confrontations, while concealed weapons were primarily carried by criminals and people who were otherwise up to no good.[25] The *Heller* decision conveniently ignored the race and gender exclusions of the amendment's original historical moment, where a "law-abiding citizen" was a white, property-owning man, who openly carried a rifle not only to defend his "hearth and home," but also to assert his dominance over enslaved labor and his access to land seized from Native Americans. Thus this 2008 Supreme Court decision divested the early emblem of "law-abiding citizenship" of its historic exclusionary connotations and reconstructed it to support our contemporary investment in DIY-security citizenship.

Yet our nation's past exclusions—ones that ensured that white, propertied men held a monopoly on lethal violence—continue to haunt the way we distribute the rights of self-defense in the present. We might observe the lopsided distribution of DIY security in the rapid spread of stand-your-ground (SYG) laws. First passed in Florida in 2005, SYG laws allow civilians who perceive themselves to be in imminent danger to use lethal force without first trying to escape to safety. The laws grant special immunities to those who claim self-defense after killing someone, as long as "the person using or threatening to use the deadly force is not engaged in a criminal activity and is in a place where he or she has a right to be."[26] They are designed to help all would-be "sheepdogs" defend themselves, their families, and their property from encroaching "wolves."

On their surface, SYG laws provide legal justification and criminal immunity to *any* person who uses deadly force in self-defense. There is significant variation among state SYG laws, but all of them emphasize the right to use lethal force when one experiences what a "reasonable person" would consider a threat, even if the person could safely retreat from the perceived danger. Another key characteristic common to SYG laws is their emphasis on each person's right to defend one's self and property from criminal violation. Proponents of the laws aim to absolve law-abiding citizens of all criminal responsibility when they respond lethally to a perceived threat.

However, as we've seen with the tragic death of Trayvon Martin, an unarmed Black seventeen-year-old gunned down by an armed citizen in a Florida suburb in 2012, perceptions of threat are in the eye of the beholder. Defensive lethal violence by armed citizens shares a historical genealogy with contemporary police violence, in that the usual targets are most commonly people of color. In 2014, police officers gunned down twelve-year-old Tamir Rice in Cleveland, Ohio, and eighteen-year-old Michael Brown in Ferguson, Missouri, because they perceived them—in the moment—as imminent threats. Neither possessed weapons, but police justified their force as necessary in the name of self-defense and the protection of the community. In these cases, as in many others, police violence against people of color takes root in the implicit biases of the larger culture. If Black men are widely perceived as intrinsically dangerous, they do not need to be armed to be seen as a threat to public safety.

But what happens when people of color, in response to the pressures of these social biases and being subject to their repeating violence, emulate the ideals of DIY security by arming themselves and standing their ground? White suspicions of Black criminality on one hand and urgent lethal self-defense on the other allow little space for people of color to serve in the growing army of DIY-security citizens. In July 2016, within a day of each other, two Black men in two different cities were killed by police. Both men were armed—following the mantra of today's armed citizen—but neither resisted arrest or made a move to use his weapon. In fact, thirty-two-year-old Philando Castile of Minnesota explained to the police who pulled him over for a broken taillight that he was carrying a concealed firearm for which he had a permit. As he tried to extract his license from his pocket, the police opened fire through his car window, killing him in front of his girlfriend and four-year-old child. In this case, it did not matter that Castile was a law-abiding citizen following the principles of armed citizenship, or that he was complying peaceably with police orders; in the eyes of the police who killed him, his blackness excluded him from the category of "law-abiding citizenship." This is not the first time this has happened, and it likely will not be the last.

While our contemporary turn to DIY security appears universal, endowing each of us with a right and an obligation to defend ourselves against criminal dangers, in fact it is based on a set of exclusions whereby enhanced security for the few depends upon vulnerability for the many. In spite of the race- and gender-neutral terms of our contemporary self-defense paradigm, the perception of threat on which it is based is rooted in ideological blind spots that have haunted this nation for centuries, particularly our historical suspicion of nonwhite strangers. According to historian Robin D. G. Kelley, from our nation's very founding, "predators and threats to [white] privileges were almost always black, brown, and red."[27] A selective right to lethal self-defense—one that privileged white (hetero-)masculine access to power and property— accompanied this nation's founding in white European settler colonialism and slavery. The exclusion of nonwhites and women from the promises of democracy shapes our seemingly egalitarian ideals of DIY-security citizenship today.

Our contemporary understandings of law-abiding citizenship and criminality are neither gender neutral nor color-blind, and self-defense is not a de facto universal right. In spite of gun advocates' claims that an armed citizenry and robust self-defense laws deter crime, states with SYG laws have seen a significant increase in homicides.[28] Further, the language of these laws promises self-defense rights to everyone, but SYG laws are adjudicated through the lens of our society's implicit racial and gender biases. The deck is disproportionately stacked against nonwhite men, who are more likely to be perceived as "reasonable threats," even when they are unarmed. Crime statistics from the past decade reveal that SYG laws have exacerbated racial discrepancies in the adjudication of self-defense: whites who kill Blacks in states with SYG laws are more than eleven times more likely to escape conviction than Blacks who kill whites.[29]

The disproportionate number of Black people killed and white people exonerated implicates our legal terrain's complicity in promoting a "reasonable" suspicion of nonwhite strangers who venture into predominantly white space. According to the journalist Ta-Nehisi Coates, "The logic [of SYG laws] incentivizes an armed citizenry where the beneficiary of justice is simply the last man standing. Your side of the story is irrelevant if you are dead."[30] Trayvon Martin was never able to tell his side of the story, and his shooter was exonerated based on widespread perceptions—and the presumed "reasonableness" of those perceptions—that Black men and boys are dangerous. Only for certain citizens are the terms of "reasonable" threat sufficiently urgent.

Likewise, female victims of heterosexual domestic violence and gender-nonconforming individuals subject to homophobic and transphobic attacks not only find themselves disproportionately vulnerable to violence but also find the legal protections of enhanced self-defense laws stubbornly elusive. In spite of widespread claims to gender equality, the "reality" of gender—the power of entrenched assumptions about femininity and masculinity as natural categories of human experience—continues to influence contemporary perceptions of threat and claims to self-defense. As witnessed in cases of women using violence to fend off attacks from intimate male partners and gender-nonconforming individuals fighting back against attackers, standing your ground remains a masculine, cisgender act. Women and gender-nonconforming people who invoke SYG laws to fend off violence face an uphill battle in court. In the words of legal scholar Mary Ann Franks, SYG laws ensure that "real men advance [while] real women retreat."[31] Especially when they are people of color, women and gender-nonconforming individuals who are subject to violence are often characterized as "unreasonable" in their perception of danger; their impulse to defend themselves dismissed as unnecessary or excessive.

At the heart of these often unspoken and unwritten exclusions rest age-old legal traditions that continue to shape our contemporary ideals of belonging and exclusion in sometimes unexpected ways. Indeed, the original doctrines of US citizenship are based on understandings of national belonging as white, heterosexual, male, and propertied. Our founding legal document, the Constitution, originally granted the rights of citizenship to white, propertied men, and the first immigration and naturalization law similarly allowed naturalization to "any Alien being a free white person."[32] As the historian Robin D. G. Kelley explains, the nation's "entire political and legal foundations were built on an ideology of settler colonialism—an ideology in which the protection of white property rights was always sacrosanct."[33] The legal scholar Cheryl Harris illustrates how whiteness itself has functioned as an especially valuable and unstated form of property in United States law. Since the nation's origins in European colonization of the Americas, argues Harris, "white identity conferred tangible and economically valuable benefits, and it was jealously guarded as a valued possession, allowed only to those who met a strict standard of proof."[34] Slavery and settler colonialism, each critical to the fortification of white masculine power and property, could succeed only with the violent repression of African-descended and Native people, and the political and legal subordination of women. But even as the legal imperatives governing citizenship were gradually amended to provide political and civil rights to nonwhites and women, the enduring exclusions persist. We bear witness today as our self-defense laws, despite their apparent race and gender neutrality, continue to protect the safety of the powerful few at the expense of the vulnerable many.

Given our present association of DIY security with good citizenship, one might suppose that the United States has always been a "shoot first, ask questions later" nation. In fact, the original English common law heritage on which our legal structure is based reserved lethal punishment exclusively for the Crown.[35] Valuing human life above property, English common law imposed a robust duty to retreat, which commanded that one "retreat to the wall behind one's back" before meeting force with force.[36] But this duty to retreat eroded quickly in the United States.

Chapter 1 covers the 1806 homicide case of Boston attorney Thomas Selfridge, who did not retreat before defending himself from the attack of a younger and stronger man. The case is notable for being among the first to address issues of lethal self-defense in the new republic, and also for its ambiguous outcome: Selfridge was exonerated in spite of the judge's instructions to the jury. This well-documented court case helps trace the history back to early liberal political theories and English common law roots of the young nation's emerging self-defense ideals. The chief exemption to the duty to retreat was the "castle doctrine," established in England in the early 1600s. Popularizing the adage "A man's house is his castle," the doctrine allowed a man to meet force with force when his home was invaded.[37] The exception was based on the assumption that a man should not have to retreat from an attacker within the space that is intended to be his haven from the dangers of the outside world and from intrusion by the government.

Since it originated at a time when women and nonwhite people were largely excluded from the rights, protections, and immunities of full citizenship, the castle doctrine exempted white, property-owning men from the prohibitions circumscribing the use of defensive violence. As it translated to the slave-holding colonies in North America, the castle doctrine did not allow people who were themselves considered property—such as enslaved Africans and African Americans—to defend themselves from white violence. Native people likewise found no protection in the castle doctrine, for settler colonialism favored the right of white Europeans to invade and seize land already populated by others. Settler colonialism, legalized slavery, and women's exclusion from most legal rights ensured that property and the power to protect it would remain in white male hands. This white male hegemony would be challenged by Emancipation, the enfranchisement of Black men, and the passage of laws giving married women limited rights to own property.

In the late nineteenth century, just as federal Reconstruction came to an end, decisions in state courts on murders involving white men killing other white men all but eliminated the obligation to retreat. Chapter 2 investigates the cultural and political context in which two pivotal court cases, *Erwin v. State* (Ohio 1876) and *Runyan v. State* (Indiana

1877), challenged the duty to retreat. Rulings in these cases held that the duty to retreat was incompatible with ideals of the "true man" and the "American mind." Shifts in gender and race ideals increasingly framed white masculinity as protective of feminized dependents and of property (often one and the same under the English common law principle of coverture, which gave men full legal control over their wives) from encroachment by nonwhite, criminalized strangers.

White resistance to the post–Civil War redistribution of socioeconomic resources and the enfranchisement of African American men foreshadowed the precipitous erosion of the duty to retreat, providing an ideological foundation for a gradual expansion of the terms of justifiable homicide for white men. Black men's postwar economic and political challenges to white supremacy were largely neutralized by popular desires to protect white feminine purity and by legal structures providing enhanced protection for white property. I situate the legal challenges to the duty to retreat in the context of the withdrawal of federal protection and support for Black citizens; the overall increase in homicide in the former states of the Confederacy; the nadir of race relations; and the emergence and circulation of the trope of the Black rapist.

In spite of post–Civil War constitutional promises of citizenship and "equal protection" under the law for African Americans, nonwhite people's self-defensive actions against white attackers were usually criminalized. Chapter 3 investigates self-defense cases originating in the West, in the "Indian Territory," a socially and racially variegated borderland where the descendants of former slaves and of forcibly relocated Native people struggled to find security and economic independence. The territory's governing judge, Isaac C. Parker, became a voice of frontier justice while fighting to retain the duty to retreat as a means of inculcating respect for life in an "untamed" land. Many of his murder convictions for defendants who "met force with force" were appealed to the Supreme Court. The uneven outcomes of these cases reveal that white masculinity defined the exclusive contours of "true manhood," and nonwhites who stood their ground against racist assaults were prosecuted. By the time the Supreme Court upheld a right to "stand [one's] ground" in 1895, Black Americans had been politically and economically disenfranchised through racist violence and the widespread implementation of Jim Crow laws.[38] Lethal self-defense thereby continued to be a right of white masculinity.

From 1877 to 1950, more than four thousand African Americans were murdered by white mobs. Chapter 4 unpacks the ideological foundations of white supremacist vigilante violence and its naturalization in the public imagination as a vital mode of protection against what was in reality an imaginary onslaught of Black criminality. Simultaneous shifts in race and gender norms contributed to the reactionary framing of what scholars have termed the "rape/lynch narrative," the belief that Black men threatened to rape white women.[39] I connect the widespread opposition to efforts to pass a federal antilynching bill to a narrative of white vulnerability and Black threat. White resistance to federal legislation was rooted in a distortion of historical reality that masked the pervasive exploitation of Black women and insisted on the overwhelming vulnerability of white women as incubators of the citizenry. Lynching was allowed to continue because of this historical sleight of hand: the seductive tale of white feminine purity in danger and the necessity of lynching as a crucial mode of white self-defense.

Chapter 5 reveals how civil rights activism and Black Nationalism shaped national ideals of self-defense in the 1950s and '60s. The Black Armed Guard and the Revolutionary Action Movement resisted white supremacist violence while drawing on and challenging existing ideals of masculine self-defense. The calls of Black Nationalists for armed self-defense ultimately enabled the successes of unarmed activists, as armed guards provided vital protection to those who boycotted racist public transportation, stood on picket lines, or sat at segregated lunch counters. Prevailing contemporary narratives of the civil rights movement of the 1960s as nonviolent and peaceful obscure this legacy of Black armed resistance. I also document how a radicalizing National Rifle Association appropriated civil rights discourse while transitioning from an orientation around gun sportsmanship and education to reactionary "gun rights" in the 1970s and '80s. Today, in a creative manipulation of history, gun rights activists critique the contemporary gun control movement by highlighting earlier state and federal efforts to disarm Black people. This rhetoric masks the white supremacist underpinnings of the reactionary, antigovernment movements for gun rights.

Chapter 6 addresses the limitations of state and feminist efforts to fight gender violence by inviting law enforcement into the previously private space of the home. The chapter reveals how widespread assumptions about race and gender inform legal definitions of "reasonable threat," excluding abused women from using self-defense against their abusers. While feminists and civil rights activists clamored for state support against white supremacist misogynist violence, the NRA was reinventing itself as a political advocate for individual rights, deploying the Second Amendment's "right to bear arms" as an individual, rather than a collective, imperative. In the 1970s the NRA's propaganda machine increasingly promoted armed self-defense by invoking the specter of Black criminality and urban riots.

In chapter 7, I explore the cultural context that enabled the rapid spread of SYG laws to more than half the states, starting in 2005, and of the active recruitment of white women to take up arms to protect themselves, their children, and their communities. The proliferation of concealed-carry permits have enabled armed citizens to fill the security vacuum created by the state's presumed inadequacies, and DIY security repels the threat of ever-encroaching "strangers." So goes the logic: if we are our own police force, then we can meet force with force whenever we feel threatened. All we need is a reasonable fear of danger to justify taking action to protect ourselves.

In spite of widespread efforts by DIY-security proponents to recruit women, nonwhites, and LGBT people to the cause of armed citizenship, the adjudication of lethal self-defense continues to privilege white hetero/cis-masculinity. The book ends by surveying contemporary cases of domestic violence survivors and victims of homophobic and transphobic violence who stood their ground, only to discover that they were not the "law-abiding citizens" the SYG laws' framers had in mind. The law's treatment of gender-nonconforming people who fight back against attackers proves the selectivity of our culture's robust investment in self-defense. Transgender people of color who defend themselves against violent attackers, even in SYG states, end up imprisoned as murderers.[40] In these cases, as in many others, the exonerating rhetoric of self-defense is revealed for what it is: a regime that creates a privileged class of citizenship for the few at the expense of the many.

The story of how we evolved from a society restrained by the duty to retreat from danger to one where some possess the right to kill is a complex, nonlinear tale. We are a nation not too far removed from institutionalized and legalized slavery and the de facto slavery of the Jim Crow system, and our collective investment in what Cheryl Harris calls "whiteness as property" still determines our access to the rights, privileges, and protections of full citizenship.[41] That contemporary celebrations of armed citizenship can *appear* to be race- and gender-inclusive attests to the power of collective amnesia. We continue to cling to comfortable narratives of a heroic past and to ignore how violence made this nation, and its contemporary power structures, possible.

Our growing devotion to DIY-security citizenship signals our willingness to turn a blind eye to the real dangers of what journalist Evan Osnos calls our "self-appointed, well-armed, lightly trained militia."[42] Furthermore, it can be difficult to see how race and gender exclusions inform our self-defense culture, even when we are faced with concrete evidence. Recently, the United States has experienced a wave of popular protest fueled by opposition to racist violence and attacks committed by police officers. Demonstrators across the country have occupied public space, lain down in streets, removed Confederate flags from public buildings, and obstructed traffic in their clamors for justice. Their voices, tweets, and posters insist that "Black Lives Matter," and challenge the nation's continued willful denial of equal protection of the law to Black citizens. Freddie Gray, Michael Brown, Sandra Bland, Walter Scott, Eric Garner, Miriam Carey, Tanisha Anderson, Rumain Brisbon, and twelve-year-old Tamir Rice—all killed by police—are just a few of the casualties of our society's effort to enforce law and order by holding blackness itself in suspicion. The rationalizations for these killings, and for the deaths of Trayvon Martin, Renisha McBride, and Jordan Davis, Black teens shot by armed civilians who stood their ground, have a common thread: our legal structures and agents deemed it reasonable to perceive (unarmed) Black people as threatening. According to the vindicating but often unspoken logic of DIY-security citizenship, lethal violence against people of color carries its own justification.

The exclusionary implications of DIY-security citizenship are often invisible, except to those who are subject to their violence. A close look at our history reveals the cracks in the democratic promise of the new armed citizen ideal. Selective appeals to safety and vulnerability have served existing power structures, shaping the terms of belonging and exclusion for hundreds of years. This book challenges our celebrations of individual self-defense by unearthing its complex legal and social histories, showing how we abandoned the duty to retreat in favor of a selective right to kill. This history is hidden in plain sight, but our contemporary appeals to race and gender-neutral armed citizenship continue to blind us to our nation's most brutal legacies.

ONE

"That Great Law of Nature"

The Origins of a Selective Self-Defense Culture

*The house of every one is to him as his castle and fortress, as well
for his defence against injury and violence as for his repose.*

—SIR EDWARD COKE, 1604

*And upon this is grounded that great law of nature,
Whoso sheddeth man's blood, by man shall his blood be shed.*

—JOHN LOCKE, 1690

When Thomas Selfridge stood trial for manslaughter in December
1806, the young nation's laws were vague on the topic of lethal self-
defense. The thirty-two-year-old lawyer had killed a man in the streets
of Boston, claiming he did so to protect himself from grave danger.
The English common law, on which US legal foundations were based,
held that one must withdraw in the face of an attack, and not retaliate
until "retreating as far as he conveniently or safely can."[1] The Crown
held the capacity of *vindices injuriarum*, of vindicating or avenging the
wrongs that citizens inflicted on one another. Accordingly, the taking
of another's life was among the most serious of crimes, one commonly
punishable by death.[2] Yet, in the United States, the idea of backing
away from a threat or of allowing the state to protect one from harm
clashed with the ideals of independence and individual rights on which
the nation was founded. And while the race of the men at the center
of this famous case went unmentioned, whiteness and masculinity,
along with property ownership, were as critical to the distribution of
political rights as to the right to defend oneself. While legal doctrine

upheld a duty to retreat, popular opinion in the young republic increasingly saw a white man's retreat from an assault, particularly an assault on his honor, as cowardly and incompatible with the values of liberal democracy.

A White Man's Castle: Coverture and Consent in the Early Republic

Sir William Blackstone's *Commentaries on the Laws of England*, published in 1769, summarized English common law in detail. The *Commentaries* provided guidance to the framers of what would become the US legal system. In his volume *Public Wrongs*, in which he discussed criminal law, Blackstone wrote, "Of crimes injurious to the *persons* of private subjects, the most principal and important is the offence of taking away that life, which is the immediate gift of the Creator."[3] The right of protecting citizens and of punishing wrongs was reserved for the Crown. If one were attacked or threatened, the king and his laws, not the individual, would avenge the injury. Moreover, under English common law, one was obligated to retreat if threatened, rather than respond with lethal violence.

Some Enlightenment thinkers, such as Thomas Hobbes and John Locke, challenged the monarchy's monopoly on lethal punishment. In 1651, Hobbes became the first to invoke an inalienable right to self-defense. He wrote in Book 1 of *Leviathan*, "A Covenant not to defend my selfe from force, by force, is always voyd."[4] Hobbes distinguished between the "state of nature," in which people had no governing structure to rein in their baser instincts, and civil society, governed by an absolute sovereign. Since citizens professed obedience to the king in exchange for protection, the right to protect oneself remained legitimate in civil society should the king fail in providing protection. In his "Second Essay on Civil Government" (1690), Locke similarly invoked self-defense as "that great law of nature" and argued, "Whoso sheddeth man's blood, by man shall his blood be shed." For Locke, one man's unlawful attack on another placed the two in a "state of war" and justified a lethal defensive response. He wrote, "He who attempts to get another man into his absolute power does thereby put himself into a state of war with him; it being . . . understood as a declaration of a design upon his life."[5] And yet, the state of "civilized England" provided circumstances quite different from a true state of nature, and men living in a civilized society were expected to defer to the law and to conduct themselves with greater consideration of each other's lives.

The chief exception to the English duty to retreat was the castle doctrine, which originated in a 1604 case involving an officer of the Crown who had forcibly entered the home of a man named Semayne. Delivering the opinion in "Semayne's Case," attorney general Sir Edward Coke established the principle that officers seeking entry into a private dwelling must first announce themselves before entering. According to Coke, "The house of every one is to him as his castle and fortress, as well for his defence against injury and violence as for his repose."[6] This decision popularized the expression "A man's house is his castle." The home was thereafter treated as a safe space for a citizen against both the intrusions of the state and the dangers of the world outside. Under the castle doctrine, a man did not have to retreat before fighting back against an intrusion on his home.

Although there was no reference to the race of the man authorized to defend his castle, in practice the castle doctrine's exception to the duty to retreat applied predominantly to *white* men. In the United States, the legal conditions that excluded most women and nonwhites from access to political and economic rights and property ownership guaranteed that the "castle" would serve as a safe haven for white men and their property. When paired with whiteness, being male determined one's access to civil and political rights. Even in cases where race and gender were not explicitly invoked in the law, the term "citizen" implied those capable of full political and economic participation. In the time of Selfridge's case, this meant propertied white men.

Except under particular circumstances, the castle doctrine exemption did not apply to women. The doctrine of coverture, also rooted in European laws, subsumed a married woman's rights under those of her husband, thereby ensuring her subordinate and dependent legal status. According to Blackstone, "By marriage, the husband and wife are one person in the law." Prior to marriage, a woman possessed some, albeit limited, legal independence, such as the ability to execute a will, enter into contracts, sue (or be sued), and own property. But marriage required the merging of husband and wife into one legal unit administered exclusively by the husband. Blackstone wrote, "The very being or legal existence of the woman is suspended during the marriage, or at least is incorporated and consolidated into that of the husband: under whose wing, protection, and cover, she performs everything."[7] At the time of Selfridge's trial, the "castle" that a married woman occupied belonged entirely to her husband.

Coverture placed women under their husbands' protective custody, thereby masking the realities of marital violence and the difficulty of fleeing abusive marriages. Under coverture, married women possessed little authority over their own or their children's lives, and divorce was extremely rare. Even in cases where husbands were recalcitrant or abusive, women who managed to secure divorces often lost custody of their children. For example, in South Carolina in 1809, Mrs. Jennet Prather sued for alimony and the custody of her children when her husband, William Prather, sent her away so that he could live with his mistress. When Mrs. Prather attempted to see her children, her husband threatened to have her killed. Because the law prohibited a wife from testifying against her husband, Mrs. Jennet had to appoint a man to testify on her behalf. In sympathy for Mrs. Prather's plight, Chancellor Desaussure declared that the "court has jurisdiction to give relief, and to allow alimony to wives, in cases of improper severity by husbands." Indeed, the court determined that Mrs. Jennet's "ill usage" by her husband was "without any default or misbehavior on her part." The chancellor declared this case "outrageous to humanity and disgraceful to civil society" but his capacity to remedy it was limited by law and custom; removing a man's children, the means by which his lineage would continue, undermined existing laws governing the distribution of property under marriage.[8] Ultimately, the court compromised by granting custody of the youngest child, a daughter, to Mrs. Jennet, while leaving the two older boys, who were vital to the endurance of the family name, in the custody of Mr. Jennet and his mistress.

Coverture had deep social implications, ensuring that a woman could not physically defend herself against her husband, even if he treated her violently. The law allowed husbands to "discipline" their wives through the right of "chastisement," or physical punishment. According to Blackstone, a husband "might give his wife moderate correction. For, as he is to answer for her misbehaviour, the law thought it reasonable to entrust him with the power of restraining her, by domestic chastisement."[9] Chastisement helped maintain a gendered social order where men and women remained in what was deemed their proper places. The same order persisted in cases of marital homicide:

> If the baron kills his feme, it is the same as if he had killed a stranger, or any other person; but if the feme kills her baron, it is regarded by the laws as a much more atrocious crime; as she not only breaks through the restraints of humanity and conjugal affection, but throws off all subjection to the authority of her husband. And therefore the law denominates her crime a species of treason, and condemns her to the same punishment as if she had killed the king. And for every species of treason, the sentence of women was to be drawn and burnt alive.[10]

A woman who killed her husband, even in defense of herself or her children, could be put to death, but a man who killed his wife was subject to a lesser charge. Although Blackstone acknowledged that time and the evolution of English civilization had softened the rough edges of marital chastisement and the violence associated with it, the law designated a man as the master over his wife, as a king was sovereign over his subjects. This hierarchical construction of marriage would enjoy a lasting legacy in the United States.

Under coverture, rape constituted a violation of a man's property, rather than a crime against a person. Since a sexually violated woman was considered damaged goods, a rapist was liable to the victim's father if she was unmarried and to the husband if the victim was married.[11] The law also granted a man the right to defend his wife's or daughter's sexual purity with lethal violence, and to sue anyone whose actions—such as rape, infliction of injury, or murder—harmed his wife's ability to perform her household labor or to contribute honorably to his lineage.[12]

The only exception to the masculine monopoly on violence existed when a white woman protected her chastity from a rapist, as long as he was not her husband. At the opening of Thomas Selfridge's trial, in December 1806, Solicitor General Daniel Davis referred to this principle. Quoting Blackstone, Davis explained that a homicide could be justified "when committed in defence of chastity either of one's self or relations" and that a woman "killing one who attempts to ravish her" may be justified, "and so too the husband or father may justify killing a man, who attempts a rape upon his wife or daughter."[13] Since a (white) woman's sexual virtue guaranteed the integrity of her husband's lineage, its lethal defense—even by the woman herself—could be legally justified.

While the law protected a woman's right to defend herself from a stranger who tried to rape her, she was defenseless against marital rape, as the concept did not exist under English law. A man enjoyed full access to his wife's body. The English jurist Lord Matthew Hale wrote that when women married, they "gave themselves to their husbands," thereby consenting to sex until the marriage ended. Hale's influential *The History of the Pleas of the Crown*, published posthumously in 1736, stipulated the following: "The husband cannot be guilty of a rape committed by himself upon his lawful wife, for by their mutual matrimonial consent a contract with wife hath given herself in this kind unto her husband, which she cannot retract."[14]

In granting men full authority over their wives and daughters, the doctrine of coverture coexisted harmoniously with settler colonialism and legalized slavery. The legal immunities of the castle doctrine and a woman's defense of chastity did not extend to Native Americans and African Americans, unless they were free property owners. Like coverture, slavery and settler colonialism rested on the belief in the supremacy of Christian men of European descent and their necessary control over other human beings. The law allowed masters liberal discretion when it came to disciplining slaves, and most slave-holding states prohibited African Americans, free as well as enslaved, from owning weapons.[15] And while some laws prohibited the outright killing of slaves, murderous or abusive masters received scant discipline.[16] The main incentive restraining a slave owner from such extreme measures was his monetary interest in the slave's labor.

Living at the intersection of white supremacy and patriarchy, enslaved women could not legally defend themselves from most forms of violence. Valued for their labor and reproductive capacities, which contributed to the owner's workforce, enslaved women played a vital role in slavery's sexual economy. A slave's sexual consent was made irrelevant by her status as chattel, as property rather than person. And just as coverture prevented the law's recognition of marital rape, the laws condoning slavery were silent on the matter of enslaved women's sexual coercion by their white masters.[17] The sexual and economic exploitation of female slaves was solidified through the legal doctrine of *partus sequitur ventrem*, "offspring follows belly," whereby children would be slave or free according to the status of their mothers, instead of their fathers. Adopted in colonial Virginia and Maryland in the seventeenth century, these laws soon spread throughout the English colonies, ensuring that children born to enslaved women would also be enslaved, regardless of paternity or skin color.[18]

The doctrine rested also on a set of suppositions about slavery and personhood whereby enslaved women could be bred like livestock. *Partus* rewarded masters who took sexual liberties with their slaves, enhancing the masters' property with the increased number of slave children. The enslaved woman—*as* property—had no claim *to* property, and thus had no power to defend herself under the common law right of self-defense of chastity. Unlike white women, who were expected to propagate a racially pure white lineage, enslaved women's chastity was without value.[19] Their inability to consent, which served as evidence of their inhumanity, rested on the notion that an African-descended woman was naturally and perpetually receptive to sex. The enslaved woman was excluded from any right to self-defense, for she owned neither her body nor the "castle" that contained her. After the criminalization of the importation of slaves in 1808, slavery's continuity relied on enslaved women's bodies to serve as the vehicles of workforce repopulation.

The 1855 murder trial of Celia, a slave in Missouri, illuminates the exclusion of enslaved women from legal protections governing self-defense against rape. Celia's efforts to ward off the sexual advances of her master ended in the man's death. Although a state law authorized women to use deadly force to protect themselves from rape, a master's right to do as he pleased with his property exceeded an enslaved woman's claim to bodily autonomy. Celia was eventually executed for murder, but the execution was delayed until she had given birth to her rapist's child, who was considered valuable property.[20] Black women's exclusion from the principle of self-defense was vital to a white supremacist economy based on unfree labor and sexual violence.

As legal systems undergirding the young nation's social order, coverture and slavery existed in structural interdependence, ensuring that the most valuable property remained under the control of white males. Legal doctrines governing the hierarchical relations of husband and wife, and of master and slave, were inextricably connected. Historian Peter Bardaglio asserts, "The sexual access of slaveholders to their wives and bondswomen provided the undergirding of patriarchy as a system that shaped both race and gender relations."[21] Neither a white man's slave nor his wife possessed the legal capacity to defend either themselves or "property" that did not belong to them. Thus law and custom conspired to exclude the nation's most vulnerable from the legal right to defend themselves.

"NOT FIT FOR BULLYING OR FISTICUFFS": THE TRIAL OF THOMAS SELFRIDGE

It was in this context that Thomas Selfridge, a devoted member of the Federalist political party, faced manslaughter charges in December 1806. Months earlier, on August 4, he had published a statement in the *Boston Gazette* calling Benjamin Austin, a Democratic Republican, "a coward, a liar, and a scoundrel."[22] It was a provocative maneuver, comparable to slapping one's nemesis with a glove. In addition to their rival political affiliations, the two were embroiled in a lawsuit involving a catering bill for a Republican Party function. The caterer hired Selfridge to file suit when Austin refused to pay. Although the legal imbroglio had been settled out of court, the two men fought over what each perceived as an unforgivable attack on his honor. The hostilities escalated.

On that morning of August 4, Selfridge received word that an incensed Austin was sending someone to settle the score. A lean man of unimposing size—court witnesses would describe him as "weak and infirm"—Selfridge armed himself with a pistol in anticipation of a conflict. He told one acquaintance that he was "not fit for bullying or fisticuffs," although he was prepared to protect himself.[23] That afternoon, Selfridge strode toward the Public Exchange on State Street, where he encountered Austin's eighteen-year-old son, Charles. Charles Austin was a sturdy, athletic young man, and he was rapidly approaching Selfridge with a cane in his upraised hand. Witnesses disagreed over who made the first assault. Selfridge and some witnesses alleged that he fired his pistol only after Charles struck him on the head with the cane. Others claimed that the younger man struck Selfridge after sustaining one shot to his chest. Regardless of whose weapon found its mark first, Charles Austin collapsed and died immediately following the encounter, and Selfridge was taken into police custody and arraigned for manslaughter.

On November 25, Chief Justice Theophilus Parsons, a prominent Federalist who had co-authored the Massachusetts constitution, delivered the charge to the grand jury. Here he designated "felonies affecting life" as either murder or manslaughter, and said that the former involved "express malice," while the latter implied accidents of human frailty.[24] Homicides committed "without malice" could be further reduced in gravity if they were ruled to be either excusable or justifiable. Solicitor General Daniel Davis, a Democratic Republican, acknowledged the complexity of distinguishing one form of homicide from another, because legal scholars had "so blended the different degrees of guilt attached to these crimes," that it was difficult to distinguish among them.[25] Davis turned to Blackstone's *Commentaries* to illustrate the specific conditions under which homicide could be either excusable, which implied less culpability on the part of the defendant, or justifiable, which implied no culpability. An example of the latter involved a blameless victim of a "forcible and atrocious crime," who uses deadly force to prevent the crime from occurring. According to Blackstone, "Where a crime, in itself capital, is endeavoured to be committed by force, it is lawful to repel that force by the death of the party attempting."

Solicitor General Davis read extensively from Sir Edward Hyde East's *Pleas of the Crown*:

> A man may repel force by force, in defence of his person, habitation, or property against any one who manifestly intends or endeavors by violence, or surprise, to commit a known felony, such as murder, rape, robbery, arson, burglary, and the like, upon either. In these cases he is not obliged to retreat, but may pursue his adversary until he has secured himself from all danger; and if he kill him in so doing, it is called justifiable self defence.

Davis also referred to Blackstone, who asserted that one could use force in self-defense only after sincerely trying to avoid the attack, "to excuse homicide by the plea of self-defence, it must appear that the slayer had no other possible (or at least probable) means of escaping from his assailant."

According to this logic, a killing could be justifiable, and a defendant ruled innocent, if it was necessary to preserve the defendant's life, and if the defendant did not provoke the quarrel. Selfridge's case thus turned on the necessity of shooting Austin and on the issues of premeditation and provocation. Solicitor General Davis argued that this homicide could *not* be ruled justifiable because Selfridge had provoked Austin's attack by publicly calling his father a coward in the *Boston Gazette*. If the jury was convinced that Selfridge's posting in the newspaper was designed to incite attack, and that he had armed himself with the intent of seeking a fight rather than defending himself, then they were likely to find him guilty of the felonious killing of Charles Austin.

When debating Selfridge's decision to arm himself in advance of a possible confrontation, the courtroom discussion turned on the defendant's vulnerability and frail health. One witness testified that Selfridge "didn't mix in manly or athletic exercises."[26] While many considered Austin "the Sampson of his class" at Harvard, Selfridge was "weak and infirm."[27] Defense attorney Christopher Gore, a Federalist, highlighted the right of an individual to protect himself from attack, suggesting that the castle doctrine's defense of habitation extended to a right to defend one's own person. Just as men were at liberty to protect their homes, he reasoned, the law allowed them to protect themselves from a violent assailant. Gore argued, "Every man is bound and ordered to defend and protect his own life, when the government cannot do it for him." Further, echoing Hobbes, the defense argued that no law created by civil society may abridge "so essential and natural a right as that of self-defence."[28]

In his closing arguments for the defense, Samuel Dexter, a well-known Federalist congressman who had served as secretary of war under President John Adams, took Gore's argument a step further, protesting that the "law has not been abundant in its provisions for protecting a man from gross insult and disgrace" and suggesting that a man therefore had a right to defend his honor. According to Dexter, if Selfridge had failed to defend himself, had simply endured the beating that Charles Austin set out to give him, the assault on his honor would have left him with nothing to live for. Dexter concluded with a dramatic flourish: "May this arm shrink palsied from its socket, if I fail to defend my own honor."[29] An unanswered assault on a man's honor left him to suffer the deepest humiliation, a fate "worse than death."[30]

Dexter's language bore a striking resemblance to contemporaneous justifications for dueling. Initiated typically among elite men, duels originated in medieval Europe as an extralegal but culturally endorsed means of restoring a nobleman's sullied honor. The dishonored man would challenge his adversary to a duel, and the two would meet at a designated time, having chosen reliable men as "seconds" to ensure honest proceedings.[31] According to political theorist Mika LaVaque-Manty, dueling offered a ritualized way to settle conflicts among elites and publicly restore their tarnished honor without the interference of the law.[32]

By the time of Selfridge's trial, dueling had come under significant criticism. Northern tolerance for the practice had diminished in the wake of Vice President Aaron Burr's infamous killing of Alexander Hamilton in a duel in 1804.[33] Judge Parker and the prosecution agreed that dueling constituted murder and that allowing a man to kill another over an assault on his honor would effectively legalize dueling.[34] In response to Dexter's assertions about his dishonored arm shrinking from its socket, Attorney General Sullivan sarcastically retorted, "I would rather that [Dexter] should retain the use of his limbs" for the defense of his country, "the true field of honor."[35]

Not only was it illegal to kill in defense of one's honor, warned Sullivan; the practice was incompatible with liberal democracy. He cautioned the jury against a society in which "the *would-be noble*, shall be allowed with his gold-hilted cane, or his elegantly mounted pistol, in defense of his honor, to play a secure but mortal game." Under such circumstances, violent chaos would reign supreme and "the volumes of laws [would] become pavement for the soles of my shoes."[36] Allowing men to kill each other in defense of their honor represented the worst kind of elitism. Such selective observance of the law would undermine a democratic republic built on equality, albeit only among white, male, and propertied citizens.

The prosecution also criticized Selfridge for carrying a concealed pistol at the time of the lethal confrontation. They reasoned that if one were trying to ward off attack, one would carry one's weapon openly. Attorney General Sullivan asserted that "such manly, open conduct, would preserve [one] from assault."[37] By contrast, Selfridge's behavior—hiding his pistol in his coat pocket—evinced suspicious intentions to catch his adversary unawares.

Moreover, according to the prosecution, Selfridge's *Gazette* ad constituted a provocation comparable to that of a woman eliciting an attack on her chastity. In his concluding remarks, Attorney General Sullivan explained:

> A robber on the highway may be killed the instant he makes the assault, so may a burglar in the attempt to rob a house, so a woman may kill a man in the necessary defence of her chastity. . . . A woman knowing her chastity is to be assaulted, must not put herself in the way of the assailant and kill him, for in that case it will be considered, that she had premeditated the destruction of the man's life, and this would

constitute the crime of murder; and in like matter, if another expects to be assaulted, he must not go in the way of the assailant with an intention of killing by a concealed deadly weapon.[38]

In the attorney general's mind, there existed a set of circumstances—commensurate with Selfridge's published incitement in the newspaper—in which a woman might know in advance if a man planned to rape her. It was therefore her responsibility not to make herself available to the would-be assailant. Self-defensive killing in such a case could be neither excusable nor justifiable because the defendant had provoked the attack. Selfridge, like a woman who knew herself to be sexually vulnerable, had likewise provoked Austin's attack by leaving the safety of his office to stroll down State Street in broad daylight.

In his closing instructions to the jury, Judge Parker asked if Selfridge could have avoided shooting Austin by "retreating to the wall, or throwing himself into the arms of friends who would protect him." He asked the jurors to ignore Dexter's plea about defending one's honor, which he claimed was incommensurable with civilized society. And while he criticized Selfridge for publicly calling Austin a "coward," the judge reminded the jury that "no words, however aggravating, no libel, however scandalous, will authorize the suffering party to revenge himself by blows."[39]

Although the defense insisted on Selfridge's "natural right" to defend both his safety and honor, Judge Parker's instructions to the jury upheld the duty to retreat. He suggested that Selfridge could have escaped Austin's attack through less lethal means. Yet his instructions, and the prosecution's logic about Selfridge's provocation, did not resonate with the jury, which swiftly returned a verdict of not guilty. Selfridge was a free man.

The trial would serve as a precedent for nineteenth-century efforts to adjudicate cases of lethal self-defense. In spite of its equivocal characterizations of justifiable homicide, this famous case provided legal foundation for the gradual decay of the duty to retreat. Selfridge's case had proven that a man violently attacked in a public place might *not* be obligated to retreat before defending himself. In practice, however, this was a right reserved only for particular men in specific circumstances.

Despite the judge's and prosecution's scorn for the defense's suggestion that a man's honor was his most valuable property, Selfridge's acquittal seemed to suggest the jury's agreement with the defense. As the nineteenth century witnessed significant challenges to traditional structures of power, law and custom gradually expanded the rules of self-defense to allow white men to fight back against perceived threats to their safety and property.

"POWER CONCEDES NOTHING WITHOUT DEMAND": NINETEENTH-CENTURY CHALLENGES TO TRADITIONAL AUTHORITY

The case was resolved just before Congress passed the Act Prohibiting Importation of Slaves, in 1807, which ended the slave trade.[40] The law stipulated that "it shall not be lawful to import or bring into the United States or the territories thereof . . . any negro, mulatto, or person of colour, with intent to hold, sell, or dispose of such negro, mulatto, or person of colour, as a slave, or to be held to service or labour."[41] The phrase "negro, mulatto, or person of colour" appeared in the act multiple times, highlighting lawmakers' recognition of breeding between supposedly separate races. Since enslaved women only gave birth to slaves, regardless of color or paternity, the law's framers acknowledged slaves' varying degrees of nonwhiteness in their effort to outlaw the traffic in human beings.

It is no accident that challenges to slavery emerged alongside other nineteenth-century struggles against white patriarchal power structures. Efforts to overthrow the foundations of slavery and coverture took shape in growing movements in support of abolition and women's rights. These overlapping social justice efforts challenged the sexual and economic exploitation at the heart of codependent systems of oppression. They also converged in a shared critique of the white masculine monopoly on the rights, privileges, and protections of citizenship. By the latter half of the century, African Americans' transition from property to legal personhood would coincide with white women's gradual acquisition of property rights. While incomplete, these transformations represented colossal challenges to traditional ideals of national belonging.

Challenges to coverture took place amid women's increasing involvement in the abolitionist movement. When the firebrand journalist William Lloyd Garrison cofounded the American Anti-Slavery Society in 1833, white women, including Elizabeth Cady Stanton, Susan B. Anthony, Lucretia Mott, Lydia Maria Child, and Lucy Stone, were among its first and most active members. For many abolitionists, there existed a clear ethical connection between race and gender oppression. Former slave Sojourner Truth canonized her simultaneous call for gender and race justice in her rhetorical challenge to a predominantly white audience in 1851, "and aren't I a woman?"[42] Harriet Beecher Stowe, the author of the influential antislavery novel *Uncle Tom's Cabin*, stated: "The position of a married woman . . . is, in many respects, precisely similar to that of the negro slave. She can make no contract and hold no property; whatever she inherits or earns becomes at that moment the property of her husband."[43] While Stowe's analogy failed to consider the crucial difference between *owning* and *being* property, it nevertheless forged a vital connection between the law's failure to recognize the humanity of all women and enslaved people.

Abolitionists circulated stories of sexual exploitation to highlight slavery's moral corruption. Many activists directly implicated white slave holders as exploiters of enslaved women's virtue. Firsthand narratives such as Harriet Jacobs's *Incidents in the Life of a Slave Girl* (1861) were published and distributed to raise awareness about slave owners' moral atrocities against Black women. Jacobs wrote: "The secrets of slavery are concealed like those of the Inquisition. My master was . . . the father of eleven slaves. But did the mothers dare to tell who was the father of their children? Did the other slaves dare to allude to it, except in whispers among themselves? No, indeed! They knew too well the terrible consequences."[44]

Jacobs's powerful autobiography also suggests the ways that white women's gradual acquisition of property rights depended, in part, on their active participation in slavery. Many of the first challenges to coverture took place in the South and West just as antislavery activism swelled in response to several major slave rebellions and their violent backlash. Lawmakers in slave-holding states proposed married women's property laws as a way to protect white patrilineal property.[45] The earliest of these laws, an 1839 Mississippi statute allowing a woman's property to remain separate from her husband's, originated in efforts to ensure that the most valuable property, human chattel, was not misappropriated by irresponsible husbands. The Lone Star Republic (soon to become the state of Texas) followed suit in 1840, passing a more robust act allowing married women to sue and be sued, to enter into their own contracts, and to file for divorce.[46] Prior to the passage of these laws, there was little protecting a woman's family inheritance from mishandling by her spouse.

Married white women gained these rights at the expense of those enslaved. Harriet Jacobs's grandmother was thwarted in her efforts to purchase Harriet's freedom by her master's protestations that Harriet did not belong to him.

> My grandmother ... tried various ways to buy me; but the never-changing answer was always repeated: '[Harriet] does not belong to me. She is my daughter's property, and I have no legal right to sell her.' The conscientious man! He was too scrupulous to sell me; but he had no scruples whatever about committing a much greater wrong against the helpless young girl placed under his guardianship, as his daughter's property.[47]

New laws granting property rights to Southern white women were ratified just as Northern women, Black and white, were joining the abolitionist cause and gaining the chance to participate actively in the public sphere, an arena dominated by men. But there were limits to the kinds of public activism women of the movement might assume. Organizers of the 1840 World Anti-Slavery Convention in London banned female activists on the grounds that respectable women had no place speaking in a public forum. A group of women who were outraged at their exclusion convened the Seneca Falls Convention in 1848 to address what Elizabeth Cady Stanton called "the degraded and inferior position occupied by woman all over the world." Joined by male allies, including the abolitionist leader and former slave Frederick Douglass, they made their critique of patriarchal domination explicit in the Declaration of

Sentiments, which ingeniously borrowed its rhetoric and structure from the nation's Declaration of Independence. This new, revised declaration enumerated the harms inflicted by men on women, including "he has made her, if married, in the eye of the law, civilly dead," and "he has taken from her all right in property, even to the wages she earns."[48]

In the same year, New York adopted a married women's property law that would serve as the model for other states. Section 1 directly addressed the property concerns enumerated in the Declaration of Sentiments: "The real and personal property of any female who may hereafter marry, and which she shall own at the time of marriage, and the rents issues and profits thereof shall not be subject to the disposal of her husband, nor be liable for his debts, and shall continue her sole and separate property, as if she were a single female."[49] In other words, any property a woman owned before marriage would remain separate from her husband's.

In spite of the Declaration's appeal to gender equality, married women's property laws were created with an eye to the *protection* of women and their property rather than to their individual empowerment as citizens with the rights, privileges, and immunities available to white men. While safeguarding patrilineal property, lawmakers also sought to protect women and their children from the actions of errant or fiscally irresponsible men. Despite their limitations, as the nation expanded westward and these laws continued to spread, they helped to secure limited financial and legal independence for married women. New states, including Kansas (1859), Nevada (1864), and Oregon (1864), guaranteed women's property rights just as the nation's battle over slavery grew increasingly bloody.

"THE FIRST LAW OF NATURE": THE POLITICS OF WHITE MASCULINE SELF-DEFENSE

As the boundaries separating white masculine safety, property, and honor blurred, and as the supremacy of white male citizenship was called into question by abolitionists and women's rights activists, laws increasingly enabled men to resort to violence in self-defense. Although all states eventually passed anti-dueling legislation, the practice continued with impunity in the South until the Civil War.[50] It became entrenched in notions of Southern chivalry, where white men of high station would go to great lengths—even risking death—to uphold their own or their family's honor.[51]

So widespread was the practice of dueling in the South that, in 1838, John Lyde Wilson, the governor of South Carolina, wrote a guidebook, *The Code of Honor*, by which he hoped to show that white men could duel with minimal loss of life. Arguing that men would duel regardless of its illegality, Wilson reasoned, "If an oppressed nation has a right to appeal to arms in defence of its liberty and the happiness of its people, there can be no argument used in support of such appeal, which will not apply with equal force to individuals."[52]

Echoing Enlightenment thinkers Hobbes and Locke, as well as Thomas Selfridge's defense team, Wilson invoked "the first law of nature, self-preservation." He acknowledged a pressing necessity for a man to seek in nature "the only remedy for his wrongs," especially where "the laws of the country give no redress for injuries received." Such rhetoric hearkened back to Samuel Dexter's concern about the law's inability to protect men like Selfridge from "gross insult and disgrace." For Wilson and many other supporters of dueling, turning the other cheek when faced with an insult to one's honor was not compatible with the "manly independence" expected of white male citizens. While such "exercise of great Christian forbearance" was laudable, it was "utterly repugnant to those feelings which nature and education have implanted in the human character."[53]

As they engaged in duels over honor, propertied Southern white men also relied heavily on the open carry of firearms to maintain their control over slaves and to assert their social dominance. According to historian Saul Cornell and legal scholar Eric M. Rubin, "Slavery, 'honor,' and their associated violence spawned a unique weapons culture. One of its defining features was a permissive view of white citizens' right to carry weapons in public."[54] While there was widespread support for white men carrying their firearms openly, courts nationwide characterized concealed carry as ignoble and duplicitous. The attorney general in Thomas Selfridge's 1806 trial had disparaged the latter's decision to conceal his pistol in his coat pocket. In 1813, Kentucky became the first state to restrict the concealed carry of firearms, followed by Louisiana, Indiana, Georgia, Tennessee, Virginia, and Alabama.[55] The 1839 Alabama statute aimed "to suppress the evil practice of carrying weapons secretly."[56] The following year, an Alabama Supreme Court decision held that "it is only when carried openly, that [weapons] can be efficiently used for defence."[57]

Open carry for white men had been established as a self-defense norm just as criminal courts nationwide increasingly allowed white men to "meet force with force" without retreating, citing the Selfridge case as precedent. For example, in Minnesota in 1859, Charles B. Gallagher was found guilty of assault and battery and fined after hitting a man, named Bailey, in a fight. After an exchange of insults and threats, Bailey approached Gallagher holding a cane in his upraised hand. Gallagher responded by hitting Bailey, causing him to fall backwards. Neither man was permanently injured, but Bailey sued Gallagher for assault and battery. The district court instructed the jury, "When any party is approached by another, with a cane raised in a hostile manner, the party thus approached is not justified in striking unnecessarily, but is bound to retreat reasonably before striking any blow." On appeal, the Minnesota Supreme Court found these instructions in error because they mandated retreat. The court determined, "Such is not the law; but the party thus assaulted may strike or use a sufficient degree of force to prevent the intended blow, without retreating at all."[58] The court granted Gallagher a retrial.

Another 1859 case, this time in the nation's capital, placed the defense of elite white masculine honor front and center in a public scandal over marital infidelity. Representative Daniel Edgar Sickles, a notorious philanderer from New York, discovered that his wife was having an affair. After she confessed, Sickles shot and killed her lover, District Attorney Phillip Barton Key, across the street from the White House and in plain view of several witnesses.[59] During the widely publicized murder trial, the district attorney described "homicide with a deadly weapon" upon an unarmed person and "under circumstances indicating cruelty and vindictiveness" as murder, "no matter what may be the antecedent provocations."[60] While a man might excusably kill his wife's lover if he caught them *in flagrante delicto*—in the act of fornication in the marital bed—it was unlawful to hunt one's wife's lover down and kill him after the fact. According to the law, explained the DA, no provocation short of an invasion of a man's castle justified killing.[61]

But public opinion was on Sickles's side, as Key had committed the unpardonable sin of violating another prominent man's bed. In an impressive stroke of legal innovation, Sickles's defense team argued that Key's seduction of Sickles's wife constituted a simultaneous assault on his home *and* his honor, and was therefore a deadly provocation. Arguing for the defense, John Graham contended, "The person or body of the wife is the property of the husband, and the wife cannot consent away her purity; and if she does, he has the same right against the adulterer as if he ravished her."[62] The defense argued that each man possessed "a natural right to protect his wife against contamination," even if this meant killing his rival.[63] Since a wife's sexual fidelity was critical to the propagation of her husband's lineage, an assault on that fidelity was commensurate with rape, a simultaneous assault on a man's property *and* his honor.

Instead of debating the particular circumstances of the case, Graham asked the court, "What was the state of the defendant's mind when he slew the man who had contaminated the purity of his wife?"[64] By turning the court's attention to Sickles's "mental condition" and "insanity in the midst of his grief" upon discovery of his wife's infidelity, Graham convinced the jury that the killing was a crime of passion rather than a murder committed in cold blood. He argued that Sickles had been temporarily incapable of reason when he killed Key. After deliberating for seventy minutes, the jury pronounced Sickles not guilty. Since "the highest provocation a man can have is the pollution of his wife," they accepted the argument that Sickles had killed Key in the heat of passion.[65]

Sickles's was the first successful plea of temporary insanity in the United States. In this watershed moment, the plea of temporary insanity granted a powerful white man immunity from criminal prosecution on the grounds that the offense committed by the deceased—the desecration of the marriage bed—had rendered him incapable of reason. To the white propertied men on the jury, the sullying of Sickles's honor justified his temporary retreat from reason. The defense had also persuaded the court that a man's right to kill his wife's lover was commensurate with a woman's right to kill her rapist, because both constituted unpardonable attacks on "the sanctity of the household."

But this right was not universally enjoyed. The exception against the absolute injunction not to kill would apply selectively to those whose claims to honor, and the social power it conferred, were considered most worthy of protection. Sickles's temporary departure from reason granted him license to kill his wife's lover, setting the stage for future invocations of provocation as a justification for certain instances of homicide. The case signified the expansion of the boundaries of certain "castles" in support of white men's ability to protect their property and social capital from encroachment.

In the nineteenth century, retreat from confrontation was increasingly considered a value incompatible with rugged independence, white masculine honor, and the nation's early investment in armed self-defense. Coverture and slavery had together solidified white masculine legal supremacy, and when these structures began to crumble, property-owning white men required additional legal fortification for the defense of their castles. Although the roots of legal challenges to coverture lay in women's protection rather than empowerment, the new laws undermined white men's mastery over their wives, while the white supremacist logic of slavery collided with growing demands for emancipation and Black civil rights. As Frederick Douglass told a crowd of abolitionists in 1857, "Power concedes nothing without a demand. It never did and it never will."[66] The resistance to activists' audacious challenges to existing power structures would be fierce, and what remained of the duty to retreat would deteriorate alongside federal efforts to reimagine the rights and protections of citizenship.

TWO

DEFENSIVE VIOLENCE
AND THE "TRUE MAN"

The End of Reconstruction and the Duty to Retreat

And I hereby enjoin upon the people so declared to be free
to abstain from all violence, unless in necessary self-defense . . .

—ABRAHAM LINCOLN, 1863

The law of self-defense is founded on the law of nature;
and is not, nor can be, superseded by any law of society.

—JUDGE WILLIAM E. NIBLACK, 1877

The tragedy of Reconstruction is rooted in this American
paradox: the imperative of healing and the imperative of justice
could not, ultimately, cohabit the same house. The one was
the prisoner of memory, the other a creature of law.

—DAVID BLIGHT, 2001

From winter 1861 to spring 1865, the nation was embroiled in its bloodiest confrontation to date, which resulted in the loss of an estimated seven hundred thousand lives and incalculable devastation. The Civil War represented the nation's bloody contest to determine how the rights, protections, and privileges of US citizenship would be distributed, and the struggle did not end with the Confederacy's defeat. After the war, the federal government instituted Reconstruction, an effort to rehabilitate the states of the former Confederacy while providing freed people with necessary rights and protections, but the expansion of rights to those previously treated as property was met by violent white resistance.

The idea of self-defense as a "natural right" lay at the heart of debates over the terms by which freed people would be admitted to full citizenship. White panic in the face of Black freedom and the association of emancipation and Black enfranchisement with "Negro Rule" continue to distort public memory, supporting contemporary associations of blackness with criminality. Historian David Blight has shown how the safety and security of newly freed citizens was sacrificed in the interest of white reunion. The simultaneous erosion of both the duty to retreat and Reconstruction was not coincidental, even if the connection has been lost in contemporary memory. Challenges to both were seeded in the desire to reunite the war-torn nation while protecting white men's political and economic supremacy. As the federal government sought to replace slavery with a free-labor economy in the South, the demands of a growing women's movement and intensifying challenges to patrilineal property were undermining coverture. By 1876, Black men were, in theory, eligible to vote, and a majority of states had adopted laws granting married women limited legal independence.[1] Considered along with larger transformations in the growing nation's population and social structure, these expansions of citizenship rights to formerly disenfranchised populations represented a potent threat to existing power structures. Starting in western border states, the legal terrain shifted after the Civil War, granting *some* citizens the right to use lethal violence in self-defense outside of their "castles."

"IN A CONDITION OF SELF-SUPPORT AND SELF-DEFENCE": RECONSTRUCTION AND CIVIL RIGHTS

After the Civil War, the process of federally mandated Reconstruction was intended to rehabilitate the former states of the Confederacy, by reconciling them with the laws of the land, chiefly the elimination of slavery, the establishment of a free labor system, and the expansion of the franchise to formerly enslaved men. A key component of this effort was the protection and empowerment of those who had lived in slavery, as policymakers reasoned that former slaves would become an economic burden if they lacked the means—such as education, land, employment, and political rights—to become self-sufficient.

After the 1863 Emancipation Proclamation outlawed slavery in the rebel states, the War Department established the American Freedmen's Inquiry Commission to investigate "the condition of the Colored Population emancipated by Acts of Congress and the Proclamations of the President." The commission surveyed all military commanders under whom freed people sought refuge, with the goal of discerning "what measures are necessary to give practical effect to those Acts and Proclamations, so as to place the Colored People of the United States in a condition of self-support and self-defence."[2] The reference to "self-defence" alongside "self-support" was evidence of the commission's recognition that former slaves would be subject to violence, from which they would need a means of protection. Governmental intervention would be necessary to counteract this violence and to mitigate the economic, social, and political disadvantages the freed people would face, particularly in the South.

Among the most vital of these interventions were the three Reconstruction or "Civil Rights" amendments to the Constitution, which outlawed slavery, radically expanded the nation's definition of citizenship, and enfranchised male citizens. Rebel states were required to approve these amendments as a precondition for readmission to the Union. These and other changes to federal laws were designed to correct what legal scholar Randall Kennedy describes as the "racially selective underprotection" of Black Americans.[3] And yet, time and time again, federal laws had limited capacity to protect Black citizens from white supremacist violence when these crimes were adjudicated in state courts.

For example, in 1864 Congress passed a law allowing African Americans to testify in federal courts.[4] At this time, all Southern states and some Northern ones prohibited African Americans from testifying against whites, which made it difficult for Black victims of white violence to obtain justice.[5] But in spite of this and other innovations designed to provide equal legal protection to African Americans, it remained difficult to challenge state legal processes. State courts, particularly in the South, would continue to exclude Black testimony and to resist prosecuting white supremacist violence. The Fourteenth Amendment's promise of "equal protection under the law" was meaningless for African Americans subject to state courts that remained opposed to the idea of Black citizenship.

In 1865, shortly before the ratification of the Thirteenth Amendment, which outlawed slavery, Congress established the US Bureau of Refugees, Freedmen and Abandoned Lands, popularly known as the Freedmen's Bureau. The bureau provided economic, social, legal, and political support to formerly enslaved people and to many poor whites at a time when state-sponsored social welfare was almost unheard of. Bureau officials also helped former slaves locate family members, reuniting children with parents and spouses who had been sold away from each other. They registered voters and negotiated labor contracts to ease freed people's transition from bondage to paid labor.

The needs and desires of most freed people were modest. Many requested land on which to live and farm, the long-awaited "forty acres and a mule" that would provide economic self-sufficiency, as well as access to an education for themselves and their children. In 1867, at a meeting billed as a "Mass Meeting of the Colored Citizens of Charleston," Black leaders discussed the terms of the federal bill allowing "former enemies of the Union"—the states of the defeated Confederacy—to regain representative power and self-government. The group formed the Union Republican Party of South Carolina to support the construction of common schools "open to all without distinction of race, color, or previous condition . . . supported by a general tax upon all kind of property." Their plans included doing away with debtor's prison and corporal punishment, and protecting "the sacred right of the elective franchise" for all loyal citizens.[6] Freed people had struggled for these basic rights, and the Union's victory brought hope that they would be guaranteed.

"Negro Rule," White Panic: The Politics of Reconstruction

White backlash against Black freedom was vicious and often state-sanctioned. In New Orleans, armed white police and civilians attacked a multiracial Republican Party convention in July 1866. Acting with President Andrew Johnson's support, Mayor Monroe declared the convention to be an "unlawful assemblage" designed to "subvert the State and municipal governments" and encouraged the attack.[7] On July 30, white citizens stockpiled firearms, depleting the stock of local gun shops. Later that day, a mob of thousands descended on the convention, promising to "clean out those damned Yankees" while claiming, "It is no sin to kill a nigger."[8] White political leaders loyal to the Union were singled out, as were African Americans, regardless of their participation in the convention. More than two hundred people were killed or seriously wounded that day.[9]

Given the widespread virulent white supremacist backlash against Black freedom, efforts to support and protect former slaves could not succeed without federal military intervention. Postwar legislation divided the former Confederacy into five military districts overseen by provisional governors. Federal troops stationed in the South supervised the institution of a free-labor economy while trying to protect Black Southerners from racist violence. Former rebel states could rejoin the Union only if they ratified the three civil rights amendments to the Constitution: the Thirteenth (abolishing slavery), the Fourteenth (providing citizenship to people born on U.S. soil), and the Fifteenth (enfranchising male citizens).

For many Southern whites, these postwar measures were coercive and punitive, fostering social and political chaos in an already battle-scarred region. Governmental expenditures on social welfare for former slaves were a particular source of alarm for whites. Detractors complained that the Freedman's Bureau supported Black citizens at the expense of overburdened white taxpayers. An 1866 Pennsylvania Democratic Party flyer depicted a cartoon of an enormous, grotesque-appearing reclining Black man whose size dwarfed several busily laboring white figures in the background; the text proclaimed the Freedmen's Bureau "an agency to keep the Negro in idleness at the expense of the white man" (see figure 2.1). The flyer praised President Johnson's efforts to dismantle the bureau, and castigated Congress for overriding his veto. The flyer offered voters a stark choice: "Support Congress and you support the Negro. Sustain the President and you support the white man."

Ratified on July 28, 1868, the Fourteenth Amendment endowed people born or naturalized in the United States with citizenship, "regardless of race, color, or previous condition of servitude."[10] Congress intended this amendment to endow freed people with the right to equal protection of the law while rescinding the political and social vulnerability that their earlier legal status as property had demanded. The new amendment overrode both the Fugitive Slave Act and the infamous 1857 *Dred Scott v. Sandford* Supreme Court ruling, whereby slaves had been determined to be non-persons ineligible for citizenship.

Figure 2.1. Pennsylvania Democratic Party flyer, 1886.
LIBRARY OF CONGRESS

In addition to providing citizens with equal protection under the law, this amendment transformed the very nature of citizenship. Before the passage of the Fourteenth Amendment, individuals were citizens if their parents were citizens, following a principle known as the law of *jus sanguinis*, "right of blood." In a radical expansion of the citizenry, the Fourteenth Amendment conferred citizenship via *jus soli*, through the "right of the soil," to all people born in the United States, regardless of their parents' citizenship. In spite of its limitations, which excluded all "Indians not taxed," the consequences of this amendment were far reaching.[11] Suddenly citizenship and its attendant rights and protections belonged to formerly enslaved people born in the United States, and they were in theory entitled to equal protection under the nation's laws.

But citizenship did not guarantee full political participation. Another amendment was needed to guarantee the rights of citizens to vote and run for public office. The Fifteenth Amendment, adopted in 1870, declared that "the right of citizens of the United States to vote shall not be denied or abridged . . . on account of race, color, or previous condition of servitude." The amendment was adopted over the vocal protest of many, particularly in unreconstructed Southern states, whose ratification was one of the requirements for reinstatement into the Union. Virginia, Mississippi, Texas, and Georgia approved the Fifteenth Amendment as a means to recuperate their congressional representation.

Many white suffragists were also critical of the Fifteenth Amendment, as they could not countenance the enfranchisement of Black and immigrant men before white women. In a rousing speech to the National Woman Suffrage Convention, Elizabeth Cady Stanton urged the audience to "think of Patrick and Sambo and Hans and Yung Tung, who do not know the difference between a monarchy and a republic, who can not read the Declaration of Independence or Webster's spelling-book, making laws for Lydia Maria Child, Lucretia Mott, or Fanny Kemble."[12]

A few months later, Frederick Douglass, a longtime abolitionist and women's rights advocate, emphasized the greater urgency of gaining political protection for Black men: "When women because they are women are dragged from their homes and hung upon lamp-posts, . . . then they will have the urgency to obtain the ballot."[13] He did not deny that Black women too were subject to systematic violence, but he argued that it was their blackness, not their womanhood, that made them targets.

The heavy resistance to women's suffrage testifies to the longevity of coverture as a cultural norm as well as a legal doctrine. Particularly in the South, beliefs in women's natural dependency, and white women's special vulnerability, would persist deep into the twentieth century. While some Western and Northern states granted women's suffrage in the nineteenth century, none of the states of the former Confederacy enfranchised women until 1920, when Congress approved a new constitutional amendment stipulating that a citizen's right to vote would not be denied on account of sex.

Intense regional anxieties surfaced in debates around the ratification of the Fifteenth Amendment, particularly as Southern states had to accept universal male suffrage in order to end military occupation and gain readmission to the Union. For many whites, the Fifteenth Amendment signaled a descent into social and political chaos. Many decried what they perceived as "martial law and negro rule" that prevailed under military Reconstruction; they characterized Black citizenship and enfranchisement as anathema to civilization. In 1867, delegates to the Conservative convention in South Carolina described Reconstruction as life "under negro supremacy . . . whereby an ignorant and depraved race is placed in power and influence above the virtuous, the educated and the refined."[14] Others accepted the inevitability of Black enfranchisement as preferable to the "the military yoke" under which the Southern states were chained: "The South can do nothing but act in the matter as a defenceless man would act in dealing with outlaws employing a like argument."[15]

Even loyal supporters of President Lincoln, such as Senator James R. Doolittle of Wisconsin, chastised Congress for holding the South "under vassalage." He characterized the proposed legislation as "white disfranchisement" and an assault on "the white people of our own blood" by compelling them "to submit to negro rule and negro domination."[16]

White backlash in response to Black male citizenship and enfranchisement represented the convergence of sex and race panic. Many whites feared a slippery slope whereby enfranchising Black men and allowing them proprietorship of their own labor would lead to political chaos, economic decline, and, perhaps more disgracefully, "social equality." Even whites who had supported abolition feared that integration of the social realm held out the alarming possibility of race mixing—miscegenation—where white women's reproductive purity would be corrupted by "Black blood."

Underlying this logic was the fear that Black men's political authority would grant them sexual access to white women. An article in the Raleigh, North Carolina, *Sentinel* decried the "insane project of elevating the Negro to political and social equality" and asked, "Whose daughter is he to marry when he shall choose to take a white wife?"[17] For many whites, social and political equality between Black and white men would lead to the dreaded state of "social amalgamation," where sexual competition from Black men would undermine the purity of white lineage.[18] White women's reproductive capacities represented a particularly powerful form of property, one critical to the reproduction of the white race. Men with political agency had exclusive access to this property, and it seemed only natural that Black men released from the shackles of slavery and endowed with political rights would demand access to these coveted bodies. An 1868 illustration in *Harper's Weekly* pictured a wedding between a white woman and a Black man, framed by a crowd of white politicians and the word "Tammany" (a reference to New York's powerful Democratic political organization). The caption asked, "Would you marry your daughter to a nigger?" (see figure 2.2). Widespread imagery like this testified to white fears that Black political power would lead to the pollution of the political process and the mongrelization of the nation.

The idea that Black political power would lead to the destruction of the white race was cruelly ironic given the widespread but silenced sexual abuse of Black women. The size of the "mulatto" population—noted upon with interest by Union generals responding to the 1863 Freedmen's Commission survey—provided physical evidence of Black

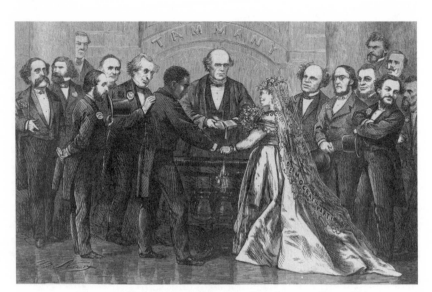

Figure 2.2. "Would You Marry Your Daughter to a Nigger?"
Harper's Weekly, *July 11, 1868*   HARVARD UNIVERSITY LIBRARY

women's sexual exploitation by white men. What African American
Studies scholar Hazel Carby describes as "the institutionalized rape of
Black women" did not end with emancipation.[19] Black women experienced continued abuse at the hands of white employers and white
supremacist vigilantes. In spite of age-of-consent legislation and other
laws protecting women's right to "defend their virtue," Black women
would continue to find scant protection in the law.[20]

In spite of hyperbolic language forecasting the end of social order,
nothing resembling "Negro rule" came about, nor were white property owners dispossessed of their land and economic power. What little
Southern land was distributed to former slaves after the war was eventually restored to its original white owners.[21] White resistance to Black civil
rights was intense, and federal enforcement woefully inadequate. After
Lincoln's assassination in April 1865, President Johnson, a Democrat,
fought against federal measures to protect Black citizens in the states of
the former Confederacy. In the absence of strong federal supervision,
new forms of quasi-slavery were allowed to thrive.

Passed in individual Southern states, "Black Codes" restricted Black freedom and mobility, and aimed to reintroduce quasi-slavery by preventing freedmen from contracting their own labor. South Carolina's Black Code, passed in December 1865, required that all people have "lawful and respectable employment," which meant employment by whites, and that Black artisans, shopkeepers, and mechanics obtain a license to pursue their trades.[22] Mississippi's 1866 Black Code similarly restricted freed people's freedom of contract, mandating that "all freedmen, free negroes and mulattoes in this State, over the age of eighteen years, found . . . with no lawful employment or business, or found unlawfully assembling themselves together, either in the day or night time . . . shall be deemed vagrants."[23]

Vagrancy laws made it a crime for Black men to be unemployed or to be self-employed, and criminalized interracial socializing while levying stiff penalties on whites who crossed the color line. Mississippi's code stated: "All white persons so assembling themselves with freedmen, free negroes or mulattoes, or usually associating with freedmen, free negroes or mulattoes, on terms of equality, or living in adultery or fornication with a freed woman, free negro or mulatto, shall be deemed vagrants."[24] The law reinforced the taboo of interracial socializing by equating "associating" with "fornication." Furthermore, in an effort to maintain white compliance with the laws of racial caste, it imposed harsher penalties on white than on Black transgressors.[25]

In order to enforce these new state-level legal codes designed to ensure Black subordination, many Southern jurisdictions recruited white men to serve in newly professionalized municipal police forces. According to the historian Keri Leigh Merritt, professional police forces had been lacking in the South prior to the Civil War. In the wake of Black freedom, uniformed white men carrying lethal weapons on official state business replaced the informal assemblage of gun-carrying white men of the antebellum period, and the rate of Black arrests skyrocketed.[26] The postwar development of professional armed police forces in the South helped codify the criminalization of Black men, while reinforcing the right of armed white men to arrest and discipline at will.

To minimize Black armed resistance, many Black Codes also re-stricted freed people's ability to own and carry weapons.[27] The Missis-sippi code stated that freedmen may not "keep or carry fire-arms of any kind, or any ammunition, dirk or bowie knife."[28] These laws also levied heavy fines on whites who provided weapons to freed people.

The authors of the Fourteenth Amendment were concerned about freedmen's right to defend themselves from racist violence.[29] In his tes-timony before Congress in 1866, Congressman Sidney Clarke of Kan-sas quoted an Alabama law prohibiting the ownership of firearms and "other deadly weapons" to "any freedman, mulatto, or free person of color in this State."[30] Lawmakers like Clarke hoped that the new federal amendment would supersede state-level Black disarmament.

Extralegal violence and repression were pervasive responses to Black freedom and citizenship. Confederate veterans seeking to restore white power to the South founded the Ku Klux Klan in Tennessee in 1865. The organization spread rapidly throughout the Southern states, as did its use of violence and intimidation to keep Black citizens subservient and disenfranchised. In response to rising violence and intimidation at Southern polling places, Congress passed the Enforcement Acts, begin-ning in 1870. Designed to protect African American voters from white supremacist mob violence, the Enforcement Acts prohibited groups of people from depriving citizens of their constitutional rights. Section 4 of the 1870 Act levied a heavy fine of $500 on transgressors who "by force, bribery, threats, intimidation, or other unlawful means, shall hinder, delay, prevent, or obstruct . . . any citizen from doing any act required to be done to qualify him to vote or from voting at any election."[31]

In spite of federal protections for freedmen's citizenship and voting rights, the popular election of Republicans—the party of Lincoln, and the party to which the vast majority of freedmen were loyal—would continue to encounter violent resistance in the South. Individual states rapidly adopted legal innovations—such as poll taxes, grandfather clauses, and literacy tests—to inhibit African American political partici-pation. On Easter Sunday in 1873, after a hotly contested popular elec-tion, a mob of whites massacred between 62 and 83 freedmen in Colfax, Louisiana.[32] Approximately 150 freedmen, some of them armed, had occupied the Grant Parish Courthouse to safeguard the election results. A mob of several hundred whites placed the courthouse under siege, eventually forcing the freedmen out by burning the building. Members of the Black militia were slaughtered, some shot in the head, burned alive, or stabbed to death even after relinquishing their weapons.

Southern newspapers framed the event as a riot instigated by the freedmen. "Fearful Atrocities by the Negroes" read a headline in the New Orleans *Daily Picayune.*[33] Ninety-seven whites were indicted under the 1870 federal Enforcement Act, for thwarting the freedmen's constitutional rights to freedom of assembly and to keep and bear arms.[34] The three who were found guilty appealed their cases to the Supreme Court.[35] In 1875, the Supreme Court ruled in *United States v. Cruikshank* that the federal government could not interfere in a case that was rightfully the domain of state courts. The most vital parts of the Enforcement Acts—those designed to protect freed people from white supremacist violence when their home states refused to intervene—were thereby incapacitated, and the three white men who had led the Colfax massacre went free.

Often considered one of the most egregious Supreme Court decisions, *Cruikshank* signaled a crass distortion of "equal protection," which undermined the federal government's ability to intervene if states failed to treat their citizens equally under the law. In the wake of *Cruikshank*, African Americans living in Southern states would have little federal protection from racist terror.

Cruikshank was also significant for its interpretation of the Second Amendment, as it held that the right to keep and bear arms was *not* endowed in individuals but rather in state militias. "The right of bearing arms . . . is not a right granted by the Constitution," explained Chief Justice Morrison R. Waite in his majority opinion.[36] Eager to keep firearms out of the hands of freedmen, Waite reasoned that the Second Amendment was designed to protect the states—which could assemble "well-regulated militias"—from a tyrannical federal government.

Elections of Black leaders in the South represented but a temporary triumph of Black enfranchisement, one that would perish along with the federal government's eventual withdrawal of military support. In the five years after the war's end, Southern states witnessed the election of Black officials, but the percentage of Black officeholders never reached beyond 15 percent, even though Black majorities existed in Southern states such as South Carolina and Mississippi. As funding dwindled, federal efforts to provide formerly enslaved people with legal, economic, social, and political rights ultimately failed, and in 1872, the Freedmen's Bureau was disbanded. The consolidation of professionalized, armed, white police forces in the South helped guarantee the subjugation of Black citizens who challenged white authority.[37] In the absence of federal protection, Black citizenship—indeed, equal protection under the law—was a lie.

In spite of these grim realities, calls for educational, social, political, and economic opportunity for Black citizens continued to provoke panic in whites, both north and south of the Mason-Dixon Line. The terms of military Reconstruction, however inadequate, were gravely threatening to whites whose political and economic supremacy had depended on the subjugation of (and denial of personhood to) African Americans. As the nation headed to the polls for the election of 1876, concerns about state sovereignty and the expansion of the rights of citizenship to formerly enslaved people were on everyone's minds. Voters from across the political spectrum knew that the nation's future hung in the balance. This election would be one of the most fiercely contested in the nation's history, and it would not be resolved without significant mayhem.

"A MAN OF ORDINARY COURAGE": THE ELECTION OF 1876

John Runyan and his brother-in-law Henry Ray were tense as they made their way to the polling station in New Castle Township of Henry County, Indiana, fifty miles east of Indianapolis. It was November 7, 1876, and Indiana was a crucial battleground in the hotly contested presidential election between Democrat Samuel J. Tilden and Republican Rutherford B. Hayes.

Runyan and Ray were white farmers longing for an end to Republican rule, and they knew they were entering a Republican stronghold where the polls might be treacherous. Under the best of circumstances, nineteenth-century polling places were rowdy, anarchic places typified by violence and drunkenness. Voter confidentiality was unknown. Men cast their votes using large slips of paper, or tickets, that were handed out by party representatives trolling the crowd. Presenting one's ticket to the election clerk was also done in plain view, and a voter was exposed to harassment and intimidation from members of the opposing party. Such roughness was acceptable as long as "a man of ordinary courage" could grapple his way to the ballot box.[38] Certainly any man lacking the necessary nerve to fight his way to the ballot box had no business voting in the first place. And the polls were especially wild this election day. The stakes were high, as a Democratic victory would bring about an end to what Runyan and Ray saw as the extreme misrule by the Republican Party of a nation struggling to heal its Civil War wounds.

Runyan, a thirty-two-year-old farmer born and raised in Henry County, was a Democrat in spite of his service as a private in the Union's Ninth Cavalry. The 1,150-man unit, with significant representation from Henry County, had faced Confederate troops on battlefields across Tennessee. Runyan was one of only 386 men to return home alive in the summer of 1865, and he bore the mark of his service in the form of a severely wounded right arm.[39] Ray was a nineteen-year-old farmhand and the brother of Runyan's wife, Charlotte.

Upon reaching the polling place, the men encountered harassment from Republican stalwarts, whose taunting ranged from verbal insults to threats of physical violence. In a small town where people made a point of knowing each other's business, some accused Runyan of treachery for supporting Tilden in spite of receiving veterans' benefits under a Republican administration.[40] Several men bullied Runyan and Ray, pursuing them around the town square and denouncing them with what witnesses would later describe as "harsh, opprobrious and threatening language."[41]

Runyan and Ray left shortly after casting their votes but returned later that evening to check the election results. Fearing for his safety, Runyan had borrowed a pistol from a friend.[42] The father of three children under four years of age, Runyan wanted to know the election results and return home safety. Yet this was not to be, because several men resumed their attacks. Witnesses testified that verbal threats turned into a physical scuffle in which Runyan and Ray became separated. Runyan tried to push through the crowd in an effort to reach his brother-in-law, and a shoving match ensued with Charles Pressnall, a twenty-seven-year-old Quaker with a combative streak when it came to politics. While some witnesses reported that Pressnall did nothing more than yell at Runyan, others testified that Pressnall punched Runyan until the latter fell to the ground. The encounter escalated until Runyan took out the borrowed pistol and shot Pressnall. As friends helped the wounded man to the shelter of a nearby hotel, a deputy hauled Runyan to jail. Pressnall died later that night, and an outraged crowd threatened to lynch his killer. The mob might have succeeded if not for an enhanced police presence.[43]

New Castle was not the only town to witness scenes of partisan violence that November. This was an especially turbulent election nationwide, and political tempers ran high. It was the second presidential election after passage of the Fifteenth Amendment, and Black voters, an overwhelming majority loyal to the Republican Party, the "party of Lincoln," met violence and intimidation in many jurisdictions with a considerable Democratic presence. In Anderson, Indiana, about twenty-five miles northwest of New Castle, a white Republican died in a fight after defending a Black voter from what one partisan newspaper described as a "Democratic ruffian."[44] Outright brawls and riots broke out in Southern polling places, where Democrats struggled to wrest control of their region from what many perceived as Radical Republican "carpetbaggers," Northerners who moved south to exploit the war-torn region and impose "Negro rule," political and social domination by newly freed and enfranchised Black men.[45]

Ultimately, this fateful election day would lead to several significant outcomes. First, there would be a seismic shift in the way self-defense would be adjudicated. Pressnall's killing eventually instigated one of two state supreme court cases to abolish the duty to retreat, paving the way for nationwide shifts toward lethal self-defense as a right of white men.[46] Second, the Great Compromise of 1877 would resolve the disputed election: the presidency was given to Hayes in exchange for an immediate end to Reconstruction. Prior to this moment, Reconstruction and the duty to retreat had endured potent challenges, and their demise was perhaps a foregone conclusion. But the events of November 7, 1876, marked their decisive decline.

For white men of voting age, such as John Runyan, the world may have appeared to be on the verge of apocalypse. The most devastating war in the nation's history (it had claimed an estimated 750,000 lives) wrought carnage across the battlegrounds of the South and the Middle Atlantic states.[47] Wartime destruction left many destitute and homeless. Race riots erupted in spaces where whites brutally vented their resentment of Black people's newfound freedom and political and economic liberty. In spite of a postwar industrial boom that sparked extensive railroad construction and the rise of newly industrialized cities, economic turmoil took hold after the devastating panic of 1873. Triggered by the intersection of industrial overspeculation, postwar inflation, and trade deficits, the panic was international in scope. The resulting depression persisted through much of the decade.

Labor unrest among industrial workers culminated in formidable strikes, eliciting violent backlash from corporate management. In an extreme show of state contempt for popular protest, the police violently subdued a crowd of seven thousand unemployed people demonstrating in New York City's Tompkins Square in 1874.[48] Economic chaos characterized by bank failures, the collapse of once-powerful railroad companies, and skyrocketing unemployment plagued the nation as the electorate headed to the polls in 1876.

As Runyan faced his antagonists on the battlefield of the New Castle polling place, the nation was at a critical juncture where many efforts converged: repairing a broken political machinery in the service of an expanding electorate, ensuring the rights of citizenship to those recently freed from bondage, and healing the rift between North and South. These desires would not be easily reconciled, as the nation abandoned its commitment to minimal protection of African American citizens in favor of the seductive promise of regional reconciliation.[49]

"IN THE HANDS OF THEIR INTENDED VICTIMS": WHITE RECONCILIATION AND TRUE MASCULINITY

The day following the election, returns showed Democrat Samuel Tilden to be the decisive winner in Indiana and the likely overall winner with 184 electoral votes. Believing Tilden the victor, the *Alexandria Gazette* declared the nation "Redeemed from Radical Misrule."[50] Yet the results would remain undetermined until early March, with four key battleground states unsettled: South Carolina, Florida, Louisiana, and Oregon. The three Southern states were the last remaining unreconstructed states of the former Confederacy, where voter intimidation and disfranchisement ran high in spite of the presence of federal troops. An Electoral Commission made up of congressmen and Supreme Court justices was assembled to determine the election's outcome. Many believed that Tilden had won the popular vote, even though many Southern states with significant Black populations might have fallen decisively to Hayes if not for systematic efforts to disenfranchise Black voters. Given widespread white resistance to the perceived Republican military occupation of the South, hopes ran high that a Democratic president would grant sovereignty to the South and end Reconstruction. So the members of the commission arrived at an agreement: they declared Hayes the victor in each of the four contested states—in spite of Tilden's winning the popular vote—in exchange for the removal of the remaining federal troops from the South. Hayes was inaugurated on March 3, 1877, having won the presidency with 185 electoral votes.

White supremacist political power swiftly reclaimed the South as the last of the federal troops departed. After twelve years of limited military, social, economic, and political protection for Black civil rights, Reconstruction came to an end, leaving African American citizens of the South on their own to face escalating violence, economic exploitation, and segregation. In the absence of federal protection, Black voters were systematically disenfranchised by literacy tests, grandfather clauses, poll taxes, and violence. Ultimately, argues historian David Blight, white supremacist backlash and desire for regional reconciliation exceeded the pull of restorative justice for former slaves.[51]

The duty to retreat had met formidable challenges long before John Runyan shot Charles Pressnall in 1876. Over the course of the nineteenth century, the law shifted selectively to allow *some* men to use defensive violence when they felt threatened outside of the protective confines of their "castle." Dating back to 1806, when Thomas O. Selfridge was exonerated in the shooting death of Charles Austin, nineteenth-century debates over self-defense implicitly centered on the urgent need to protect white masculine honor. In their final deliberations on Selfridge's guilt, Judge Isaac Parker and Attorney General Sullivan had vigorously discredited the notion that a man might kill in defense of his reputation. Yet widespread understandings of white manhood as tethered to honor triumphed when Selfridge was acquitted of manslaughter. Echoes of this case's invocation of white men's honor in dire need of legal protection would reverberate through the century, as when Daniel E. Sickles was acquitted of murder after shooting his wife's lover in the streets of Washington, DC. Claiming their client's temporary insanity, Sickles's defense team capitalized on pervasive concerns over perceived threats to elite white masculine honor and procreative legitimacy.

Anxieties over white male vulnerability loomed large in the case of Ohioan James W. Erwin. In January 1872, fifty-five-year-old Erwin killed his twenty-year-old son-in-law, David Lawless, in a squabble over the use of a storage shed on Erwin's property. The two had argued over how the shed would be used, after which Lawless removed all of Erwin's tools, replaced them with grain, and locked the building to prevent Erwin's entry. The older man retaliated by breaking the locks, removing his son-in-law's stash of grain, and putting his tools back in the shed.[52] According to Erwin, Lawless entered the shed and threatened him with an ax, provoking Erwin to shoot in self-defense.[53]

Erwin was convicted of second-degree murder and appealed his conviction to the Ohio Supreme Court. The court overturned the lower court's decision and remanded for a retrial in 1876. The court's decision rested on Erwin's "faultlessness" in instigating the conflict. According to Judge George McIlvaine, "A true man, who is without fault, is not obliged to fly from an assailant, who by violence or surprise maliciously seeks to take his life, or to do him enormous bodily harm."[54] Even though there were no living witnesses who could testify as to whether Lawless's actions provoked in Erwin a reasonable fear for his life, the higher court gave Erwin the benefit of the doubt. Similar to Selfridge's case, Erwin's involved an alleged attack by a stronger, larger man against a weaker, older man, in a location outside the defendant's "castle," and thus not exempted from the duty to retreat. This landmark case established the right of the "true man" to stand his ground against an attacker, even if the attack took place outside of the man's home.

The judge's instructions to the jury and the true man doctrine derived from Sir Matthew Hale's *Pleas of the Crown* (1736), which asserted, "If a thief assaults a true man either abroad or in his house to rob or kill him, the true man is not bound to give back, but may kill the assailant, and it is not felony." In Hale's account, "giving back" was shorthand for retreating until one's back was against the wall, and it did not matter where the confrontation took place. For Hale, retreat was not necessary for a man maliciously assailed by a *thief.* But the criminal element of "thief" dropped out of Judge McIlvaine's 1876 interpretation, where he claimed to act on the rule "best calculated to protect and preserve human life." For McIlvaine, the "surest [way] to prevent the occurrence of occasions for taking life" was "by letting the would-be robber, murderer, ravisher, and such like, know that their lives are, in a measure, in the hands of their intended victims."[55] Lethal self-defense was a right of "true manhood," and would serve as a deterrent to crime. On retrial, Erwin's conviction was reduced from second-degree murder to manslaughter.

Erwin's manslaughter conviction was delivered just one month after John Runyan shot Charles Pressnall. In February 1877, Runyan was tried, found guilty of manslaughter, and sentenced to eight years in the penitentiary.[56] Runyan appealed his case to the Indiana Supreme Court, which ruled that he was entitled to a retrial. According to Judge William E. Niblack, the lower court had improperly instructed the jury that Runyan was obligated to retreat in the face of a threat.[57]

Judge Niblack reasoned that retreat was incompatible with American values of rugged independence and self-sufficiency. He asserted, "The tendency of the American mind seems to be very strongly against the enforcement of any rule which requires a person to flee when assailed." For Niblack, retreat in the face of danger ran counter to human nature: "The law of self-defense is founded on the law of nature; and is not, nor can be, superseded by any law of society."[58] The *Runyan* court echoed the Ohio Supreme Court's declaration that a "true man" does not back away from danger. This watershed moment saw a decisive shift in support of a white man's "natural" right to defend himself violently without backing away. On retrial, John Runyan was acquitted, and allowed to return to his family and farm.

Runyan's acquittal and the reduction of Erwin's charge turned on dominant constructions of violent self-defense as natural and essential to white masculinity. The legal documentation does not contain explicit reference to the race of the men involved in the cases, but these pivotal appeals to self-defense must be considered in the context of the nation's pursuit of regional reconciliation at the expense of Black citizenship, and the accompanying systems of race and gender policing that emerged after emancipation. When Judge Niblack invoked the "law of nature" in arguing that a person should not be forced to "flee when assailed," he did not intend his decision to apply to women or nonwhites. The three Reconstruction amendments promised state-mandated redistributive justice and equal protection, providing formerly enslaved people with citizenship, and enfranchising all male citizens, regardless of "race, color, or previous condition of servitude." But the liberalization of self-defense would not apply to Black citizens.

A white man's obligation to use lethal violence to defend himself, his dependents, and his honor became enshrined in nineteenth-century legal terrain, just as the preeminence of white patriarchal power was being challenged by abolitionists and suffragists. The expansion of limited legal, economic, and political rights to women and nonwhites accelerated the erosion of the duty to retreat as the "true man" needed legal justification to defend his "castle"—and himself—from further encroachment. By the 1870s, the command that self-defense require one's "retreat to the wall" was incompatible with the belief in a true man's natural right to stand his ground and meet violence with violence. Whiteness and masculinity would remain the primary qualifications for the acquisition and protection of property, codified in appeals to the (white) man's "castle."

David Blight observes that "sectional reunion . . . was a political triumph by the late nineteenth century, but it could not have been achieved without the resubjugation of many of those people whom the war had freed from centuries of bondage."[59] The contested 1876 election and the "great compromise" of 1877 precipitated government withdrawal of military oversight along with the redistributive and legal redress services intended to support formerly enslaved citizens. The compromise resulted not only in the retreat from the promise of "forty acres and a mule" and any other redistribution of property to Blacks; it also fortified the whiteness of the American "true man."

The true man doctrine was forged in the fire of willful collective amnesia. The landmark state cases idealized the honorable citizen— "without fault," according to the *Erwin* case—who protected his home and helpless dependents from the figure of the newly enfranchised Black male intruder and potential rapist. Both the *Runyan* and *Erwin* cases involved white men killing other white men, so the faultlessness of the true man might go unquestioned. And the true man's chivalrous protection of white women's virtue lay at the ideological core of post–Civil War national reconciliation, serving the needs of white supremacy while effacing the violence of slavery.

By necessity, the true man was a white man, and the *Erwin* and *Runyan* decisions provided legal justification only for white men's ability to "meet force with force" at a time when national reconciliation hung in the balance. Therefore, it is not accidental that the most precipitous legal challenges to the duty to retreat coincided with the demise of Reconstruction. In the wake of civil war and economic turmoil, intensified by the depression of 1873, state supreme courts echoed the concerns of the larger culture by delivering decisions that championed lethal self-defense over retreat. Taken together, the *Runyan* and *Erwin* decisions eradicated white men's obligation to retreat by reinforcing the ideology of the true man, and the tendency of the "American mind" to perceive white masculine retreat as cowardice.[60]

A few years after the Great Compromise ended Reconstruction, Texas passed its first state penal code, which defined justifiable homicides as those committed "in necessary defense of person or property." The code did not require retreat in cases where one's person or property was unlawfully attacked. Furthermore, decades after slavery's end, a man still held a property interest in his wife's body. Under Article 567 of the Texas Penal Code, a homicide was justified when "committed by a husband upon the person of any one taken in the act of adultery with the wife," provided the killing took place before the parties to the act of adultery have separated.[61] There was no similar allowance for women who discovered their husbands in the act of adultery. This and similar legislation made it increasingly difficult to see where the law drew the line between white masculine honor and property, as both might be legally defended with deadly violence.

The economic, political, and social status of African Americans would remain tenuous, their access to socioeconomic and political power constrained by legalized exclusion from the protections of the law and by white supremacist terror. Until 1910, migration north and westward would be possible for a relatively small majority who possessed the means to relocate, away from family, cherished social networks, and a known way of life. The vast majority of African Americans, approximately 90 percent by 1910, would continue to reside south of the Mason-Dixon Line until the Great Migration of some six million out of the South, between the years of the First World War and 1975.[62] In spite of widespread segregation and exclusion from state-funded schools, Black citizens made significant strides in education; in 1870, almost 80 percent of African Americans over fourteen were illiterate, but by 1900, that percentage had fallen to 45 percent.[63]

The erosion of the rule of retreat had an immediate impact on homicide rates, which increased dramatically, especially in the states of the former Confederacy.[64] And while the lynching of African Americans was rare before the Civil War, extralegal murders—most of which went unpunished and/or took place with the tacit approval of law enforcement—increased after the end of Reconstruction, reaching a crescendo in 1892.[65] Between 1877 and 1930, white lynch mobs claimed the lives of approximately 3,220 African Americans.[66] While lynchings took place everywhere, most were concentrated in the states of the former Confederacy, with Mississippi, Georgia, Texas, and Louisiana witnessing the most egregious loss of Black life.[67] The majority of those killed were Black men, and although rape was rarely the actual provocation for the lynchings, whites maintained that these punishments were necessary to prevent Black men from raping white women. These public, quasilegal spectacles of Black suffering were intended to be traumatizing and instructive for those who might question the rigidity of the color line.

The *Erwin* and *Runyan* decisions—both occurring in border states where skepticism about federal Reconstruction ran high—legitimated a "true man's" right to use lethal violence in self-defense, even in spaces beyond his "castle." Given the simultaneous withdrawal of federal protection for freed people, and the legal innovations intended to return Black citizens to a state of quasi-slavery, the right of lethal self-defense would remain a right of white men.

THREE

"A Mighty Power in the Hands of the Citizen"

Justice and True Manhood
in the Western Borderlands

The frontier is the outer edge of the wave—
the meeting point between savagery and civilization.

—FREDERICK JACKSON TURNER, 1893

A person who has an angry altercation with another person,
such as to lead him to believe that he may require the means
of self-defence in case of another encounter, may be justified,
in the eyes of the law, in arming himself for self-defence.

—*GOURKO V. UNITED STATES*, 1894

Debates over who possessed the right—and the need—to defend them-selves lethally reflected a complex tangle of beliefs about criminality and vulnerability, and white anxieties over the expansion of the rights of citizenship. While dueling fell out of favor after the Civil War, its legacy persisted in the form of greater legal tolerance for lethal violence in the South. After the *Erwin* and *Runyan* decisions challenged the duty to retreat, most Southern states followed suit in allowing white men to stand their ground when faced with an adversary that could be seen (by a white, male jury) as a "reasonable" threat.

While most states eventually challenged the duty to retreat in the wake of *Erwin* and *Runyan,* others proved resistant to the rhetoric of the "true man's" right to lethal self-defense. Harvard law professor Joseph Beale claimed, in 1903, "It is undoubtedly distasteful to retreat; but it is ten times more distasteful to kill."[1] Others echoed Beale's concern about the consequences of permitting men who felt threatened to use lethal force outside their homes. Alabama Supreme Court judge George Washington Stone was among a small number of Southern judges who fought to maintain the duty to retreat in his state's adjudication of homicide. Stone saw a slippery slope from justifiable homicide in self-defense to legally sanctioned murder, and his court resisted pressure to excuse defendants who killed in mutually instigated fights.[2] Except for Alabama, Florida, and the Carolinas—where the duty to retreat before using deadly force, *except* in one's home, persisted—most of the other states that resisted the expansion of justifiable homicide were in the Northeast.

Those in favor of expanding the terms of justifiable homicide argued that advancements in firearm technology made safe retreat impossible. From the Civil War until the turn of the twentieth century, innovations in gun technology developed rapidly, evolving from the single-shot flintlock to the rotating-cylinder revolver, which could fire up to six shots in relatively quick succession. The Winchester rifle was invented following the war, and quickly became popular because of its efficient lever-action repeating-fire system.[3] The postwar invention of cartridges also allowed for firing multiple shots without reloading.[4]

During the postbellum period, a rapidly growing population and shifts in the racial and ethnic composition of the citizenry contributed to beliefs that the nation's racial purity was under siege. In spite of the catastrophic loss of life in the Civil War, the population grew from approximately thirty-one million in 1860 to seventy-six million by 1900.[5] Immigration, primarily from the European continent, accounted for approximately 14 percent of the population during that time. By the turn of the twentieth century, the science of eugenics—popularized by Theodore Roosevelt—promoted the selective breeding of white, native-born citizens as a way to counteract what was seen as the excessive fecundity of the immigrant and nonwhite masses.

As the US population grew, the nation expanded westward. While most immigrants arriving during the nineteenth and early twentieth centuries settled in the urban spaces of the Northeast, the American West experienced radical shifts in racial and ethnic composition. Native Americans were increasingly forced westward to make way for white settlement. After the Mexican-American War, and Mexico's 1848 forced cession of 529,000 square miles, the territory now comprising the US Southwest was home to approximately eighty thousand Mexican nationals and thousands of Native people. While the US government originally promised Mexican nationals the benefits and protections of US citizenship, white settlers immediately began seizing land for cotton plantations and cattle ranching.[6] Violence against nonwhite inhabitants of the western territories was common from 1848 until 1930; historians William Carrigan and Clive Webb estimate that thousands of Mexican and Native-descended people were lynched in the struggle over control of this profitable land.[7]

White violence was also common against Chinese men, who had begun arriving in the West in the 1850s to seek their fortunes in gold mining, construction, and the railroad industry. Some companies, like the Central Pacific Railroad, began actively recruiting Chinese men as laborers to build the transcontinental rail.[8] While their numbers amounted to no more than three hundred thousand by 1890, and though many of them eventually returned to China, their arrival set off a wave of racist panic that culminated in the nation's first racially exclusionary immigration law in 1882.[9]

Concerns about the impact of nonwhite masculinity on US civilization were also expressed in anti-miscegenation laws, which prohibited marriage between whites and nonwhites. Marriage exclusions depended on the fantasy of discrete racial categories. Designed to safeguard the purity of white lineage, the laws were amended in response to the arrival of other communities of people considered nonwhite when they appeared to encroach on white economic and political power.[10] In 1878, the California anti-miscegenation law, which had originally prohibited African Americans from marrying whites, was amended to include the Chinese as a prohibited category.[11] Native Americans too would find themselves prohibited from marrying whites in many states where they constituted a significant presence.[12] Those labeled "Mexicans" were not explicitly prohibited from marrying whites, but their precise racial status would remain suspect. They would continue to find access to the full rights and immunities of US citizenship elusive.

Suspicion of nonwhite men in the West found voice in nineteenth-century popular literature, like the 1854 serialized novel, *The Life and Adventures of Joaquin Murieta*, which characterized the "Wild West" as lawless and hostile to civilization. Similar stories, such as James Fenimore Cooper's *Leatherstocking* series, romanticized the ruggedness of the frontier while reinforcing popular mythologies of nonwhite masculinity as violent and unruly. Popular fiction in the form of widely selling dime novels of the time characterized the West as wild and untamed, a refuge for bandits and criminals. Tough, virtuous white heroes such as Buffalo Bill, Kit Carson, and Cooper's Natty Bumppo battled the elements, criminal outlaws, and savage Indians to rescue innocent damsels in distress while taming the land for "civilized" white settlement.[13]

If western regions with relatively sparse white populations were rife with lawlessness, then white men establishing homes there would need to protect themselves, their property, and their dependents (see figure 3.1). If the young nation's European-descended "original stock" were to fulfill the promises of Manifest Destiny and to populate the nation "from sea to shining sea" (see figure 3.2), laws would have to shift, if only selectively, to ensure that self-defense became nothing less than a "divine right."[14]

In the late nineteenth century, most western courts supported a man's right to stand his ground against a violent attack, with decisions that reflected the logic of *Erwin* and *Runyan*: robust self-defense rights in situations where "faultless" men found themselves under attack by violent perpetrators. The 1879 Texas Penal Code stated, "The party whose person or property is so unlawfully attacked is not bound to retreat in order to avoid the necessity of killing his assailant."[15] While the Lone Star State was unusual in its energetic protection of property, other states embraced similarly expansive rights of self-defense. Decisions in Kansas in the 1890s established that one may "stand his ground and use

Figure 3.1. New Home Sewing Machine Company trading card, 1881.

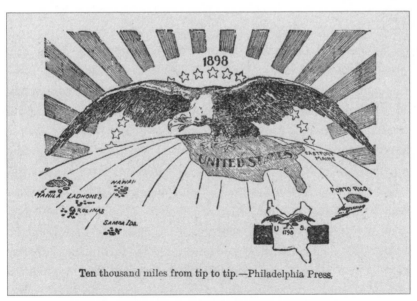

Figure 3.2. "Ten Thousand Miles from Tip to Tip," 1898.

such force as reasonably appears necessary to repel the attack and protect himself" whenever "one is unlawfully attacked by another."[16] Missouri (1902) and Wisconsin (1909) followed with cases that disparaged the duty to retreat as an outmoded doctrine.[17]

"IF HE CAN SAVE A HUMAN LIFE": JUDGE ISAAC C. PARKER'S RESISTANCE TO LETHAL SELF-DEFENSE

In spite of western challenges to the duty to retreat, the "true man's" prerogative to kill an assailant would face a considerable opponent in Judge Isaac C. Parker, who oversaw the US District Court for the Western District of Arkansas from 1875 to 1896.[18] Known as a defender of Native American rights, Parker was appointed by President Ulysses S. Grant to oversee what many called "The First White Man's Court in the Indian Territory" and to adjudicate criminal cases involving US citizens in the 74,000 square miles of land west of the Mississippi River, then designated for Native people.[19]

By the 1890s, the decade in which many of Judge Parker's most famous self-defense cases took place, the territory was home to a multiracial and multicultural population in flux. Much of the northern part of the Indian Territory, which bordered Kansas, was a socially liminal borderland in which increasingly dispossessed Native people, African Americans, and white migrants from the East struggled to carve out a living. Law in the Indian Territory fell under the jurisdiction of the tribes who lived there, but the United States maintained jurisdiction over crimes involving non-Native US citizens. The region, with its indeterminate legal status and relatively small population, drew criminals trying to escape justice. Judge Parker saw it as his duty to "tame" the region by instituting law and order, particularly where violent crime was concerned. He also saw himself as a protector of human life as well as "friend to the Indian," whose interests the US government had failed to honor.[20] He fought to defend Indian land rights, and made a special effort to ensure that whites who exploited Native people by stealing their property or selling them alcohol received maximum sentences.

Judge Parker worked to provide equal protection for Native people, particularly when they were victims of crimes by white men. In the winter of 1895, James Davenport, a well-known white lawyer and landowner, shot and killed William Goforth, his Cherokee tenant, claiming he acted in self-defense. Since Davenport's wife was Cherokee, he was considered a member of the tribe, but his status as a US citizen placed him under Judge Parker's jurisdiction. At trial that spring, Judge Parker reminded the jury that, regardless of social status and public esteem, "All men stand upon the same plane before [the law]."[21] He also invoked the jury's responsibility to provide justice to William Goforth, who was "as much entitled to the full power of this protecting agency called the law as you are, or I."[22]

While it was up to juries to determine whether the conditions under which a homicide took place constituted actual danger to the defendant, it was a judge's duty to instruct the jury on the distinctions between different types of homicide. Although many of his contemporaries perceived it a man's "natural right" to meet force with force, Judge Parker saw things differently. For him, lethal self-defense clashed with the law's respect for human life. In the Davenport case, his instructions to the jury took up fifty-five pages of the stenographer's court record.[23] He explained that a defendant's perceived "state of real danger or actual danger, or deadly danger, or danger of great violence to the person . . . must be actual" in order for a lethal crime to constitute justifiable homicide. In Parker's eyes, a defendant could not claim self-defense unless the deadly danger was imminent, "then and there impending and about to fall, so near thereto as that the defendant could not avoid it."[24]

Invoking the much-maligned obligation of retreat, Parker explained that a faultless individual attacked "in a violent way—under such circumstances which denote an intention to take away his life, or to do him some serious bodily harm . . . may lawfully kill his assailant, *provided he use all means in his power otherwise* to save his life or prevent the intended harm, *such as retreating as far as he can* or disabling his adversary without killing him, if it be in his power." Nowhere in his instructions did the judge acknowledge a right to "stand one's ground" and meet force with force if assailed. In fact, Parker believed that one's duty to retreat—to avoid conflict to the best of one's ability—triumphed over one's right to self-protection: "All the time that he is seeking to protect this great right that belongs to him, *there is never a moment* when this duty leaves him. The duty of using less violence than that which produces death . . . the duty of *getting out of the way* of the deadly danger . . . because if he can save a human life his duty to society calls him to do so."[25] Parker's instructions suggested that Davenport had not done all in his power to avoid the violent affray, and the jury found him guilty of manslaughter. He was sentenced to seven years in prison and fined five hundred dollars.[26]

Davenport appealed his case to the Supreme Court, which found Judge Parker's instructions on the duty to retreat to be in error.[27] The case was remanded for retrial in 1897, and Davenport was acquitted of murdering Goforth.[28] This homicide case did not hinder the future success of "Sunny Jim" Davenport, later celebrated for his kind disposition and sense of humor. He joined the Cherokee National Council and was elected mayor of Vinita, Kansas, before serving in Congress as a Democratic representative from Oklahoma, from 1911 to 1917. After returning to Vinita to practice law, Davenport was elected as a judge on the Criminal Court of Appeals, where he served until his death, in 1940. Oddly, Davenport's 1895 killing of William Goforth receives no mention in the popular histories documenting his life.[29] This historical silence attests to the established nature of a white man's right to use deadly force to protect himself, and perhaps also to the lesser value ascribed to the short life of William Goforth.

While Judge Parker's jury instructions invoked the sanctity of human life, he was known as the "Hanging Judge" for sentencing over 160 people to the gallows. Parker's supporters attributed his punitive attitude to his determination to impose law and order in a persistently lawless region where "criminal elements" ran rampant. According to attorney S. W. Harman, Parker took seriously his duty "to run down and ferret out those of the criminal classes in the Indian Territory who were too much hardened."[30]

And yet, some of the young men who came before Judge Parker in the 1890s were a far cry from "hardened criminals." Alexander Allen was a relative newcomer to this part of "Indian Country," having recently moved from his parents' home some twenty miles to the north to work on the farm of Albert Marks. Alexander had just turned fourteen when he came before Judge Parker's court for the murder of eighteen-year-old Phillip Henson in May 1892.

It was a warm spring morning when Alexander set off to locate several horses that had wandered away from the farm. Twelve-year-old James, one of Marks's sons, accompanied Alexander on his journey. The sight of two Black boys, carrying horse halters with a length of rope for a lead, would not have seemed unusual to residents of the borderlands where southern Kansas and northern Cherokee Territory met. In spite of the land's allocation for Native people forcibly relocated from the Southeast following the Indian Removal Act of 1830, non-Native people began settling on the land long before the Civil War. Many had purchased tracts for farming, establishing permanent settlements along the borders in what would later become the state of Oklahoma.

This territory had particular appeal for "exodusters," Black migrants fleeing the white supremacist violence and disenfranchisement of the Deep South following the end of Reconstruction. The triumph of "Redemption"—the white South's recovery of power in the wake of the Compromise of 1877—resulted in Black repression in the form of state-level exclusionary innovations that effectively undermined the three Reconstruction amendments. Along with the widespread threat of violence, vagrancy laws, poll taxes, literacy tests, and quasi-slave-labor conditions helped maintain a system of racial caste in which African Americans remained excluded from the rights, privileges, and protections of full citizenship. Albert Marks and his family were among the estimated forty thousand African Americans who left the South in the 1870s to venture west, hoping to find relative safety and economic opportunity on the Great Plains.[31] It was through this cultural and geographical borderland—a space of racial intermingling and social fluidity—that Alexander and James searched for the missing horses. Before long, they encountered three white youths: eighteen-year-old Phillip Henson, planting watermelon seeds on his family's farm, and his cousins, George and Willie Erne, who lived nearby. The proximity of the Henson farm to Marks's—just a few miles apart—made it likely that the boys were familiar with each other.

It is clear from the outcome of their exchange that there was significant ill will, at least on the part of Phillip. When Alexander asked the three boys if they had seen the missing horses, Phillip's response betrayed his animosity. He approached the two younger boys, shouting insults and threats. He did not wish to be addressed familiarly by presumptuous "niggers," whose work was of no concern to him. Perhaps he also resented the boys' freedom of mobility and access to property. For though both the Henson and Marks families leased, rather than owned, their farms, there is evidence that Alexander was better educated and possibly better dressed than the white boys. The son of a North Carolina farmer who moved west in search of a better future for his children, Alexander had learned to read and write before taking the job on the Marks family farm. Case evidence suggests he was also wearing shoes, while the white boys were barefoot.[32]

Phillip and his companions responded to Alexander's query by chasing him and James with sticks, threatening to "kill a nigger" and to seek them out on Saturday "to settle with [them]."[33] Later, in court, the Erne boys would confirm that insults were exchanged in this first encounter, but they would not expound upon the precise content.

The details of what happened between Phillip and Alexander two days later would become the subject of much debate in the western circuit court of Fort Smith, Arkansas. Conflicting witness testimonies make it difficult to know for certain who instigated the confrontation. When the pair met again, this time on the outskirts of the Marks farm, a lethal fight ensued. Alexander fired several shots from a pistol he had borrowed that morning, after which Phillip Henson lay bleeding to death on the ground.

Alexander Allen's homicide case came before Judge Parker and was appealed to the Supreme Court three times before its resolution in December 1896.[34] The case's back-and-forth journey between the western circuit court and the Supreme Court coincided with several other significant cases, including James Davenport's, involving lethal self-defense. According to legal scholar David Kopel, *Allen v. United*

States was among several key self-defense cases in the 1890s that helped pave the way for the 1921 Supreme Court case of *Brown v. United States*, which effectively eliminated the duty to retreat.[35]

But Alexander Allen's case was unique. While other cases that appeared before the Supreme Court supported a man's right to use lethal violence against an attack, the outcome of Allen's case would appear to challenge this right. As an African American teenager claiming self-defense in the killing of an older, white youth, Allen's actions collided with the nation's preoccupation with white masculine vulnerability. His case illuminates the racial implications of violence and criminality at the turn of the century, where Black masculinity, even in an adolescent, signified pathological violence in the white imagination. At a time when "true manhood" evoked white, property-owning citizenship and belonging, race shaped the complex boundaries differentiating legitimate self-defense from murder.

Allen's case was in many ways similar to the hundreds of other homicide cases that came across Judge Parker's desk during his twenty-one-year tenure, in that the judge did all in his power to discredit the defendant's right to use lethal self-defense, regardless of the defendant's race. During this time, 344 capital cases came before Judge Parker's court, resulting in 161 murder convictions; and 79 people met their deaths on the gallows of Fort Smith.[36] Taken in the context of other capital cases appealed before the Supreme Court during this time, Allen's stands out, revealing the contested status of self-defense ideals in this western, racially variegated borderland. In spite of Judge Parker's efforts to curtail the use of lethal self-defense, the right to stand one's ground was becoming more widespread, but only for a select few.

"Mere Words Alone Do not Excuse Even a Simple Assault": Race and the Perception of Threat

Alexander Allen was unarmed when he set out to perform his chores on May 12, 1892. Both he and James Marks testified in court that Phillip Henson used "threats and oaths" and language of "great bitterness" in their first encounter.[37] By the time they met again, two days later, Alexander was carrying a six-shooter. Earlier that morning, James's grandfather had instructed Alexander to retrieve a pistol from his overcoat and to take it with him during his errands. James or Alexander must have told him about the earlier encounter, and he took seriously the threats Phillip had made against the younger boys. Having lived most his life in the Deep South, Mr. Marks no doubt was well acquainted with white-on-Black violence and the law's persistent failure to protect African Americans from lynching and other forms of routinized, extralegal violence. For his part, Alexander complied with the older man's suggestion, and took the pistol along on his errands.

On May 14, when the boys met on the boundary of the Marks farm, Alexander was accompanied by eleven-year-old Harvey Marks. Witnesses' testimony clashed on the matter of who instigated the conflict, but a scuffle between Phillip, the Erne boys, and Alexander ensued, in which the latter shot and killed Phillip. Alexander fled to Edna, Kansas, where he was arrested and brought to Arkansas to be tried for murder. He was held in the Fort Smith jailhouse to await his trial, set for February 1893.

In the courtroom, Judge Parker's lengthy instructions to the jury made clear his position that his court would treat this and all homicide cases with gravity. He asked:

> When can a man slay another? When can he sit as a judge passing upon the law, and a jury passing on the facts, ... and then going out as a marshal or sheriff and executing that judgment, all at the same time— determining the law, determining the facts as judge, jury, and executioner all at the same time?[38]

For Parker, the assumption of these manifold responsibilities constituted "a mighty power in the hands of the citizen," one that was only to be used on behalf of "the law of necessity" when one's "own life is either actually or really in deadly peril from which he cannot escape except by the use of that deadly means."[39] The "law of self-defense" in a civilized world was only to be "execute[d] for the sake of society, for protection ... against the acts of violence of the wicked, which would destroy their rights to their property, jeopardize their liberties, and destroy their lives."[40] The judge's instructions emphasized the extreme nature of the conditions under which such a "mighty power" could exist. In Judge Parker's eyes, the conditions of "deadly peril" were not present when Alexander Allen took Phillip Henson's life.

Court records attest to the difficulty of establishing Alexander's culpability beyond a reasonable doubt. According to Harvey Marks's testimony, he and Alexander had been working near the Markses' hog pen when Phillip and the Erne brothers approached them with sharpened sticks. When Alexander asked what they wanted, Phillip said they had come to "kill a nigger."[41] Harvey testified that the white boys approached him and Alexander aggressively, crossing over the property line into Marks territory and then attacking them with sticks. According to Harvey, it was only when the three white boys were on top of Alexander that he fired the pistol, killing Phillip.

Thirteen-year-old Willie Erne, who took the stand for the prosecution, testified that it was Alexander who had pursued him and the other two boys, and that they had merely "crossed north of the [Markses'] yard" on their way to go fishing. According to Willie, they had been searching near the Marks farm for frogs to bait their fishhooks when Alexander climbed over the Markses' fence and threatened them with his pistol. The court established that Alexander and Phillip had "exchanged words" several days before the deadly encounter, but only James referred to any explicitly threatening content in Phillip's remarks. Conflicting stories of instigation and different scales of weaponry and perceived threat dogged this jury, which nevertheless convicted Alexander of murder and sentenced him to the gallows. He appealed the case to the Supreme Court.[42]

Just as Alexander was appealing his murder conviction, a similar case arrived in Judge Parker's court. Seventeen-year-old Thomas Thompson was a Creek Indian who lived and worked on the farm of Sam Haynes, also of the Creek nation. In June 1893, Thompson shot and killed a white man named Charles Hermes in Creek Territory, about one hundred miles south of where Alexander Allen shot Phillip Henson. Like Allen, Thompson claimed self-defense and insisted that he had armed himself in response to prior threats from the deceased. Like Allen, Thompson was performing errands for his employer when his deadly confrontations took place, and he also reported having been taunted with racial epithets and threatened with death in an earlier encounter with the deceased. In Thompson's case, too, Judge Parker urged the jury to reject the defendant's self-defense plea, and the jury found Thompson guilty of murder.[43] Thompson, too, appealed to the Supreme Court, and his case was remanded for a retrial.

When Thompson set out on horseback on the afternoon of June 8 in 1893, he was carrying a package that Mrs. Haynes had asked him to deliver to a neighbor a few miles away. About half a mile into his ride, Thompson encountered Jacob Hermes and his two grown sons, planting corn in a field next to the road. Hermes was a white farmer who rented his land from Sam Haynes, and he had several times expressed animosity toward Thompson. He suspected that Thompson had injured his hogs, and witnesses testified that the older man had threatened to "chop his head open" if he "came acting the monkey around him any more."[44] As Thompson approached on horseback, Hermes and his sons shouted insults and accusations. Knowing little English, Thompson nevertheless recognized their threats and accusations about killing hogs. He sped off to his destination, delivered the package, and then deliberated on how to return safely since the only viable path home was by the Hermes farm.

Thompson made a detour to borrow a Winchester rifle from a friend. Like Alexander Allen, he did not want to face his adversaries unarmed. As he neared the Hermes farm, Thompson saw the two sons plowing the field, and heard their father shout something about a gun. Charles, one of Hermes's sons, started toward a gun that was leaning in the corner of the fence, and Thompson shot him before speeding away on horseback. The elder Mr. Hermes gave chase, firing his rifle at the fleeing man.

As in Allen's case, the jury found Thompson guilty of murder and sentenced him to hang. He also appealed to the Supreme Court. In both cases, the higher court ruled Judge Parker in error in his jury instructions. In Allen's first appeal in 1893, the Supreme Court took issue with

Judge Parker's reference to the possible state of mind of the defendant, which was "to hazard the substitution of abstract conceptions for the actual facts of the particular case as they appeared to the defendant at the time."[45] For the majority of the court, Judge Parker's lengthy rumination on lethal self-defense was "too metaphysical" and distracted the jury from the facts at hand.

The Supreme Court's 1894 decision on *Thompson v. United States* found Judge Parker in error on several points, some of which overlapped with errors stated in Allen's case. The judge had argued that Thompson relinquished his claims to self-defense when he armed himself and rode near the Hermes farm. Given Mr. Hermes's earlier threats and the fact that the road was the only available route home, the Supreme Court took issue with Parker's suggestion that Thompson's actions were necessarily evidence of "malice aforethought."[46] Further, the court affirmed the relationship between "previous threats" made against the defendant and the defendant's decision to arm himself. Thompson's case went to retrial at Fort Smith, where the jury acquitted him of murder.[47]

Although many of the circumstances were similar to Thompson's case, Allen's retrial that same year yielded a very different result, a murder conviction, and again he appealed to the Supreme Court. This time, the Court found Judge Parker in error in his instructions that one who arms himself in advance of the deadly encounter has demonstrated "a purpose to kill." Further, Judge Parker had "misled the jury" by suggesting that the sharpened sticks the three white boys had used to threaten Allen could not be considered deadly weapons.[48] Once again, the court remanded a retrial.

In Allen's third trial, Judge Parker instructed the jury that "mere words were not sufficient to reduce the crime from murder to manslaughter," and that, in order to qualify as self-defense "something more than an ordinary assault" had to have been made on the defendant to justify his shooting Henson. While he did not invoke a duty to retreat, Judge Parker explained that an assault made on the defendant "would lead a reasonable person to believe that his life was in peril" before he could legally fight back with lethal violence.[49] For the third time, Allen was convicted of murder.

All told, Allen appealed his case to the Supreme Court three times. On the third appeal, in 1896, the court affirmed the lower court's decision. In the eyes of the Fort Smith jury, and in the eyes of the nation's highest court, the verbal taunts Alexander had received from Henson did *not* constitute a reasonable threat. Nor was it "reasonable" for Allen to have believed his life was in danger when Henson and the Erne boys approached him with sharpened sticks on that morning in May. The Supreme Court affirmed the lower court's guilty verdict, and Alexander Allen was sentenced to death.

Less than twenty years earlier, the *Erwin* and *Runyan* cases had established lethal self-defense as a natural right, beyond the boundaries of a man's home, as long as the defendant occupied a space where he had a right to be. And in Runyan's case, it was deemed acceptable to arm oneself after being threatened. But the exculpatory claims of "true manhood" would apply selectively. The limitations on African Americans' and women's access to the rights and protections of full citizenship helped code self-defense as a right of white masculinity. Following these landmark decisions, individual states began expanding the boundaries of justifiable homicide, removing it from the confines of one's home and chipping away at the duty to retreat. By the early twentieth century, most states had determined that "a man who is without fault need not retreat but may stand his ground and, if necessary to preserve his life, kill his adversary."[50] Francis Wharton, a specialist in criminal law, wrote in 1907 that "the law of self-defense is founded upon necessity," and one's "reasonable" perception that one's life is in imminent danger.[51] For Wharton and many others at the turn of the century, the "true man's" right to protect himself, as well as his family and property, hinged on beliefs that lethal violence was necessary to protect oneself in a rapidly changing, increasingly dangerous nation.

Yet the *Thompson* and *Allen* cases stand out for shedding light on the racial implications of self-defense at the turn of the twentieth century. Both defendants were nonwhite youths who shot and killed older white men in territory far outside either's "castle." In fact, neither defendant was in possession of a "castle" as both were propertyless employees on other men's farms. While they could not claim to have been protecting

property, they did invoke self-defense as their right, given the dangerous circumstances they had found themselves in prior to the deadly
encounter. Unarmed in that first encounter, they borrowed weapons
only after being threatened by the deceased. In each case, witnesses testified that the deceased threatened to kill the defendants, and that their
threats had contained racial epithets.

But Judge Parker did not consider these prior threats relevant to
the defense. In fact, the existence of prior threats subjected the defendants to harsher scrutiny, as the judge suggested that both homicides
resulted from the defendants' desire for retribution. In instructions to
both juries, he argued that "mere words alone do not excuse even a
simple assault." His dismissal of threats as "mere words" and emphasis on retribution downplayed the menacing effects of language against
racially targeted people. And while the Supreme Court took issue with
Judge Parker's logic in Thompson's case, they affirmed it in Allen's. Ultimately, neither Allen nor Thompson would be executed or lynched
for having killed white men. President Grover Cleveland commuted Allen's death sentence to life imprisonment in February 1897. Thompson
eventually went free after his successful appeal to the Supreme Court.

"A MIND DELIBERATELY BENT ON MISCHIEF": PREMEDITATION AND THE POLITICS OF MASCULINE VULNERABILITY

While the outcomes of the cases diverged significantly, the Supreme
Court's decisions reflect prevailing beliefs in self-defense as a natural
right and its disapproval of Judge Parker's efforts to discredit that right.
In both cases, the higher court found Judge Parker in error in his assertions to the jury that having previously armed oneself with a deadly
weapon disqualified one from a self-defense plea. They cited the case
of *Gourko v. United States*, which also took place in Indian Territory
and went before Judge Parker's court. In November 1892, two men "of
Polish nativity" quarreled in a public space before one shot the other.
Similar to Allen and Thompson, nineteen-year-old John Gourko had
armed himself only after being threatened and verbally harassed by a

larger, older man. Forty-year-old Peter Carbo allegedly threatened "to shoot John like a dog" after a heated encounter outside a post office. Court records described Carbo as an intimidating man and "a dangerous character."[52]

Parker's instructions to the jury suggested that Gourko's decision to arm himself after his hostile encounter with Carbo amounted to "malice aforethought necessary for murder." According to Parker, "Where deliberation, premeditation upon a purpose to slay, where previous preparation to execute that purpose exists, there is banished from the case that condition known as manslaughter, because that grows into existence upon sudden impulse, without previous impulse to take life." For Parker, arming oneself and killing after a verbal squabble evinced "a heart regardless of social duty, and a mind deliberately bent on mischief."[53] In Parker's mind, Gourko's actions made him a murderer, rather than a law-abiding citizen trying to protect himself.

As in Allen's and Thompson's cases, Gourko was initially pronounced guilty of murder, and he appealed to the Supreme Court. In April 1894, Justice Harlan's opinion held Parker's court in error: "A person who has an angry altercation with another person, such as to lead him to believe that he may require the means of self-defence in case of another encounter, may be justified, in the eye of the law, in arming himself for self-defence."[54] The highest court determined that arming oneself after being threatened did not automatically disqualify one from justifiable homicide in self-defense.

The Supreme Court ruled similarly in both Allen's and Thompson's cases, finding in error Judge Parker's instructions that arming oneself after a confrontation constituted malice aforethought. While Parker had instructed all three juries similarly on the defendants' decisions to arm themselves, he addressed the issue of prior threats differently. Parker urged both Allen's and Thompson's juries to discount the verbal threats made against the defendants. In Thompson's case, he argued, "You cannot kill a man because of previous threats. You cannot weigh in the balance a human life against a threat. There is no right of that kind in law."[55] And in both cases, the judge depicted the threats from white men against Allen and Thompson as provocation for the youths' violence and "spite," rather than justification for their decision to arm themselves.

In a book published shortly after Judge Parker's death, attorney S. W. Harman, a close friend and admirer of Isaac Parker, described both Allen and Thompson as aggressors, as young criminals looking for trouble when they heartlessly gunned down their victims. In Harman's account, "Thompson rode by the [Hermes] field and gave a shout, which was meant as a challenge, a sign of defiance. Then he rode away and armed himself and returned to the vicinity and while Charles Hermes was in the act of turning his horse at the side of the field, Thompson shot him."[56] This characterization contradicts witness testimony, which portrayed Thompson as a peaceable young man, responsibly fulfilling his duty when the first confrontation occurred.

Harman similarly described Allen as the aggressor in his confrontation with Henson. Allen, as a "member of a despised race," was at fault:

> Believing everybody his avowed enemy, without a mind development capable of analyzing the intent of any who might attempt to approach him, he resented every speech that seemed like undue familiarity, misconstrued every act of a stranger, imagined that his rights were being imposed upon, and from out the morose disposition thus developed his first thought, where other and better trained boys would have laughed heartily at a joke, was to kill.[57]

It was, in short, Allen's inability to see Phillip Henson's threats as harmless jokes that provoked him to seek vengeance.

In stark contrast to his descriptions of Allen and Thompson as aggressors rather than targets, Harman depicted James Davenport, the white landowner who shot and killed the Cherokee tenant farmer William Goforth, as "a fine looking white man [who was] considered a good citizen."[58] Davenport was eventually acquitted on appeal, for witnesses testified that Goforth's actions suggested intent against Davenport in the moment that the two scuffled. The *Davenport* case saw a white, propertied "good citizen" killing a Native American tenant farmer in legitimate self-defense. The *Allen* case reversed the direction of deadly threat with a Black boy shooting an older white youth in an act that was ultimately judged to be murder.

Characterizations of the defendants' malicious intent toward the deceased were not present in *Gourko*. The threatening speech and superior size of the deceased, Peter Carbo, were recurring themes throughout. The *Gourko* jury was swayed by several witnesses' claims about his vulnerability as "a teenager in delicate health who weighed about 135 pounds," being threatened by "the deceased, who was over 200 lbs and possessed extraordinary physical strength."[59] Court records indicate that—as in the *Allen* and *Thompson* cases—the deceased threatened the defendant's life while applying to Gourko "epithets of the most degrading kind, and which need not be here repeated." Gourko, Allen, and Thompson had all been subject to verbal threats prior to their deadly encounters. In Gourko's appeal, as in Thompson's, the Supreme Court considered prior threats not as evidence of "malice aforethought" but as legitimate grounds for arming oneself. Testimony about Gourko's relative physical vulnerability and the fact that many believed him to be "a quiet, peaceable boy" likely swayed the jury.

After the Supreme Court found Judge Parker's instructions in error, Gourko's case was retried, and he was found guilty of manslaughter and sentenced to four years in prison. James Davenport, who had killed William Goforth in 1895, was acquitted on retrial after the Supreme Court held Judge Parker's court in error for mandating retreat in the face of an attack. In contrast, Alexander Allen's case was appealed to the Supreme Court three times, the third confirming the lower court's murder conviction. Judge Parker would not live to see the case carried through to its conclusion, as he died in November 1896, having served on the Fort Smith circuit court for twenty-one years. Acting on the recommendation of Judge Parker's own court and the Fort Smith district attorney, President Cleveland spared Allen the death penalty. It is likely that the defendant's youth at the time of the shooting played a significant factor in this decision.[60]

In another 1895 case appealed from Fort Smith, the Supreme Court appeared to contradict its opinion in *Allen*. This case involved a white man named Babe Beard, who killed his nephew Will Jones in a fight over a cow. The defendant claimed self-defense based on prior threats from Will Jones that he would kill Beard if he did not relinquish the cow. On the day of the confrontation, Will Jones and his brothers, one carrying a shotgun, approached Beard on his own property and demanded the cow. In the struggle that ensued, Beard hit Jones on the head with his shotgun, inflicting a wound that resulted in the latter's death. In court, Judge Parker remained true to his consistent opposition to lethal self-defense, instructing the jury that the defendant had an obligation to try to get out of the way of danger. Beard was convicted of manslaughter and sentenced to eight years in prison.

On appeal to the Supreme Court, Justice Harlan countered,

A man may repel force by force, in defence of his person, habitation or property, against one who manifestly intends or endeavors, by violence or surprise, to commit a known felony, such as murder, rape, robbery, arson, burglary, and the like, upon either. In these cases he is not obliged to retreat, but may pursue his adversary until he has secured himself from all danger; and if he kill him in so doing it is called justifiable self-defence.[61]

Beard's case was remanded for retrial, and he was acquitted in February 1896, several months before the Supreme Court affirmed the Fort Smith court's murder conviction for Alexander Allen.

As with the cases of Allen, Thompson, Davenport, and Gourko, Beard's case turned on notions of a man's right to "repel force by force" outside the confines of his home. Beard's was the only case in which the killing occurred on the defendant's property, but the others involved a different but equally authoritative form of property—the exonerating power of white masculinity itself. Contemporary legal scholars remain confounded by the contradictions inherent in the Supreme Court's numerous challenges to Judge Parker's invocation of the duty to retreat but in the end to allow Alexander Allen, just fourteen years old when he shot his older assailant, to be convicted for murder.[62] In the end, although the Supreme Court took seriously the business of providing a fair hearing for all citizens, justice was far from color-blind.

In spite of his oft-celebrated reputation for consistency in his defiance of liberal self-defense, Judge Parker's instructions to the third Allen jury betrayed his biases against the defendant. In his explication of manslaughter versus murder, Parker characterized the former as the absence of "malice aforethought," whereas murder evinced "a heart void of social duty, and a mind fatally bent upon mischief." For Allen's crime to have qualified as manslaughter rather than murder, Henson must have "offer[ed] some provocation to produce a certain condition of mind." Further, that provocation could not have been in the form of "mere words," such as the ones uttered at their earlier encounter. Parker reasoned that Henson's threats to "kill a nigger" and to seek Allen out later and "settle with him"—based on testimony from two young Black witnesses—did not constitute a legitimate provocation to downgrade Allen's sentence from murder to manslaughter. What had been for Beard and Carbo a reasonable response to verbal threats had been proof that Allen's mind was "bent on mischief."[63] The jury confirmed its assent by convicting Allen for murder for the third and final time.

According to legal scholar David Kopel, the successful appeals of self-defense cases like Allen's and Thompson's stand as evidence that the Supreme Court "stood up again and again for the rights of Blacks, American Indians, and other outsiders" in the same era when their infamous *Plessy v. Ferguson* decision legalized racial segregation.[64] The Supreme Court's inclination to find the Parker court in error twice on Allen's case suggests that the justices considered self-defense an inviolable right. Yet the cases' divergent outcomes—Allen's lifetime imprisonment for murder compared to Gourko's four-year sentence for manslaughter and Beard's and Thompson's acquittal—suggest wider perceptions that self-defense was a right only for certain men under particular circumstances.

By the early twentieth century, propertied white men were granted increasing liberty in lethal self-defense, even when their confrontations took place on public property. In 1921, the Supreme Court would effectively eliminate the duty to retreat in *Brown v. United States*. Delivering the majority opinion, Justice Oliver Wendell Holmes ruled that "if a man reasonably believes that he is in immediate danger of death or grievous bodily injury from his assailant, he may stand his ground and that if he kills him he has not exceeded the bounds of lawful self-defense." He famously added, "Detached reflection cannot be demanded in the presence of an uplifted knife."[65] This rhetoric would appear to vindicate Allen, who was a forty-four-year-old resident of the federal penitentiary in Fulton County, Georgia, at the time. Then again, legal interpretations of the highest court's mandate to excuse homicides committed under "reasonable belief" of threat would be upheld only selectively, and the right of citizens to protect themselves restricted to a privileged few.

FOUR

"Queer Justice" and the Sexual Politics of Lynching

Fundamentally men have an inherent right to defend
themselves when lawful authority refuses to do it for them.

—IDA B. WELLS, 1891

Have mercy on the poor, the weak, the innocent and defenseless,
and deliver us from the body of the Black Death. In a land of light
and beauty and love, our women are prisoners of danger and fear.

—THOMAS DIXON, 1905

As state and federal courts affirmed lethal self-defense as a necessity for "true" white masculinity, extralegal, racist violence became routine, particularly in the South. From 1877 to 1950, approximately four thousand African Americans lost their lives to lynch mobs.[1] And while most victims were men, very few of whom were formally accused of a violent crime, women and children were also victims of mob violence. In 2015, the Equal Justice Initiative (EJI), a nonprofit organization created to provide underserved communities with legal support, compiled an in-depth study of lynching in twelve Southern states. Their findings suggest that "racial terror"—the effort to fortify the color line and maintain the social and economic subservience of Black people—was the primary motivation of lynching.[2] The practice of extralegal racist violence depended on African Americans' exclusion from the equal protection of courts and law enforcement, which in turn prohibited them from defending themselves against white supremacist violence. Lynching served both as a means of maintaining African American submission to white supremacist power structures and of disseminating the propaganda of white vulnerability.

The EJI's emphasis on terror highlights the ways in which mob violence isolated citizens from equal protection and justice. Stories of lynchings and their aftermaths circulated widely in Black public memory, serving as enduring reminders of the distorted justice that criminalized African Americans while excluding them from the rights, privileges, and protections of full citizenship.[3] And while most lynchings occurred in the states of the former Confederacy, the practice received the tacit approval of the North as necessary to the defense of white womanhood. White supremacist reinventions of public memory were vital to maintaining a sexualized fantasy of African American criminality and white vulnerability.

"THE PROPAGANDA OF HISTORY": COLLECTIVE MEMORIES OF REVERSE VICTIMIZATION

W. E. B. Du Bois named the final chapter of his foundational work *Black Reconstruction* "The Propaganda of History" to show how "the facts of American history . . . have been falsified" to convince the population that the Civil War and Reconstruction had subjugated white Southerners.[4] Many white authors of the time, such as William L. G. Smith, Thomas Nelson Page, Mary H. Eastman, and William Gilmore Simms, romanticized the Old South as a place of peaceable social order, governed gently by benevolent whites. Confederate president Jefferson Davis also wrote popular histories propagating the myth of the "Old South" as an idyllic space in which whites and Blacks lived in symbiotic harmony.[5] His multivolume work *The Rise and Fall of the Confederate Government* echoed popular plantation literature and characterized slavery as a benign institution that rescued enslaved people from "heathen darkness" and "the torrid plains and malarial swamps of inhospitable Africa."[6] Once transferred to the American South, these unfortunate souls were "trained in the gentle arts of peace and order and civilization; they increased from a few unprofitable savages to millions of efficient Christian laborers. Their servile instincts rendered them content with their lot." According to Davis, "A strong mutual affection was the natural result of this life-long relation" between master and slave, and "never was there a happier dependence of labor and capital upon each other."[7]

In contrast to the peaceful spirit of the old plantation, Reconstruction signified a "hostile demonstration against the people and States of the deceased Confederacy."[8] For Davis and many other authors of popular history, the emancipation of slaves had been achieved only at the cost of "the enslavement of the free citizens of the South."[9] According to these narratives, the federal government trampled on the Constitution by challenging slavery and seeking to prevent its spread into the western territories. Furthermore, argued the Democratic statesman and popular historian Claude Bowers, freed people's natural barbarity made them a threat to themselves and to civilized society. According to Bowers, whose primary source was Southern newspapers, "The Southern people [were] literally put to the torture" and subject to "poisonous propaganda" under Reconstruction.[10]

Northern-born William Dunning would become one of the most influential American historians of the turn of the twentieth century. He helped found the American Historical Association and became its president in 1913. His work contributed to widespread beliefs that Reconstruction was a violation of Southern citizens' rights and safety.[11] He also praised the institution of Black Codes, disenfranchisement, and other methods of instituting de facto slavery. His work minimized Southern violence against freed people while emphasizing the harm done by federal military reconstruction in the South. In spite of Du Bois's efforts to expose the white supremacist roots of these and other betrayals of history, the Dunning school of thought on the Civil War and its aftermath enjoyed popularity and intellectual hegemony throughout much of the twentieth century.

Histories of imperiled whiteness spurred the establishment of organizations to honor the Confederacy. The United Daughters of the Confederacy (UDC) was created in 1894 by Southern white women who had supported Confederate soldiers during the war. Among the oldest of the nation's "patriotic lineage organizations," the UDC memorializes the heroism of the Confederate cause. Since its founding, the UDC's objectives have included "historical, benevolent, educational, memorial, and patriotic" goals, as well as an effort "to honor the memory of those who served and those who fell in the service of the Confederate States" and "to collect and preserve the material for a truthful history of the War Between the States."[12]

Over the years, the UDC's "true history" has emphasized Southern self-determination and the heroic struggle to defend the region's independence, while obfuscating the brutal realities of slavery. UDC and other Southern heritage organizations, like the Sons of the Confederacy, have erected hundreds of monuments celebrating Southern heroism and defiance. An obelisk erected in 1911 in Montezuma, Georgia, carries a plaque that reads "Macon County holds in proud and grateful remembrance her brave and loyal sons who preferred death to betrayal of her principles."[13] Another monument constructed that year consists of a figure of a Confederate soldier atop a twenty-foot pedestal in the Star City, Arizona, town square. More recently, in 2010, the Confederate Secret Service Camp sponsored a monument memorializing "Arizona's Confederate Veterans Who Sacrificed All in the Struggle for Independence and the Constitutional Right of Self-Government."[14] The memorials celebrate bravery, honor, loyalty, and sacrifice; they omit any mention of slavery.

Intentionally placed in spaces of civic activity, usually in town squares and in front of courthouses, the monuments provide persistent reminders of a glorious past that never existed. Bryan Stevenson, founder of the EJI, grew up in Montgomery, where fifty-nine monuments celebrate the "courage" and "tenacity" of Confederate leaders. In the process of romanticizing the bravery of Confederate heroes, explains Stevenson, who is descended from slaves, "we have completely eliminated the reality that created the Civil War." Taken together, the war memorials, popular histories, and literature depicting a benevolent Old South idealize the "architects of slavery, the defenders of slavery."[15]

According to historian David Blight, reimagining the war and masking the violence of slavery were vital to forging national reconciliation.[16] A manufactured memory of heroic white Southerners—who had sacrificed their lives in defense of their honor—laid the ethical foundation for white reconciliation at the expense of Black citizenship. The defeated South, analogized as a dishonored but defiant white woman, became a familiar image that whites on both sides of the Mason-Dixon Line understood.

"HISTORICAL ROMANCE": WHITE
SELF-DEFENSE IN POPULAR CULTURE

Much of the literature and popular culture of the early twentieth century, such as films and novels, equated white femininity with sexual vulnerability and Black masculinity with sexual violence. The association of lynching with the prevention of sexual violence ensured that the law would turn a blind eye as thousands of African Americans met their deaths for imagined crimes against white women.

Thomas Dixon's famous trilogy *The Clansman: An Historical Romance of the Ku Klux Klan* depicted a culture teetering in the balance, challenged by the chaos and criminality of Blacks liberated from the civilizing influence of slavery. Dixon's work helped Northern readers identify with the terrible suffering of white Southerners during Reconstruction, and his sensational depictions of Black men as constantly pursuing white women supported the prevailing mythology.

Dixon's 1905 novel narrates the postbellum story of white Southern political displacement through the lurid lens of sexual exploitation. The story takes place in a South ravaged by war and overrun by "Negro rule" and corrupt white sympathizers. The narrative crescendos when a Black man rapes a virtuous young white woman, who commits suicide rather than live with the stain of her violation. Dixon frames this crime against Southern white womanhood as the primary motivating force behind the Ku Klux Klan's emergence after the Civil War. In this retrospective story of the Civil War and its aftermath, the Klan provided a vital self-defensive response to so-called "Negro rule." The white woman's virtue, indeed the honor of the Old South itself, could only be avenged by the valiant hooded knights of the KKK.

Dixon's version of plantation romance was eventually adapted to film in 1915 by D. W. Griffith. The first American-made motion picture screened at the White House, *The Birth of a Nation* was an instant success across the nation, grossing more than any prior motion picture. In spite of nationwide protests by the NAACP, white audiences throughout the nation enjoyed the romantic depiction of the Old South. Whites also appreciated the compellingly comfortable retelling of the history of the Civil War, wherein the South's uniquely chivalrous way of life had supported a "natural" racial order that kept Black barbarity in check. The movie also played to white longings for national reconciliation, as the film ends with two marriages that unite families across the Mason-Dixon Line. The film retained the novel's salacious linkage between racial violence and rape, making the white supremacist backlash of the time seem both natural and necessary. Its success was at once a major contributor to and consequence of the Jim Crow regime of racial separation that prevailed nationwide. And the Ku Klux Klan would enjoy a resurgence, riding the tide of popularity fostered through the literary and filmic retelling of history.

"To Protect Woman's Dearest Possession": The Sex and Race of Lynching

Lynching's utility as a solution to white status anxiety was based on what historian Crystal Feimster calls the "rape/lynch narrative," which characterized Black men as sexual threats to white women. In spite of its inaccuracy, this prevalent myth united white men across class lines to protect their property interests, just as it elevated all white women to the status of "ladies," entitled to chivalric protection and respect.[17] Historian Nell Irvin Painter highlights the tight connection in white Southerners' minds between "social equality"—the inclusion of Blacks on an equal footing with whites—and the supposed sexual exploitation of white women by Black men.[18] This popular story resonated with nostalgia for a mythological Old South, where a rarely questioned social order prevailed. It also provoked race panic and mob violence among whites determined to maintain the racial hierarchy.[19]

The law carried few protections for Black self-defense against white supremacist violence as long as police, judges, and juries remained all white men. Further, mob violence designed to disfranchise and terrorize Blacks was often state-sanctioned and instigated, as in the New Orleans riot of 1866 and the Colfax Massacre of 1873 (discussed in chapter 2). In these and other cases, state and federal officials tasked with protecting the citizenry betrayed their obligations to uphold equal protection in order to discipline those who challenged white supremacy.

Under these circumstances, Black women remained especially vulnerable to sexual violence. In the wake of the war, Black women claimed new citizenship rights, such as the right to contract their own labor and to receive the equal protection of the law, but the states did little to enforce these new legal protections. State laws no longer imposed different sentences depending on the race of perpetrators and victims, but white men accused of raping Black women could expect to be acquitted.[20]

Even vicious gang rapes of Black women went unpunished when the perpetrators were white, as in the case of Rhoda Ann Childs in Henry County, Georgia. In 1866, Childs was abducted from her home by eight white men and brutally beaten and raped. Her rapists threatened to shoot her and her children since her husband had served in the "God damned Yankee Army."[21] During its initial heyday from 1866 until 1871, the Klan regularly engaged in sexual torture of Black men and women, often castrating men and raping women.[22] In spite of the Freedmen's Bureau's efforts to bring the perpetrators of such violent crimes to justice, white male law enforcement, judges, and juries resisted investigating and prosecuting white crimes against Black citizens.[23] The small numbers of white men who were convicted often appealed successfully and were exonerated.[24]

Conversely, Black men accused of attacking white women were almost always found guilty. Crystal Feimster argues that "a convergent set of racial and sexual fantasies" framed the Black man as a perpetual sexual threat to white women.[25] Rape statutes allowed juries tremendous leeway in determining whether a convicted rapist received the death penalty or life imprisonment, and Black men were punished much more harshly when convicted of raping white women.[26] Most Southern states imposed the death penalty for rape, but in practice, this penalty was most often reserved for Black men accused of raping white women.[27] Legal scholar Jennifer Wriggins asserts that "thirty-six percent of Black men who were convicted of raping white women were executed" between 1930 and 1967, compared with 2 percent of all defendants convicted of rape.[28] The rape/lynch narrative thus validated both a legal and an extralegal system to defend white women's sexual purity from perceived Black violations.

Rebecca Latimer Felton, a white suffragist from Georgia who later became the first woman appointed to the US Senate, expressed this sentiment in an August 1897 address to the Georgia Agricultural Society. Entitled "Women on the Farm," Felton's speech addressed the unique dangers facing poor white women and girls living unprotected in rural areas. Foremost among them was the Black man whose newfound political power and economic independence gave him "license to degrade and debauch" white women. She exhorted white men to seek justice beyond the courthouse and to "put a sheltering arm about innocence and virtue." For Felton, and for many others who contributed to the popularization of the rape/lynch myth, extralegal violence was an essential answer to the onslaught of Black men against white women: "If it needs lynching to protect woman's dearest possession from the ravening human beasts——then I say lynch, a thousand times a week if necessary."[29] While Felton's incendiary remarks received some criticism, the belief in Black men's predatory nature was already widespread.[30] The turn-of-the-century popular press regaled readers with stories of "Negro Rapists" and "Lustful Brutes," guilty of heinous crimes against white femininity.[31] Against this cultural backdrop, falsified claims against Black men were adjudicated by mobs of white men while violent crimes against Black women were rarely brought to justice.

"THE OLD THREAD-BARE LIE": IDA B. WELLS AND BLACK SELF-DEFENSE

Born to enslaved parents in 1862 in Holly Springs, Mississippi, Ida B. Wells was among the first to speak out publicly about the correlation of racial terror with false accusations of sexual violence and would become a preeminent opponent of lynching. Wells came into her activism at a young age, suing a railroad for forcing her from her seat in the first-class car and winning a temporary victory. She was active in the struggle for woman's suffrage and spoke out about the simultaneous impact of racism and sexism on Black women. Some of her early writings addressed Black women's resistance to their "wholesale contemptuous defamation" in a white patriarchal world.[32] Wells's experience suing the railroad—after her initial triumph, the railroad was acquitted on appeal—shook her faith in justice and American law. She wrote in 1887 about her mistaken belief that "the law was on our side and would, when we appealed to it, give us justice."[33]

Her cynicism regarding the law's failure to protect the rights of African Americans grew as she witnessed white supremacist violence in the South. In 1891, she published an editorial in the *Free Speech* commending the Black community's "retaliatory measures" in response to a lynching in Georgetown, Kentucky. Whites responded to her editorial by demanding that the *Free Speech* be closed down for supporting violence and lawlessness. Wells decried her white critics' hypocrisy, arguing that "fundamentally men have an inherent right to defend themselves when lawful authority refuses to do it for them. . . . The way to prevent retaliation is to prevent lynching."[34] For Wells, it was only "human nature" to defend oneself when the channels of justice remained selectively closed.

But it was in Memphis, Tennessee, that Wells witnessed the atrocity that transformed her into a public crusader against lynching. In 1889, one of Wells's friends, a successful businessman named Thomas Moss, opened the People's Grocery Company in a Black neighborhood near Memphis. By 1892 he had created robust competition with white-owned businesses. On March 5, a group of white men led by police officers attacked Moss's store.[35] In response, Moss's allies fired their guns, shooting three. Moss and thirty other Black men were charged with "rioting" and taken to jail.[36] Fearing reprisals, the county judge confiscated all firearms from the Tennessee Rifles Company, the city's Black military unit that had tried to defend the grocery store.[37] At the same time, white men and boys were told to arm themselves in preparation for confronting a Black mob, and they stormed into the Black neighborhood, loot-ing Moss's store.[38]

Early on March 9, a mob of white men broke Moss, Calvin McDow-ell, and Henry Stewart out of jail and lynched them. While white newspa-pers covering the event alleged that the victims had incited the violence, Wells and many other African Americans knew why the lynching took place: Moss and his colleagues had competed for a share of economic prosperity, and attempted to defend themselves from racist violence. Taken together, the men's defiant challenge to white economic power *and* to the white monopoly on lethal self-defense constituted unforgiv-able crimes. This event prompted Wells to publish her first antilynching article in the *Free Speech and Headlight*, in which she encouraged Black citizens to boycott white businesses and to "leave a town which will nei-ther protect our lives and property." Many followed her advice.[39]

Moss, McDowell, and Stewart had all been respected members of the Black community, and no one had accused them of rape. Yet even the editors of the "progressive" *Chicago Daily Tribune* responded to the tragedy by urging "the colored people of the South" to "warn their own people 'against the commission of those offenses which arouse popular passion.'"[40] Such elliptical references to rape as the unspeakable crime that necessitated white violence depended on public recognition and consent to the rape/lynch mythology, a shared agreement that white "popular passion" was justified in defense of white womanhood. In this distorted logic, lynchings served as both punishment for and deterrence against rape.

But Wells brazenly called out the rape/lynch association as mere camouflage. After the tragedy in Memphis, she asserted, "Nobody in this section believes the old thread-bare lie that Negro men assault white women. If Southern white men are not careful they will over-reach themselves and a conclusion will be reached which will be very damaging to the moral reputation of their women."[41] Her suggestion that white women willingly pursued relationships with Black men sub-verted the narrative of Southern chivalry, which placed white women on pedestals as virtuous upholders of racial purity. The white outcry against this allegation was fierce, and an angry mob burned the *Free Speech* headquarters. Wells was forced to leave the city or else face her own death by lynching.

Lynching rates peaked in 1892, with more than two hundred victims, the same year Wells published "Southern Horrors: Lynch Law in All Its Phases" in the *New York Age* under the pseudonym Exiled. So deeply entrenched was the idea of Black male criminality that even Frederick Douglass, before reading Wells's work, took for granted the Black man's commission of "the peculiar crime so often imputed to him."[42] But Wells attacked these claims, and the pernicious white supremacist logic that supported them. Her piece received international attention and was published later as a pamphlet.[43] According to Wells, "the South is shielding itself behind the plausible screen of defending the honor of its women." She reiterated her challenge to the sexual mythology behind whites' urgent "need" to lynch Black people, asserting that "white men lynch the offending Afro-American, not because he is a despoiler of virtue, but because he succumbs to the smiles of white women."[44] She described several cases where consensual relations with a white woman led to a Black man's incarceration or death.

Wells also highlighted cases in which Black women and girls were assaulted by white men, only to find the channels of justice closed to them. On an evening in Baltimore in 1891, "three white ruffians" attacked and raped a Black girl who had been out walking with "a young man of her own race." Although "it was a deed dastardly enough to arouse Southern blood, which gives its horror as an excuse for lawlessness," the perpetrators were all acquitted.[45]

The pamphlet *Southern Horrors* also called for armed Black self-defense, asserting that "the only times an Afro-American who was assaulted got away has been when he had a gun and used it in self-defense." She insisted that "a Winchester rifle should have a place of honor in every black home."[46] Wells eventually purchased a pistol so that she could defend herself against violence, "determined to sell [her] life as dearly as possible if attacked." She explained, "I felt if I could take one lyncher with me, this would even up the score a little bit."[47]

Her forced exile from the South placed Wells in the national spotlight as she embarked on a speaking tour throughout the North and eventually to Europe, where she worked to educate sympathetic whites. Historian Gail Bederman explains that, since most lynchings took place in the South, many Northerners were distanced from their actual brutality. Wells and other antilynching activists therefore shared detailed, often gruesome narratives with Northern audiences.[48] Wells was disappointed to discover that her audiences were predominantly African American. Even progressive whites did not wish to hear the ghastly details of white supremacist violence against Blacks, for it implicated them in racism and inaction. It was only when she embarked on her British speaking tours that Wells succeeded in applying pressure to Northern whites. Speaking to English audiences, Wells portrayed the United States as "uncivilized" and "unmanly" in its tolerance of lynching. She used public humiliation to hit a nerve, revealing the lies and the reverse victimization at the heart of the rape/lynch mythology.[49]

Wells has been credited with influencing President William McKinley's views on lynching and encouraging him to speak out against it. In his 1897 inaugural address, he proclaimed, "Lynchings must not be tolerated in a great and civilized country like the United States; courts, not mobs, must execute the penalties of the law." He called for "the preservation of public order" and "the orderly administration of justice."[50] While the president urged citizens to respect and uphold the law, he ultimately failed to take formal steps to challenge mob violence. Like many politicians of the time, he was afraid of alienating Southern white voters.

"JUSTICE PASSES THROUGH THE LAND ON LEADEN SANDALS": LYNCHING AS VENGEANCE AND PREVENTION

Judge Isaac C. Parker was similarly eager to end mob violence, although his approach represented a distinct departure from Wells's. He was nearing the end of his long career when he published an article in the *North American Review* titled "How to Arrest the Increase of Homicides in America." It was 1896, and the judge was still awaiting the Supreme Court's ruling on Alexander Allen's homicide case, growing increasingly frustrated with the sluggishness of the appeals process and what he perceived as a miscarriage of justice in favor of criminal defendants. For Parker and many others, such legal indolence occurred at the cost of law-abiding citizens. But Parker's greatest concern was a spike in homicides, from 4,290 in 1890 to over double that figure in 1895. From 1890 to 1896, asserted Parker, there were 43,902 homicides, along with "723 legal executions and 1,118 lynchings."[51] Separating lynchings from homicides, the judge implied that lynchings and legal executions held in common a similar appeal to justice. Each represented a group of citizens gathering—in one case on a jury; in the other, as members of a mob—to deliver justice to a violent criminal. For Parker, mob rule, as well as individual acts of homicidal vengeance, occurred when people "band themselves together as mobs to seek that protection which they fail to obtain under the forms of law."

According to Parker, good citizens could not trust the slow and inefficient system of criminal justice, which allowed violent criminals to appeal their sentences, so they naturally resorted to extralegal means to ensure that criminals were punished. He cited an 1889 address to the American Bar Association in which the speaker complained about how difficult it was "to convict and punish a criminal" in the United States. The speaker asserted, "Truly we may say that justice passes through the land on leaden sandals." At this point in Judge Parker's career, he had witnessed numerous appeals in which men charged with capital crimes had escaped punishment or received a lighter sentence due to the "corrupt justice" of the US legal system. Such leniency in appeals processes made "the man of crime . . . the despotic ruler" of the land.

Parker's solution to mob violence was "full, fair, and rapid vindication of the law by honest people." Courts capable of delivering swift justice to criminals could "teach an object lesson of the most important character to the bad, the vicious, and the criminal." And swift delivery of justice through courts would reassure law-abiding citizens that "they can depend upon the law for protection and security." Parker proclaimed,

"Let capture be sure and punishment certain, and crime is in a measure destroyed." Punishing criminals swiftly would restore citizens' faith in the legal system, and "mobs [would] be entirely destroyed."

Parker's rhetoric mirrored Ida B. Wells's criticism of corrupt justice, but their ideological similarities ended there. Both surmised that if citizens could not trust the law to deliver justice or to protect them from crime, they would turn to extralegal, violent measures. But while Wells exposed the failure of the nation's criminal justice system to protect Black citizens from white violence, Parker insisted that (white) mob violence was a natural result of the law's failure to protect "good citizens" from violent criminals. Although Parker did not implicate the race of the actors in his analysis of legal failure, "good" or "law-abiding" citizenship meant *white* citizenship in the popular imagination.

THE NEGRO DESPERADO AND THE POSSE: CRIMINAL JUSTICE AT WORK

When the criminal justice system was allowed to determine whether a Black man had the right to stand his ground against a white man, more often than not, the answer was a resounding no. This was the case for Frank Richardson in Tuscaloosa, Alabama. In October 1911, a reportedly drunk white man appeared at Richardson's house demanding to borrow a saddle. The man, who happened to be a deputy officer, became violent and shoved his way into the house when Richardson refused. In an effort to protect his home and family, the latter opened fire, killing the deputy. Had Richardson been white, his case would have turned on the castle doctrine's preservation of a man's right to use lethal force in defense of his home.

But as a Black man, Richardson feared the inevitable lynch mob and fled the scene. He later shot and killed a member of the white posse assembled to catch him. A *Times-Picayune* headline declared "Two White Men Dead. Negro Desperado Eludes Posse in Swamps Below Tuscaloosa. Had Dispute with a Deputy over Saddle and Killed Him, Then Shot Posse Leader."[52] After his capture, Richardson was brought to trial, where the white jury found him guilty of murder and sentenced him to hang in July 1912. While Richardson was spared the torture of the lynch mob, his and other cases proved that the law would not protect a Black man's right to defend his home and property.

Far more frequently, Black citizens accused of killing whites did not get their day in court. Many whites saw vigilantism as an antidote to politicians who were considered too soft on crime. Some elected officials, like Governor Lee Cruce of Arkansas, had a reputation for commuting the sentences of convicted criminals; from 1911 to 1915, he spared twenty-two convicted criminals from the death penalty.[53]

In spite of his opposition to capital punishment, Cruce remained unwilling to challenge the practice of lynching. After Laura Nelson and her fifteen-year-old son were lynched by a mob in Okemah, Oklahoma, on May 25, 1911, the NAACP accused white Oklahomans of barbarism and challenged the governor to condemn and investigate the tragedy. Cruce defended the whites of his state, claiming that "our people are just as highly civilized as the people of New York; in fact, more highly civilized than the masses of your people."[54] While he acknowledged the lynching as an "outrage" and convened a grand jury to investigate, he claimed that Nelson and her son "had wantonly shot to death" a white officer named George Loney. By many accounts, Loney and a posse of white men had come to Nelson's house to investigate the theft of a cow. In the course of that investigation, one of the white men reached for the family's Winchester rifle, and the Nelsons' teenaged son used a different shotgun to prevent them from taking it. The gun went off when Laura tried to disarm her son, hitting Loney in the hip.[55]

After Loney died from his wounds, the family was taken to jail and sentenced. Mr. Nelson confessed to stealing the cow to feed his family and was sent to the state prison. While Laura and her son were imprisoned locally to await their trial for murder, a mob came in the night and kidnapped them, raped Laura, and then hanged both mother and son from a bridge just south of Okemah.[56] Onlookers photographed the horrific scene of a mother and her son suspended by their necks from a bridge with what appear to be a hundred white people looking on. In his letter to the *Crisis*, the newspaper founded in 1910 by W. E. B. Du Bois,

Governor Cruce argued that this tragedy and lynchings more generally were provoked by African American "outrages" against whites.[57] In his reasoning, Nelson and her son had assaulted a white officer, so their violent death-by-mob was a natural retaliatory gesture; the only means of stopping lynching remained in the hands of Black citizens themselves.

Another lynching in Arkansas garnered much media attention. In the early morning of March 31, 1914, seventeen-year-old Marie Scott, accused of stabbing Lemuel Peace, was dragged from her jail cell in Wagoner County, Oklahoma, by a mob of between fifty and a hundred white men. Most of the mob were wearing masks as they broke into the jail, overpowered the jailer, and looped a rope around Scott's neck as she struggled. Purportedly several months pregnant, she was dragged down the street before being hoisted above the heads of her captors and hanged from a telephone pole. Having delivered justice for the murder of nineteen-year-old Lemuel Peace, the mob dispersed and allowed the sheriff to cut Scott's body down.[58]

Newspaper coverage of the event testifies to the ambivalence with which the public perceived the lynching of a young Black woman and the nature of the crime that allegedly provoked it. Some mainstream white newspapers, like the *Muskogee Times-Democrat*, expressed support for the mob and opined, "The people appear to be satisfied with the way of justice as administered."[59] Others condemned mob violence but nevertheless characterized Scott as a "murderess" and a prostitute whose violent nature and loose morals justified her execution. The Anaconda, Montana, *Standard* announced "Mob in Oklahoma Hangs Negro Woman. Murderess Is Dragged Unceremoniously from Cell." The article described how, several days earlier, Scott had killed a young white man by "driving a knife through his heart."[60] The *Hobart Daily Republican* declared, "Mob Hangs Negress for Killing White Boy."[61] And while the *Tulsa Star* condemned the "beastly cowardly brutes who killed a poor defenseless woman," it depicted Scott's lethal attack on Peace as unprovoked.

Other public accounts complicated the matter of culpability by suggesting that Peace had instigated Scott's attack. According to an article in a white-owned Kansas newspaper, the *Emporia Gazette*, "Oklahoma

Chivalry: Colored Woman Taken from Jail by Mob of One Hundred Men," Peace, accompanied by "other young white fellows," had "made trouble in the Negro section of Wagoner" before Scott killed him.[62] The *Tulsa Star*, an African American–owned paper, suggested that Peace was in the habit—as were many white men "from good families"—of "continually trespassing the 'color line,' with the lowest type of Negro woman prostitutes." In these accounts, Peace had invited danger through his regular transgressions of the color line.[63] The articles depicted a crisis in white masculinity: white men who strayed into such places as "the Bottoms" of Wagoner County courted disaster; and those who participated in lynching, particularly when the victims were women, undermined the legacy of chivalry.

Some narratives of Marie Scott's murder were even sharper in their critique of white men's exploitation of Black women. According to accounts in the Associated Press and the *Crisis*, Peace and his friends had forcibly entered Scott's home and sexually assaulted her. The AP reported that Scott's brother had killed Peace after hearing his sister's screams for help.[64] Unable to locate her brother, the mob lynched Scott to avenge Peace's death.

Other accounts in the Black press portrayed Scott as having killed Peace in self-defense. The *Cleveland Gazette* hailed Scott as a martyr who "lost her life as the result of her effort to protect her virtue."[65] The *Appeal* (St. Paul) similarly proclaimed, "To defend herself she killed him."[66] An article in the *New York Age*, another influential African American newspaper, demanded to know what Lemuel Peace was "doing in the society of Marie Scott on Sunday night" and why he was "not at home with his alleged white family." Asking rhetorically, "Did Marie Scott rape Lemuel Peace and shoot him after she did it?" the author asserted that Scott killed Peace "to protect her honor or to avenge it." This author urged the "Negroes in Oklahoma" to expose the facts of the story, bringing to light the "hundred masked cowards guilty of this crime against womanhood and the queer justice of the laws of Oklahoma."[67]

The Black press placed white men's crimes against Black womanhood front and center, framing Scott as a victim who tried to defend herself against a white rapist. These and other pointed critiques of "queer justice" highlighted the failure of American legal structures to protect Black citizens from white supremacist violence. "Queer justice" also signaled white society's invocation of Black criminality to conceal widespread Black victimization and exclusion from equal protection.[68] The rape-lynch mythology framed white women as the *only* victims of rape and Black men its *only* perpetrators, thus rendering the violence perpetrated against Black women invisible.[69] Marie Scott's blackness made any act of self-defense unthinkable in the popular white imagination. Her crime of killing a white man was unforgivable by early-twentieth-century standards, and for that she paid the ultimate price.

"A MOB OR RIOTOUS ASSEMBLAGE": THE FAILURE OF FEDERAL ANTILYNCHING LEGISLATION

The federal government's sluggish response to mob violence reflected widespread conflation of lynching with white self-defense. The first federal response to a lynching originated in the 1891 killing of eleven Italian men in New Orleans. A mob broke into the local jail and killed prisoners who had been arbitrarily rounded up in the wake of the murder of the city's police chief. Members of the lynch mob included some of the city's leading citizens, including a well-known lawyer, who reportedly shouted to the crowd before the massacre, "Shall you protect yourself?" to which the crowd responded "Yes!" and "Self-preservation is the first law of nature!"[70] Theodore Roosevelt, then a member of the Civil Service Commission, reportedly called the lynching "a rather good thing." An editorial in the *New York Times* branded the victims "sneaking and cowardly Sicilians, the descendants of bandits and assassins."[71]

But international newspapers condemned the act, shaming the United States for allowing mob violence to triumph over law. The United States stood accused of outrages against citizens of a peer nation in Europe, not to mention one in possession of a superior navy. To save face and prevent hostilities, President Benjamin Harrison paid reparations of $25,000 to Italy.[72] Nevertheless, Italian immigrants were the second most frequently lynched minority group in the United States between 1870 and 1940. Their visibility as a population whose culture, language, and religious practices appeared threatening and "foreign" sparked suspicion and hostility among acculturated Americans.[73] The fact that Italian immigrants in the South often socialized with African Americans also did not endear them to the defenders of white supremacy.[74]

The nation's aspirations to become a global power for democracy stood starkly at odds with the practice of mob violence. In spite of his earlier promotion of the film *The Birth of a Nation*, President Woodrow Wilson issued a public statement in 1918, characterizing lynching as "a blow at the heart of ordered law and humane justice."[75] The same year, Congressman Leonidas C. Dyer, Republican from Missouri, introduced the Dyer Anti-Lynching Bill, the first federal antilynching bill. In recognition that many states were unlikely to prosecute white mob participants, the bill would charge lynchers with capital murder and try all cases in federal court. Developed in collaboration with the NAACP, Dyer's bill also proposed to fine not only the jurisdictions in which lynchings took place but also any officials who failed to make a reasonable effort to prevent them.[76]

The bill gained momentum in the early 1920s, largely through the efforts of a group of women affiliated with the NAACP and the National Association of Colored Women (NACW). Led by Mary Burnett Talbert, an educator who had helped establish the NAACP, the Anti-Lynching Crusaders worked tirelessly to promote the Dyer bill in 1922. Like Wells before them, the Crusaders assiduously gathered data and publicized the details of lynchings to raise public awareness.[77] But unlike Wells, the Crusaders adopted a more conciliatory and reformist tone. They actively sought the support of white women by emphasizing the impact of lynching on women and children, with the goal of convincing one million women to donate one dollar each to the campaign to pass the Dyer bill. The organization was short-lived, lasting less than a year, and they were unable to recruit a critical mass of white women or to reach their ambitious fund-raising goals. The Dyer bill never passed, and the Anti-Lynching Crusaders disbanded in spring 1923 when the organization was subsumed into the NAACP.

The Dyer bill failed because it ran into vehement resistance from Southerners, who claimed that it represented an assault on the Constitution and on Southern states' ability to protect their (white) citizens. A Methodist pastor named C. M. Ledbetter complained in 1922 that "the north . . . has abused the whites of the south far more for lynching criminals than they have censured the negroes for the crimes that furnished the excuse for lynching." In a similar vein he ranted that "negro papers and preachers have censured the white man a great deal more for lynching the negro rapist than they have censured the rapist."[78]

In spite of the lack of any evidence pointing to Black men's sexual threat to white women, Ledbetter and other lynching apologists continued to appeal to widespread fears of rape. Protecting (white) women from (Black) rapists became a collective project in historical obfuscation and mass forgetting, with white supremacist violence posed as vital to national identity and self-defense. Consequently, each of the antilynching bills introduced in Congress from the twenties through the forties was stalled in Congress when Southern congressmen filibustered or threatened to do so.[79]

In 1933 another federal antilynching bill was proposed in response to the lynching of two white men arrested for kidnapping and murder in California.[80] In response to nationwide outrage, Senators Robert F. Wagner (D-New York) and Edward Costigan (D-Colorado) cosponsored a bill that would provide payment of up to $10,000 for families of lynching victims, to be paid by the county in which the lynching took place. In an echo of the Dyer bill, officers on duty in jurisdictions where lynchings took place would lose their jobs, and federal rather than state courts would try those accused of lynching.[81]

In April 1935 the bill reached the Senate, only to be defeated by the powerful resistance of Southern senators, who deemed the bill an "invasion of the sovereign rights of the states." One South Carolina senator argued that the bill undermined states' rights and that "southern womanhood must be protected."[82] Others similarly fought to maintain states' rights to address the issue without federal interference. So urgent were the dominant white culture's invocations of white feminine vulnerability that even otherwise progressive leaders such as President

Franklin Roosevelt did not support the proposed legislation. The nation ultimately failed to pass a federal antilynching bill.

In his analysis of this failure, the historian Harvard Sitkoff emphasized states' suspicion of federal intrusion into what they perceived as local criminal matters. The passage of the civil rights acts in the 1960s provoked Southern states to prosecute lynchings in their own courts rather than risk inviting federal intervention.[83] According to the Equal Justice Initiative, the decline of lynchings in the mid-twentieth century can also be attributed to the migration of many African Americans out of the South and to the expansion of the criminal justice system's use of capital punishment. Bryan Stevenson argues, "The death penalty's roots are sunk deep in the legacy of lynching."[84] One way to subdue the passions of the mob was to ensure a speedy execution for those accused.

Popular skepticism about the efficiency and effectiveness of the criminal justice system recurs in contemporary calls for citizens to take up arms individually against violent criminals. Calls such as Judge Isaac Parker's for the criminal justice system to deliver "swift justice" have echoed through history, stoking suspicions of our nation's judicial system and doubts about its ability to protect "law-abiding citizens" from violence.

In spite of our contemporary condemnation of lynching, we see the echoes of the rape/lynch mythology in our criminal justice system's unbalanced adjudication of rape, in the disproportionate punishment of nonwhite men accused of rape, and in the persistent dismissal of such accusations when the victims are women of color.[85] Moreover, the mythical association of Black men with rape continues to haunt popular understandings of "reasonable threat." The nation's failure to face the formidable impact and ubiquity of white supremacist violence is in part the legacy of collective amnesia that favors a romantic past of Southern chivalry while denying the racist violence that constituted it. Today, organizations like the EJI work to lay markers on the places where African Americans lost their lives to lynch mobs in a battle to call attention to a brutal past that continues to shape our present. The effort to restore collective memory around lynching continues to be an uphill one.

In spite of the efforts of Ida B. Wells, Mary Talbert, and other activists to illuminate the lies at the root of the rape/lynch mythology, lynching and the generalized apparatus of racial apartheid continue to place armed self-defense within the jurisdiction of white men. In response to nationwide systemic racial exclusion and violence, militant African American activists would heed Wells's warning to keep their Winchester rifles on hand, but they risked exposure to the horrific violence of lynching if they ever pulled the trigger.

FIVE

"AN AMERICAN TRADITION"

The Black Paramilitary Response to White
Supremacist Terror and Unequal Protection

*The principle of self-defense is an American
tradition that began at Lexington and Concord.*

—ROBERT F. WILLIAMS, 1962

*Gun control laws were originally promulgated by Democrats
to keep guns out of the hands of blacks. This allowed the
Democratic policy of slavery to proceed with fewer bumps and,
after the Civil War, allowed the Democratic Ku Klux Klan to
menace and murder black Americans with little resistance.*

—ANN COULTER, 2012

The filter of memory is used to contour the politics of the present.

—RANDALL KENNEDY, 2015

Black paramilitary organizations, like Monroe, North Carolina's Black
Armed Guard and, later, Louisiana's Deacons of Defense and Mississippi's United League, took root in a twentieth-century South stubbornly
resistant to the full inclusion and citizenship of African Americans.
Quasilegal state innovations such as literacy tests, poll taxes, the
convict-lease system, and debt peonage excluded Black citizens from
social, political, and economic freedom. And when they stood up to
these flagrant injustices, the Klan, White Citizens' Councils, and members of an all-white law enforcement system used intimidation and violence to force Black submission. In spite of the efforts of activists and

progressive officials to defend the Fourteenth Amendment's promise of equal protection, racist aggression and exclusion retained a powerful presence nationwide. While many activists sought what they perceived as the moral high ground of nonviolent resistance, others took up arms to confront white supremacist violence head on, meeting force with defiant force.

Although popular memory privileges the work of nonviolent civil disobedience as popularized by Martin Luther King Jr., recent scholarship has revealed the extent to which the armed support of Black paramilitary organizations was critical to the advances of the modern civil rights movement.[1] By 1965, armed self-defense was key to the civil rights agenda in the Deep South, and many ostensibly nonviolent activists, such as Fanny Lou Hamer and Daisy Bates, kept weapons for their personal protection. The peaceful strategies of the Congress of Racial Equality (CORE), the Southern Christian Leadership Conference (SCLC), and the Student Nonviolent Coordinating Committee (SNCC) went only so far in gaining justice in a region colonized by racial terror. Particularly in places where Black citizens encountered white violence on a daily basis, the use of what the North Carolina activists Robert and Mabel Williams called "armed self-reliance" proved critical to basic survival. Without armed protection, a Mississippi farmer named Hartman Turnbow warned Martin Luther King Jr., in 1964, "this non-violent stuff" could get people killed.[2]

In their demands for social justice and racial equality, the more militant voices of the modern civil rights movement irrevocably reshaped broader ideals of self-defense. Robert and Mabel Williams, leaders of the Black Armed Guard, linked citizenship rights with armed self-reliance, providing an ideological foundation for later organizations, such as the Revolutionary Action Movement and the Black Panther Party for Self Defense, in the 1960s. These militant antiracist organizations drew on existing ideals of self-defense while challenging their white supremacist foundations. They did so against a political backdrop of radical protest, challenging the nations' racist, patriarchal, and capitalist exclusions, while proving that armed self-defense was necessary in a world lacking legal protection for Black citizens. Where the nation's tacit approval of lynching was based on a spurious myth of white vulnerability to Black criminality, Black militancy was rooted in the actual history of racist violence and state complicity. This chapter traces the history of militant responses to white supremacist terror, with an eye to understanding how our nation's selective memory of historic movements for Black civil rights serves destructive ideological structures today.

SOUTHERN HISTORIES OF BLACK MILITANCY

Mabel Robinson was born in North Carolina in 1931, eleven years after the Nineteenth Amendment expanded full suffrage to all citizens, regardless of sex. Yet Black women and men in the South remained largely prohibited from exercising their right to vote by a combination of exclusionary laws, poll taxes, white primaries, and intense intimidation. In 1934, only twenty-two of several thousand eligible Black citizens were registered to vote in Robinson's home county.

Compared to other Black families in Monroe, the Robinsons were relatively well off.[3] They worked as servants to the wealthy white Belk family, and their loyalty was compensated in the use of a small house, a steady wage, and clothing passed down from the Belk children to Mabel and her siblings.[4] Her family's comparatively elevated status enabled Mabel to attend high school, instead of working as a domestic servant.

The world in which Robinson grew up was one of pervasive Black poverty, political and social exclusion, and labor exploitation. Although slavery had been abolished, the Jim Crow South found many ways to circumvent the terms of twentieth-century legal protections and leave Blacks scarcely better off than they had been under slavery. Sharecropping and debt peonage kept African Americans propertyless and dependent on white landowners, while the convict-lease system consigned thousands of Black men to live out their lives in bondage and forced labor.[5] Under the convict-lease system, Southern Black men could be arrested on trumped-up charges such as vagrancy or spitting in public, and then sold into de facto slavery to corporations, where their labor would swell the coffers of white capital. Southern prisons made a fortune selling the labor of Black prisoners to both Northern and Southern companies, laying the foundation for a contemporary collusion known as the "prison-industrial complex," between racially skewed mass incarceration policies and corporate profit.[6] Contrasting convict laborers with their enslaved precursors, Angela Davis argues that the workers' disposability—the fact that each convict laborer could be replaced by another convicted putative "criminal"—differentiated this system from slavery, where slaves had been valuable commodities.[7]

Expendable and criminalized Black labor continued to be a powerful source of white profit, while Black personhood and citizenship remained largely outside the nation's distribution of rights and protections. Widespread perception of Black criminality and the need to protect white property from Black competition guaranteed that systems of unfree Black labor could function well into the twentieth century. That African American freedom constituted a threat to white power was a given, and the unquestioned operation of white-overseen local courts lent credence to the notion that the law protected the worthy while punishing, and consigning to bondage, the guilty.

Mabel Robinson was a teenager when Lena Baker, a forty-five-year-old mother of three, was executed for killing her white male employer in rural Georgia. Originally hired as a maid, Baker had tried to escape the sexual slavery in which sixty-seven-year old Earnest Knight had trapped her. As she struggled to break away, Baker shot Knight with his own gun, and she was charged with murder. In spite of her plea of self-defense, she was convicted by an all-white, male jury after a one-day trial. Her execution by electric chair on March 5, 1945, proved yet again that Black women could not legally defend themselves against the onslaught of racist sexual violence.[8]

A deep reservoir of frustration and rage over Black women's continued sexual subjugation by white men added urgency to civil rights mobilization. Historian Danielle McGuire contends that the Montgomery Improvement Association—the organization that launched the famous 1955 bus boycott—was the culmination of "a decades-long struggle to protect Black women . . . from sexualized violence and rape."[9] Black women's sexual vulnerability was a legal and cultural fact, one obscured by the rape/lynch myth and perpetuated by a criminal justice system designed to concentrate power and property in the hands of white men.

By the time Mabel Robinson married Robert Williams in 1947, lynching was on the wane, but white supremacist violence was nationally widespread. Having served in the segregated US Army during the war, Robert experienced firsthand the white backlash that greeted Black military veterans.[10] Race riots took place wherever whites suspected Blacks were stepping out of their "proper place," whether sharing in spaces of recreation, like public pools and beaches; patronizing businesses designated for whites only; or simply insisting on humane treatment. In the summer of 1943, the city of Detroit flared into a riot when white youths attacked groups of African Americans trying to enjoy a day of leisure at Belle Isle Park. The fights escalated into rioting when whites attacked predominantly Black neighborhoods, killing thirty-four people while destroying Black homes and businesses.[11]

While lynchings became somewhat more rare at midcentury, in part as a result of the Great Migration of African Americans out of the Jim Crow South, the malignant view of Black masculinity as a threat to white womanhood retained its power. In August 1955, fourteen-year-old Emmett Till, while visiting relatives in the South, was tortured and murdered by white men after allegedly flirting with a white woman in Money, Mississippi. The woman, who was the wife of one of Till's murderers, reported that Till had groped her and called her "Baby."[12] The more likely story, and the one supported by Black witnesses, was that Till had wolf-whistled at her to get a laugh out of his friends.[13] A few days after the incident, Till was kidnapped from his uncle's house by two white men, and he was not seen again until fishermen discovered his body in the Tallahatchie River. The kidnappers stood trial for murder but were swiftly acquitted by an all-white jury, on the spurious grounds that the body was so badly mutilated that no one could prove whose it was.[14] Indeed, Till's bereaved mother, Mamie Till-Mobley, chose to display her son's battered body in an open casket at his funeral, because she "wanted the world to see what they did to my baby." Widely circulated photographs of the teen's mutilated face shamed the nation, galvanizing support for the cause of racial justice while raising public awareness of white supremacist terror.

The murderers later confessed in an interview for *Look* magazine, explaining that Till had failed to show humility or to beg forgiveness.[15] One of them explained, "As long as I live and can do anything about it, niggers are gonna stay in their place. Niggers ain't gonna vote where I live. If they did, they'd control the government. They ain't gonna go to school with my kids. And when a nigger gets close to mentioning sex with a white woman, he's tired o' livin'."[16] In the minds of his white captors and their jury, Till's alleged transgression of the color line had earned him a just sentence.

In spite of the Supreme Court's *Brown v. Board of Education* decision in 1954, which overturned the infamous "separate but equal" doctrine of *Plessy v. Ferguson*, jurisdictions nationwide defiantly refused to take steps to integrate schools and other public accommodations. Nonviolent resistance to achieve the aims of the civil rights movement were championed by most civil rights organizations and became the prevailing method of challenging the racist Jim Crow laws and customs. Peaceful protesters organized voter-registration drives, sat at "whites only" lunch counters awaiting service, and marched in the streets demanding basic rights. As nonviolent activists challenged the most resistant structures of segregation, they were subject to violent backlash.

The 1955 bus boycott in Montgomery, Alabama, is an iconic example of the long, arduous road civil rights activists traveled in the struggle for equal citizenship. A Montgomery city ordinance required that Black passengers ride in the back of the bus and yield their seats to white passengers if the white section became full. The moment that sparked the boycott has been emblazoned in the nation's imagination: a diminutive, well-dressed woman named Rosa Parks was thrown off a bus and arrested for refusing to cede her seat to a white man. The brutal treatment of an innocent, respectable lady was the last straw and sparked the yearlong boycott in which Black customers withheld their patronage from the racist bus system. Historians have added nuance to this narrative, highlighting Mrs. Park's established leadership as an anti-rape activist and particularly her militancy in resistance to white supremacy. The nation's partial memory of Mrs. Parks's activism stems from collective denial of the pivotal role of militancy in Black struggles for civil rights.[17]

The bus boycott—which used economic pressure to force a change in municipal policy—could not have succeeded without the support of the innovative Montgomery Improvement Association, which assembled a fleet of station wagons to transport people throughout the city. Many of the drivers were Korean War veterans, whose experience driving military vehicles proved vital to the effort to transport Black citizens safely through a hostile city. Widespread knowledge that the drivers possessed military training and that many of them were armed helped prevent the Klan and others who opposed the boycott from attacking the Black passengers and their drivers.[18]

"THIS SOCIAL JUNGLE CALLED DIXIE": CONTESTED LEGACIES OF CIVIL RIGHTS

Prevailing histories of nonviolent activism also obscure the persistence of racial terror. The Till case was just one example of the complicity of law enforcement and criminal justice in maintaining white supremacist intimidation and violence. Nationwide, the police and courts refused to defend the safety, property, or rights of African Americans.[19] Instead, police, juries, and judges continued to be drawn exclusively from a population that had a vested interest in maintaining the structures of white privilege.

An episode in Monroe, North Carolina, helped ignite the militancy of Robert and Mabel Williams. In May 1959, an all-white male jury acquitted a white man accused of the beating and attempted rape of Mary Ruth Reed, who was pregnant. Even though a white witness testified that the man had attacked Mrs. Reed, the jury's sympathy lay with the accused. During his instructions to the jury, the white judge described the defendant's wife as "this pure white woman, this pure flower of life" and asked why a man in possession of such a wife would "have left this pure flower," then gesturing to Mrs. Reed, "for *that*?"[20] Reed's attacker went free.

Once again, traditional legal structures had failed to protect Black women from racist sexual violence. This time Robert Williams took action. His public statement, as president of the local chapter of the NAACP, decried the Reed case as a betrayal of the nation's Constitution, which "cannot be enforced in this social jungle called Dixie." In the absence of law enforcement and equal protection, Williams declared it "time for Negro men to stand up and be men and if it is necessary for us to die we must be willing to die. If it is necessary for us to kill we must be willing to kill."[21]

The call for self-defense often sat uneasily with the paradigm of nonviolence that was foundational for many civil rights activists. An outspoken opponent of violence, Martin Luther King Jr. nevertheless expressed ambivalence about forceful self-defense. In response to Robert Williams's public declaration, he wrote, "There is more power in socially organized masses on the march than there is in guns in the hands of a few desperate men." King worried that armed self-defense would provoke white backlash while tainting the legacy of civil rights. Should violence define the movement, warned King, the "legacy to the future will be an endless reign of meaningless chaos."[22]

King's invocation of the civil rights movement's nonviolent legacy proved historically ironic. Ultimately, the story of nonviolence would triumph in the minds of future generations of Americans, to the partial obfuscation of alternative, more militant memories of "Negroes with guns," the title of the 1962 memoir Williams wrote with his wife. King's critique illuminated a battle over historical truth, a competition between two divergent narratives of an event from the recent past in Monroe.

The event in question involved Black women standing up to white supremacist terror in order to protect a beloved Black doctor from lynching. Dr. Albert E. Perry was widely revered and respected in Monroe, especially by Black mothers, who felt gratitude to the kind doctor for his unflagging care. In 1957 Dr. Perry was arrested for allegedly performing an abortion on a white woman, but eventually he was freed unharmed. According to King's version of the event, the "aroused people of Monroe" crowded into the police station and secured the doctor's release "without use of arms or threats of violence."[23]

But Mabel Williams, who participated in the action, told a different story. According to Williams, the Black women of Monroe were determined to protect their beloved doctor from lynching, given white hysteria over his alleged violation of white femininity. The women stormed the county jail, armed with meat cleavers, rolling pins, brooms, and anything they could find and wield against the white police.[24] This display of armed and dangerous feminine strength forced the police to release Dr. Perry on bond.

King wrote that his account of the episode came from Dr. Perry himself. Yet the doctor was imprisoned in the jailhouse basement when the women stormed the building, and he did not personally witness the events that resulted in his release. Further, Perry may have been hesitant to share the militant details of his rescue with King, who was known for his advocacy of nonviolence. These divergent narratives of one story illustrate the extent to which Black militancy, particularly Black women's open defiance of white supremacy, could be downplayed or effaced in popular memory.

They also illuminate conflicting understandings of self-defense in the context of racial justice advocacy. In spite of his critique of Williams's militancy, King nevertheless expressed limited support for "violence exercised in self-defense, which all societies from the most primitive to the most cultured and civilized, accept as moral and legal." He cited Gandhi as having "sanctioned [self-defense] for those unable to master pure nonviolence."[25]

In contrast to King's ambivalence, the Williamses characterized "armed self-reliance" as a necessity and a right for those unable to secure the state's protection against racist violence. After Dr. Perry led an effort to integrate the public swimming pool in 1957, he received death threats from the Klan, and the white police refused to provide protection. Under Robert Williams's leadership, a group of sixty armed Black men took turns standing sentry outside Perry's home, each holding a loaded rifle, in vigilant compliance with the jurisdiction's open-carry laws.[26] In the 1950s and '60s, the North Carolina law allowed one to carry a gun as long as it wasn't concealed. This group of armed protectors would become the Black Armed Guard, a paramilitary association to defend a community struggling for basic access to equal citizenship and protection.

The Williamses' leadership in this movement for armed self-defense made them targets of white supremacist threats, as well as victims of trumped-up charges from law enforcement. After Robert was accused of kidnapping a white couple in 1961, he and Mabel went into exile in Cuba. Written shortly thereafter, *Negroes with Guns* invokes a history where armed self-defense had "always been an accepted right of Americans." In an echo of earlier appeals to self-defense as a right, the Williamses wrote, "The citizens can, and must, act in self-defense against the lawless" in the absence of legal protection.[27] This rhetoric would have resonated with Judge Isaac C. Parker six decades earlier or with members of the mob that seized and killed Marie Scott in 1914, except that the vulnerable citizens the mob wished to protect were *not* the Black victims of violence. For the Williamses and other African American activists, self-defense was a right, but, more crucially, it was a vital necessity for the disenfranchised and powerless to fend off the relentless violence of the powerful.

"That Had Been Our History": The Power in the Story

The Williamses argued that the mainstream embrace of nonviolence had resulted from the fact that "the majority of white people in the United States have literally no idea of the violence with which Negroes in the South are treated daily—nay, hourly." They wrote, "This violence is deliberate, conscious, condoned by the authorities. It has gone on for centuries and is going on today, every day, unceasing and unremitting." History itself justified the actions of the Black Armed Guard: "One hundred years after the Civil War began, we Negroes in Monroe armed ourselves in self-defense and used our weapons. We showed that our policy worked."[28]

The turn to weaponry represented a last resort for a community beset by racist violence. Mabel Williams explained in 2005, "We didn't know when we started fighting that the FBI [and] the federal government [were] supporting the power structure. We were asking for what we thought were simple things, like the right to have a job ... but they wouldn't give us that." Activists' efforts to pursue non-violent channels to justice had failed. Even though many Black citizens owned guns, explained Mabel Williams, they would not use them for self-defense: "When the Klan would come out, people would be afraid. That had been our history."[29] The rhetoric of armed self-defense encouraged those targeted by racist violence to unite under the banner of their shared history of exclusion from equal protection of the law.

Contrary to popular contemporary understandings that have framed Black militancy as criminal and violent, gun safety and adherence to the law were of critical importance to the Black Armed Guard and other paramilitary organizations. Mabel Williams explained, "The only reason you would ever pick up a gun is for self-defense and not for anything aggressive or not to scare off anybody."[30] When Black activists took up arms, they did so in close observance of legal codes governing gun ownership and how and where one could legally carry them. In a 1999 interview with historian David Cecelski, Mabel Williams stated that the activists who carried weapons "knew how to use [them]."[31] When Robert organized an armed resistance, according to Mabel, "He was very much one for obeying the law. So he would go around with a luger on one side," and they always kept a gun in their car. "What he knew but did not accept is that the law wasn't meant for us," explained Mabel. She meant that the laws allowing for the ownership and open carry of firearms were not intended for Black citizens. However, she added, Robert "was going to make it be for us." The Williamses' efforts rested on a call for equal justice, where Black citizens could carry weapons in collective self-defense in the absence of the state's protection. In Robert's mind, the risk of backlash was worth it because "he would rather die just five minutes standing up like a man than crawling at the feet of his oppressors."[32]

In the late 1950s, Robert Williams applied for and was granted a National Rifle Association charter for a rifle club in Monroe. At the time, the NRA was an apolitical sporting organization that focused on hunting, marksmanship, and firearm safety, and its membership was chiefly composed of white men. In 1934, the NRA had supported the National Firearms Act, which levied fines on the types of weapons most often used among bootleggers and other participants in Prohibition-era organized crime.[33] For the Williamses and other members of the Monroe Black Armed Guard, the NRA appeared as a law-abiding, pro-government organization through which they might gain legitimacy and vital information on gun laws and safety.

However, the NRA leadership did not know they were granting membership to a Black rifle club, and Robert did not disclose the group's racial identity. According to Mabel, "I'm sure when we joined and the years after then, had they known we were a Black group, they would have revoked our charter."[34] When asked why it would have concerned the NRA to know that their group was Black, she answered that whites "knew that if a large number of Black people should take up arms that . . . it may lead to a . . . civil war." Whites had "control of the police department and of the state troopers, the National Guard. And they didn't intend to release that power. And they felt that [Blacks taking up arms] was a threat to the power."[35] As a mainstream, white, male-dominated organization, the NRA did not knowingly support the controversial effort to promote gun ownership and use among Black Southerners, so the Black Armed Guard became "stealth" members of this legitimacy-conferring organization.

Armed self-defense proved necessary for many other civil rights activists, even those who espoused an agenda of nonviolence in their public activism. When white supremacists targeted her after her prominent role in the 1957 integration of the public school system in Little Rock, Arkansas, Daisy Bates carried a pistol and enlisted armed guards to patrol her home.[36] Fannie Lou Hamer, prominent in the Student Nonviolent Coordinating Committee (SNCC) and the Mississippi Freedom Summer, also kept a rifle at the ready in case of racist attacks on her home.[37]

In Jonesboro, Louisiana, the Deacons of Defense and Justice was formed in 1964 to protect nonviolent demonstrators from police and Klan violence. The group's goal was to protect CORE activists who were trying to register Black citizens to vote. When the group was founded,

Blacks were a majority of the population in Claiborne County, but only 7 percent were registered voters, and the county had no Black elected officials.[38] The all-white local police force included many Klan members, so Black activists formed their own carefully organized group of armed protectors. The Deacons of Defense provided a recognizable armed presence, identifiable by their white shirts, overalls, and black hats, as well as by the rifles they carried openly.[39]

Without armed self-defense, argues historian Akinyele O. Umoja, peaceful demonstrations, voter-registration drives, and economic boycotts might not have succeeded against a white supremacist backlash tacitly supported by the state. Boycotts of white businesses constituted a "principal form of insurgency for Black activists" in the 1960s and '70s. White supremacist groups found it more difficult to suppress boycotts and voter-registration drives when activists carried weapons openly.

As in North Carolina, Louisiana's liberal open-carry laws served the strategy of the Deacons, who could legally carry loaded weapons in public. The visibility of uniformly dressed Black men holding firearms conveyed a powerful message to white supremacists, who responded with a proposal, in September 1967, to outlaw the group's possession of firearms. As laws were changed to prevent Black activists from carrying weapons, activists adapted so that they could operate in adherence to the law. For example, when new gun laws made it a crime to transport arms inside a vehicle, people added gun racks to the outside of their trucks' cabs.

The armed militancy of the Deacons of Defense and the Black Armed Guard in the South helped inspire the creation in 1966 of the Black Panther Party for Self Defense (BPP) on the West Coast. Envisioned by Huey P. Newton in Oakland, California, the BPP was a revolutionary answer to the continued political, economic, and social oppression of Black citizens. While earlier militant interventions had taken root in the rural South, Black Power originated in urban spaces on the West Coast and in the North among Black communities created largely during the Great Migration. Echoing earlier instances of Black armed resistance, the BPP invoked self-defense to differentiate their philosophy from the mainstream civil rights movement's emphasis on nonviolence. The BPP constituted a radical approach to systemic white supremacy, supporting Black citizens in underserved communities while defending them from rampant police violence.

On October 15, 1966, Huey Newton and Bobby Seale, the BPP's founders, drafted a succinct ten-point party platform that included demands for survival basics including "land, bread, housing, education, clothing." The ten points exemplified the party's critique of interlocking systems of power that historically subjugated Black Americans. They highlighted the interdependency of capitalism and white supremacy in relegating Black citizens to low-paying, exploitative jobs that extracted Black labor while failing to provide for basic human needs. In recognition of the web of structures that led to the disproportionately high rate of incarceration of Black men, point 8 attacked the criminal justice system, demanding the release of Black inmates from prison, "because their constitutional rights have been violated." This point was in response to the complex state apparatus that channeled Black men and boys into state surveillance and control, which was being constructed in the 1960s. Historian Elizabeth Hinton reveals how President Lyndon Johnson's War on Crime constructed an alliance of social welfare and antipoverty efforts with nationwide juvenile delinquency programs concentrated in underserved urban neighborhoods. According to Hinton, a result of the state's marriage of social welfare and crime prevention was the expansion of the "carceral state" in the interest of controlling Black youth.[40] BPP leaders were well aware of the tragic consequences of the state's efforts to combat urban crime through punitive measures that intensified racially biased law enforcement. Other points in the BPP manifesto emphasized the connection between white supremacist power and police violence. At the core of the party's mission lay an urgent need for armed self-defense in a world where Black lives were simultaneously undervalued and criminalized.

The BPP created "people's survival programs," including hot breakfasts for children and public health services.[41] In spite of the masculine iconography commonly associated with the movement today, women made up close to two-thirds of the BPP and were among its most devoted rank-and-file members.[42] The BPP's vision for collective self-defense included holistic support and social welfare for vulnerable populations. Sociologist Tressie McMillan Cottom describes how the BPP's emphasis on basic services laid a crucial foundation for the provision of state responses to alleviate inner-city poverty: "When a poor kid eats school breakfast or the local ambulance is obligated to respond to inner-city victims of violence, they owe a debt to the Black Panther Party." According to Cottom, the state's "bureaucracies absorb disruptions, like labor movements and community programs, to stifle dissent and protect its legitimacy as the 'official' provider of public services."[43] Even as it bolstered its carceral apparatus in the 1960s and '70s, the state co-opted selective elements of the BPP's social justice mission and in the process effaced their Black Nationalist roots.

Restorative history was also key to Black community empowerment. Point 5 of the BPP manifesto demanded education on "our true history and our role in the present-day American society." The organization's founders possessed a keen sense of the power of popular memory—and its absence—to shape people's lived experience in the present. As W. E. B. du Bois had written decades prior, the racist "propaganda of history" had formidable material implications for African Americans and other targeted groups. The BPP's expansive call for justice and "true history," and their critique of the white supremacist state enjoyed great popularity among the younger generation of civil rights activists, who had to search far and wide for an empowering sense of personal history. Many were persuaded by the BPP's eloquent appeal to self-defense and collective armed resistance. The BPP peaked in 1970, when it had chapters in sixty-eight cities. But as the organization's influence spread nationwide, so did the intensity of the racist backlash.

The self-defense vision of the BPP posed a major threat to white supremacy, and resistance from various state power structures was fierce. The FBI's secret Counter Intelligence Program (COINTELPRO) had been created in 1956 with the goal of eliminating Communism and other traces of internal political radicalism. To achieve this goal, it surveilled and intimidated civil rights and Black Power activists, characterizing them as subversive and antigovernment. The covert organization's intimidation tactics intensified along with the growing visibility of Black Power and antiwar activism in the late 1960s. FBI director J. Edgar Hoover led the charge to isolate the BPP from more moderate civil rights organizations and to portray the leadership as a threat to public safety. As they criminalized the BPP, the federal antisubversion apparatus set out to assassinate BPP leaders.[44]

In response to Black armed self-defense, conservative leaders also worked to criminalize the open carry of firearms. California's Republican governor, Ronald Reagan, told reporters that he saw "no reason why on the street today a citizen should be carrying loaded weapons."[45] Governor Reagan later enacted the Mulford Act of 1967, which prohibited the open carry of firearms in California. Similar gun-restriction efforts during this time emerged in response to the visibility and proliferation of armed Black self-defense in American cities.[46] Where state laws had earlier supported the open carry of firearms—based on the assumption that a visibly displayed gun was the optimal way to prevent an attack—the practice fell out of favor as Black activists engaged in open carry to defend their rights, property, and personal safety against systemic racist violence.

Covert federal violence and infiltration eventually had the desired effect. Roiled by internal struggles among leadership, and under steady assault by federal and local law enforcement, the BPP experienced major setbacks in the 1970s. The collective armed resistance that proved such a compelling component of its public image ultimately contributed to its breakdown. The nation could not countenance the widespread visibility of "Negroes with guns."[47]

A 1970 editorial in the NRA's *American Rifleman* sheds light on widespread white suspicions of Black militancy. The author posits the BPP as a "primarily racist," "activist political organization," in juxtaposition to the "non-political and non-partisan" NRA. According to the author, the NRA's primary goal was "to preserve America by peaceful means for the sake of all good Americans" in contradiction to the BPP's politically polarizing "racism" against whites.[48] But the definition of "good Americans" depended on white supremacist understandings of criminality.

While the author of this editorial celebrated the NRA's political neutrality, the organization had become a reactionary voice for armed, white self-defense by the late 1970s. And in spite of Reagan's earlier zeal to eliminate the open carry of guns—specifically, to disarm and criminalize Black activists—he soon thereafter joined the crusade for "gun rights" for "decent law-abiding citizens," while promising a decisive "crackdown on crime."[49] Catapulted to the presidency in 1980 in part thanks to the NRA's growing strength as a political force, Reagan graced the cover of the July 1983 issue of *American Rifleman.*

BLACK GENOCIDE AND URBAN RIOTS: LEGACIES OF A CARCERAL NATION

From 1963 to 1969, more than 250 violent uprisings took place in American cities.[50] Urban civil disturbance often followed police brutality against Black citizens and resulted in hundreds of civilian deaths. Called riots in the press and by policymakers, these clashes between white police and Black citizens became conflated in the public imagination with militant civil rights activism, to the point that any show of armed Black resistance was viewed as a threat to public safety and white property. Urban "riots" became the pressing menace against which white politicians could solidify their legitimacy by appealing to "law and order." Elizabeth Hinton describes how President Johnson's Great Society programs took shape in response to these urban disturbances, linking anti-crime legislation and heightened surveillance with social welfare.[51]

In the fall of 1967, a Black journalist named Robert C. Maynard worked to challenge the stereotypes of urban violence by pursuing a study of five cities in which so-called rioting had taken place: San Francisco, Los Angeles, Detroit, Chicago, and New York. He investigated the sources of urban violence, and what he described as the "angry and violent mood . . . nearing the explosion point in the Black communities of America's largest cities."[52] According to Maynard, Black Nationalists made up a small minority of activists yet were a persuasive voice among those who feared the intensification of white repression. Maynard quoted the Reverend Albert C. Cleage from Detroit's West Side, who linked white supremacist violence and repression to Hitler's Final

Solution, suggesting that whites would stop at nothing to annihilate Blacks. He also interviewed activists who believed that the nation was on the cusp of a racial war and that violent resistance would be necessary for Black survival.

Maynard framed the phenomenon of Black violence within the context of systemic poverty and urban ghetto life, which fed "this mass of trapped humanity, fixed and frozen in yesterday's dream." He declared Black ghettoes to be "immune to wars on poverty, civil rights laws and liberal rhetoric," predicting that "this other, yesterday country threatens to explode now." For Maynard, Black rage was at a boiling point, threatening to wreak havoc.[53] Black citizens' disappointed dreams of finding safety and sustenance in the cities of the North had given way to growing anxieties that "the white man is readying concentration camps and ovens for the Blacks." "The word genocide is used regularly now," explained Maynard, quoting H. Rap Brown, who said in Los Angeles, "'If America plays Nazi, we ain't goin' to play Jews.'" Unrelenting police brutality, combined with federal and state recalcitrance in addressing urban poverty, convinced Black citizens "that whites have a will to murder them."[54]

Maynard discovered that this message especially resonated with the young Black man, who "in violent struggle against this society may be free at last to pursue life without fear of death from the white man." Echoing the words of Robert Williams, urban activists told Maynard they "would rather 'die like men' than live as they are."[55] Some invoked the historical resonance of the movement: "It is not just slavery to which they point, not just the lynchings that multiplied in the years after the collapse of reconstruction, not just the years of deprivation in the cities and abuse in the rural South." Black Nationalists recognized that white supremacy was not confined to the past. In spite of recent civil rights gains—including federal legislation passed in 1964 to outlaw racial discrimination and in 1965 to prohibit voter discrimination—and the national War on Poverty, Black poverty, unemployment, disenfranchisement, and political exclusion persisted. Further, in the name of restoring "law and order," federal law enforcement legislation passed in response to urban riots laid the foundation for the hyperincarceration of Black men.[56]

White insecurity in the face of urban crime drove the creation of neighborhood watch programs. The system originated in response to the failure of neighbors to intervene on behalf of Kitty Genovese, a twenty-eight-year-old white woman who had been attacked by a Black man in the Kew Gardens neighborhood in Queens, New York, in 1964. Although several people heard her screams as she was stabbed and raped, few tried to help, except to yell from their windows. No one called the police until it was too late. Genovese ultimately died from multiple stab wounds. The failure of "good people" to intervene on Genovese's behalf sparked outrage at what psychologists would term the "bystander effect," and public indignation over the case influenced the 1972 creation of the National Neighborhood Watch Program.[57] Overseen by the National Sheriffs' Association, the program epitomized state-sanctioned DIY-security citizenship by engaging citizens in monitoring and policing their own communities. In spite of their emphases on individual empowerment and community engagement, Neighborhood Watch programs intensified the already excessive policing of people of color and others who appear to be "out of place" in particular communities. Decades later, interdependent systems of class, race, and gender bias would continue to frame nonwhite men and boys as potential criminals against whom idealized law-abiding citizens must arm themselves.

Collective Black armed resistance to white supremacist violence would continue long past what many consider to be the height of the civil rights movement. In 1978, the United League—a self-protection organization in northern Mississippi, led by Alfred "Skip" Robinson—resisted racial terror with an armed show of force. The grassroots movement eventually boasted seventy thousand members across the state.[58] At a time when coverage of civil rights mobilization had faded in the popular press, the group provided organized, armed protection against Klan harassment and police brutality.[59] The United League's motto, "Jobs, Land, and Freedom," echoed the multipronged approach to social justice of the Freedman's Bureau and the Black Panther Party, and emphasized the links between economic opportunity, safety, and Black freedom. Like the BPP, the United League drew inspiration from earlier efforts in "confrontational protest" that placed armed self-defense on the front line in the struggle for Black civil rights.[60]

TRAPPED IN HISTORY

James Baldwin wrote in 1955, "People are trapped in history and history is trapped in them."[61] The story of Black paramilitary self-defense illuminates the ways in which people become trapped in partially remembered popular histories, which in turn help perpetuate systemic inequality. As in the case of misremembered stories of Reconstruction as white subjugation, collective memories of Black civil rights activism shift to accommodate the majority population's need for reassurance that all is as it should be. Many long for comfortable historical truths that justify, rather than challenge, existing power structures. Prevailing narratives of civil rights emphasize civil disobedience and peaceful resistance to racial terror, often omitting the bold militancy that made other methods of social-justice work possible.[62] Today we witness a multitiered betrayal of civil rights history: one that holds up nonviolent, peaceful resistance as the exemplar of racial justice activism, and the other that co-opts Black armed militancy in the service of justifying the contemporary armed citizen.

Originally founded to support marksmanship, hunting, and gun safety, the NRA underwent a radical transformation in the late 1970s, when its leaders embraced what we now call "gun rights" activism. Ironically, this ideological shift in favor of reactionary, armed citizenship was made possible by the co-optation of rights discourse popularized by civil rights activism.[63] Grounded in an uncompromising interpretation of the Second Amendment as protecting each American's right to own and bear arms, the turn to "gun rights" signaled an urgent need for individual citizens to own guns for self-defense.

The change in the NRA's focus was in large part driven by an alliance of the reactionary right—eager to roll back the accomplishments of recent struggles for social justice—and gun manufacturers concerned about the nation's waning interest in hunting. The latter capitalized on white fears of urban crime, sparked by the so-called riots of the 1960s and '70s and the "war on drugs" that disproportionately targeted and criminalized underserved communities of color, to motivate people to purchase firearms for self-defense. Starting in the late 1970s, disproportionately white gun rights activists framed individual, armed self-defense as a necessity against the threatening figure of the armed and dangerous Black man, depicted in media coverage of urban riots and conflated in the popular imagination with the Black Panther Party and other militant civil rights organizations.[64] While the NRA and its political allies used race-neutral language to rally public support, their efforts were designed to protect white property and power against the threat of Black criminality. In practice, gun rights were intended to be enjoyed by the powerful few in self-defense against the socially, economically, and politically vulnerable.

The history of the NRA's reactionary politicization is difficult to reconcile with contemporary efforts to anchor gun rights to the ongoing struggle for minority groups' safety and civil rights. Today, the stories of armed Black militants such as Mabel and Robert Williams have been appropriated by a contemporary gun lobby badly in need of a historical makeover. Decades after Robert Williams secured a charter from the NRA for his Black Armed Guard, the NRA's support for Black civil rights became a point of pride for an organization struggling to position itself as color-blind and race neutral. In the mid-1990s, as Robert fought a losing battle against cancer, the NRA invited him to their annual meeting to describe how the organization had helped protect the Black community from white supremacist violence. Mabel Williams laughed as she described how the NRA leadership "talked about Robert Williams and how his rifle club allowed them to survive in the racist state of North Carolina."[65] The irony was not lost on Mabel Williams. Today the NRA celebrates itself as a crusader for Black civil rights against racist federal gun regulations—racist because, per the NRA and other supporters of armed citizenship, gun control laws deprive vulnerable citizens of their right to bear arms. Under this logic, contemporary gun control laws share the same genealogy as the nineteenth-century Black

Codes that disarmed freedmen, leaving them helpless against white supremacist backlash.

John Bender, executive director of Seniors United Supporting the Second Amendment, has similarly characterized gun control as racist and elitist. He asks, "How many people know that the NRA helped train Blacks in Monroe, N.C. and the local NRA chapter mounted an armed defense against the Klan, routing them in a gun battle?"[66] He fails to mention that the NRA conferred a charter on the Black Armed Guard without knowing the members were Black. Bender's version of history celebrates the "role guns played in securing the victories blacks achieved in the civil rights movement of the 1960s" and frames the NRA as the nation's "oldest civil rights organization."[67] Narratives like this reinvent the past to associate contemporary gun control efforts with Black political subjugation. This version of history also elides the fact that the ideological core of the Black Armed Guard and other Black paramilitary groups of the 1950s, '60s, and '70s was a call to *collective* self-defense against pervasive white supremacist power. It also conveniently ignores the particular historical and political context in which Black citizens had no choice but to arm themselves against the violent subjugation of state-sanctioned racial terror.

The historical manipulations are not without their creative turns. For example, one-time Republican presidential hopeful Dr. Ben Carson invoked the Nazi dictatorship's disarming of Jews as evidence that gun control in the United States is a fascist plot against freedom. Had the Jews been armed, argues Carson, the Holocaust would never have happened.[68] His logic echoes that of Jews for the Preservation of Firearm Ownership (JPFO), which calls itself "America's most aggressive civil rights organization." They similarly compare gun control with Nazism and racist terror, while holding up gun rights as the cry of freedom and democracy.

We might witness a similarly history-bending gesture in the conservative commentator Ann Coulter's contemporary advice to Black citizens to "join the NRA" and disavow support for the Democratic Party. Coulter reasons that since nineteenth-century Democrats—the party of choice for supporters of the Confederacy and for those who opposed Black freedom and the Reconstruction amendments—sought to keep weapons out of the hands of African Americans, the party's gun control efforts are similarly racist today.[69] She conveniently fails to mention the mid-twentieth-century political realignment that consolidated the Republican Party under the banner of limited government and states' rights, and—in the wake of Richard Nixon's "Southern strategy"— assembled a base of Southern white support by appealing to fears of Black Power. When the NRA supported Republican Ronald Reagan for president, it was only after he had passed state legislation in California to keep firearms out of the hands of Black militants in the 1960s. For Reagan and other leaders who later supported gun rights, armed citizenship was intended for whites only.

Civil rights militancy occupies an ambivalent position in the contemporary imagination. Although armed self-defense was essential to the success of the movement, dominant historical narratives of the civil rights movement as nonviolent and peaceful obscure more militant legacies.[70] History textbooks celebrate Martin Luther King Jr. and Rosa Parks as exemplars of peaceful resistance, often effacing the contributions of armed activists such as Mabel and Robert Williams and Huey Newton. The emphasis on nonviolent resistance downplays Dr. King's eventual tolerance of armed self-defense, as well as Rosa Parks's militant ideological background that led to her historic confrontation on a Montgomery bus on December 1, 1955.[71]

Dominant portrayals of the modern civil rights movement as peaceful, not militant, serve our nation's dependence on reassuring histories in which goodness inevitably triumphs over evil. The established narrative of Black civil rights activism locates white supremacy—captured in images of cross-burning KKK gatherings and young activists being doused by fire hoses—comfortably in the past. According to this reductionist logic, white supremacist brutality was perpetrated by isolated bad guys who existed in the past, rather than being systemically embedded in the nation's power structures.

Given the nation's appeals to color blindness and multiculturalism, and the election of the first Black president, today's denizens of

DIY-security citizenship must distance themselves from explicit white supremacy. Even when the larger ideological structure of DIY-security citizenship promotes security measures such as stand-your-ground and concealed-carry laws that fail to protect people of color, the gun rights narrative appropriates contemporary claims for social justice by invoking a distorted past.

The false historical conflation of civil rights with gun rights masks both the specificity of the past and the continued racist harms of the present. Today's gun rights activists ignore the particular circumstances under which armed Black militancy constituted a *collective* response to the state's recalcitrance and wanton denial of equal protection. Perhaps more destructively, the historical narrative masks the ways in which contemporary appeals to DIY armed citizenship perpetuate, rather than challenge, white supremacist effects. In the prevalent gun rights narrative, "All lives matter" is the defiant response to "Black lives matter."[72] White supremacy becomes something we read about in history textbooks, and Black citizens needn't be dissatisfied with existing legal protections.

Spurious claims to a manufactured civil rights legacy reassure today's DIY-security citizen that being armed and standing one's ground are racially neutral rights, even if such measures contribute to the criminalization of blackness. If we look to the Black Panther Party for Self-Defense as a legacy not of an enduring aspect of the history of Black responses to white supremacy and violence, but rather as a defiant model of antigovernment militancy, then we need not question why our contemporary calls for DIY-security citizenship actually contribute to racial inequality, rather than challenge it. The language of SYG laws and the NRA's "Armed Citizen" campaign promise that any and all citizens may invoke the law to stand their ground. But in practice, only some enjoy this right.

Today we remain trapped in history, attached to collective memories that perpetuate DIY-security citizenship in the service of white property and power. As in decades past, the law is not a neutral apparatus intended to protect all citizens equally. It continues to serve the reigning power structures, sometimes subtly but always with an eye to the larger society's understandings of "reasonableness," which at their core depend on social blindness and historical amnesia. Our contemporary reverence for the narrative of peaceful civil rights protest sanitizes the violence of the twentieth century, while distracting us from the centrality of Black militancy to civil rights successes. In addition, historical actors such as Mabel and Robert Williams become contemporary models of armed citizenship, helping connect gun rights with freedom and civil rights, while equating federal gun regulation with white supremacy.

SIX

"THE STUFF OF PULP FICTION"

Unreasonable Women, Vigilante Heroes,
and the Rise of the Armed Citizen

*Assessments of reasonableness essentially turn on
a balancing of values, making the term "reasonable"
itself a value-laden expression.*

—JODY D. ARMOUR, 2000

*The one thing a violent rapist deserves
to face is a good woman with a gun.*

—WAYNE LAPIERRE

In the 1960s and '70s, feminist activists rallied around the battle cry "The personal is political" to expose the pervasiveness of gender violence. They emphasized rape and domestic violence as twin consequences of a heteropatriarchal order, but many mainstream solutions to these issues failed to address the simultaneous influence of poverty and racism in women's lives. Efforts to criminalize domestic violence invited law enforcement into the previously "private" space of the man's castle, disproportionately subjecting poor women and women of color to amplified policing while criminalizing their efforts to protect themselves.[1] Indeed, the state's unequal treatment of gender violence has a long history, where women's continued legal subjugation colludes with the preeminence of the white man's castle to make it very difficult for women to secure protection from violent male partners. Moreover, in spite of gun rights lobbyists' efforts to entice women to find empowerment and safety through firearms, those who fight back against their abusers find themselves excluded from the exculpatory language of "reasonable" fear.

"Privacy" in Defense of
the White Man's Castle

According to popular wisdom, threats to women's safety lurked outside of the home, not within it. Throughout the first half of the twentieth century, the home was viewed as a haven or refuge for women and children, with men serving as their natural protectors.[2] Absent their husbands' protection, white women were thought to be at greatest risk from violent intruders and burglars who breached the home's boundaries. Manufacturers of the Savage Automatic handgun in 1907 (see figure 6.1) capitalized on anxieties about home intruders in advertising that appealed to the insecurity of the white wife and mother in her husband's absence. The gun's small size and simplicity of use—"Ten Quick Shots!"—rendered the otherwise vulnerable woman and her "little ones and property" "SAFE!" during a home break-in.

The ad's urgent depiction of white womanhood in danger masked the ongoing vulnerability of Black women, who struggled at the intersection of sexual and white supremacist violence. Through much of the twentieth century, all-white male juries continued to vindicate white men accused of raping Black women, and activists like Ida B. Wells, Fannie Barrier Williams, Anna Julia Cooper, and Rosa Parks made anti-rape activism a critical part of their broader civil rights platforms.[3] The simultaneous gender, race, and class analysis provided by women of color would prove crucial to later feminist interventions against rape and domestic violence.

The Savage ad also veiled the reality of domestic violence, which was by far a more significant threat to women's safety than home invasions by strangers. As the boundaries of a man's castle expanded to allow certain white men to engage in lethal self-defense outside the home, women of all races and classes remained powerless against violent husbands. Even as coverture and laws supporting a man's right to "chastise" his wife

Figure 6.1. The Savage Automatic pistol, manufactured from 1907 to 1920, was advertised in the popular press. This ad appeared in Cosmopolitan *in 1913.*
UNIVERSITY OF MICHIGAN LIBRARY

eroded during the late nineteenth century, the state allowed domestic relations between husbands and wives to remain largely unregulated.[4] Obtaining a divorce remained difficult without proof of a spouse's excessive abuse or nonsupport. Furthermore, wives who managed to separate from abusive husbands struggled economically in a world where women's unpaid labor was considered part of their "natural" roles as caregivers who were the dependents of male heads of households. For many women, remaining with an abusive spouse was preferable to the stigma and economic insecurity of divorce.[5]

Appeals to the privacy of the home made it difficult to justify state intervention in any but the most egregious cases of domestic battery. In 1890, Boston attorneys Louis Brandeis and Samuel Warren proposed the existence of a right to privacy in a *Harvard Law Review* article that reinforced popular beliefs that the government should neither regulate nor interfere with citizens' private business—and domestic violence came under that rubric.[6] Their introduction of privacy as a right suggested the exclusion of state and federal law enforcement from intervening in matters taking place within the home. Under this perspective, the home was a private space, whose governance fell to the man of the house. Women subjected to violent treatment by their spouses had little recourse, and domestic violence was not considered an issue of public concern.

Given the wider society's support for home privacy and the absence of systemic measures to address domestic violence, little reliable data exists on its prevalence in the first half of the twentieth century. A study of family violence in Boston by historian Linda Gordon reveals that abused wives often sought aid from child abuse agencies in an effort to protect themselves and their children from violent husbands.[7] When women did seek support from local agencies, the help they received was limited by dominant perceptions of family violence as an individual, rather than a larger, social issue. Legal scholar Claire Houston explains that psychological theories emerging in the 1920s and '30s portrayed family violence as a problem of abnormal personalities rather than a result of persistent structural inequalities.[8] Domestic relations courts attempted to foster spousal reconciliation, but they did nothing to protect women from ongoing violence. The effort to preserve marriage remained at the heart of therapeutic, individualized responses, which maintained the privacy of the home by keeping the government out of domestic affairs.[9]

"THE PERSONAL IS POLITICAL": FEMINISTS RESPOND TO RAPE AND DOMESTIC VIOLENCE

The widespread appeal to privacy as a veil for gender violence came under attack in the 1960s, when intersecting social justice efforts, including antiwar, civil rights, New Left, and second-wave feminist movements, ushered in an era of pervasive critique and protest. Under the rallying cry "The personal is political," feminist activists worked to expose the roots of sexual and gender violence, particularly that which took place in the supposedly protective spaces of the home. Radical feminists such as Kate Millett and Del Martin spoke out against the myth of the "safe home," revealing the heterosexual family as one of the many structures fostering and masking patriarchal oppression.[10]

Women of color contributed incisive analyses of gender violence, focusing on multiple, simultaneous axes of oppression, including race, ethnicity, and class, in addition to gender and sexuality. Long before second-wave feminists turned a public lens on sexual and domestic violence, activists such as Rosa Parks worked to draw attention to Black women's ongoing subjugation to white supremacist sexual violence. Demands for justice for Black rape survivors helped influence the wider struggle for civil rights, eventually providing a critical intellectual foundation for radical feminist interventions in the 1960s.[11]

The Third World Women's Alliance (TWWA), formed in 1968 as a branch of the Student Nonviolent Coordinating Committee, similarly brought a critical feminist lens to racial justice struggles.[12] The TWWA's newsletter, *Triple Jeopardy: Racism, Imperialism, Sexism*, addressed multiple forms of gender violence afflicting women of color worldwide, including forced sterilization, police violence under fascism, and generalized sexism.[13] The Combahee River Collective, formed in Boston in 1974, likewise addressed "the manifold and simultaneous oppressions" that historically subjected women of color to intersecting strains of violence.[14]

The first public demonstrations against sexual violence took place in New York City in 1971 under the leadership of the New York Radical Feminists and featured individual women speaking out about their experiences with rape and other forms of gender violence.[15] Participants at this and other public rallies depicted intimate violence as a systemic, widespread social problem, which flew in the face of prevailing beliefs that rape was an act of individual, sexually pathological men. In 1975, Susan Brownmiller depicted sexual violence as a means of maintaining patriarchal privilege and reinforcing women's status as quasi-property.[16]

The critical advocacy work of feminists of color was vital to the push to bring previously "private" violence into the public spotlight. The Women of Color Task Force developed from the National Coalition Against Domestic Violence in the late 1970s, building collaboration among community leaders and fostering support services for victims of domestic violence.[17] Other organizations designed for immigrant women and women of color, like the South Asian group Asha, focused on the particular vulnerabilities of poor, non-English-speaking women trapped in abusive relationships. Mending the Sacred Hoop, organized in the 1980s, supports Native American survivors of sexual violence.[18] The Chicana Service Action Center, founded in California in 1978, addressed women's vulnerabilities holistically, establishing women's shelters as well as employment, child-care, and educational initiatives.[19] For these organizations and their leadership, domestic violence was one of many sinister consequences of widespread systematic exclusions of the poor, people of color, and women from the promises of equal protection.

In the late 1970s, states responded to the growing pressure by women's antiviolence advocates by disallowing certain forms of evidence in rape trials, such as testimony about a woman's past sexual experience, and passing mandatory-arrest laws that required police to arrest perpetrators of domestic violence, regardless of whether the victim consented to the arrest.[20] Given the complexity of intimate-partner violence, in which survivors often continue to harbor feelings of attachment to their abusers and/or fear reprisal should they cooperate with law enforcement, many resist the arrest and prosecution of their abusers and refuse to testify against them. In 1980, Michigan passed comprehensive anti-rape legislation to help protect rape survivors from having their sexual history admitted as evidence in court.[21] By 1981, twenty-one states permitted warrantless arrests in domestic violence cases involving misdemeanors.[22] According to feminist legal scholar Jennifer Nash, this policy "shift[ed] the injury of domestic violence from the victim alone to the victim and the citizenry," effectively transforming domestic violence into "a crime worthy of public attention."[23]

While anti-domestic-violence initiatives led by white feminists tended to focus on patriarchal power as the root of inequality, those created by women of color addressed gender violence as also embedded in systemic classism and racism, as well. Feminists of color, including Angela Davis, Kimberlé Crenshaw, Gloria Anzaldúa, bell hooks, Dorothy

Roberts, Audre Lorde, and Barbara Smith, have shown how the struggle against patriarchal violence must be grounded in an equally robust opposition to racist and classist structures that disproportionately harm poor women of color.[24]

Many feminists have also cautioned against an overreliance on the government to address problems of systemic oppression. Given the government's complicity in systems of domination that favor white masculinity, Angela Davis writes, "It is difficult to envision the state as the holder of solutions to the problem of violence against women of color."[25] Indeed, efforts to enlist law enforcement in eliminating gender violence have often resulted in what political scientist Marie Gottschalk calls "unsavory coalitions" between women's advocates and conservative sponsors of "law and order" policing.[26] Like the selective policing of underserved communities and the historic targeting of people of color—exemplified in the "war on drugs"—mandatory-arrest policies tend to disadvantage the poor and people of color, even if domestic violence is a problem that transcends racial and class boundaries. Even as feminists have worked to expose and eliminate domestic violence, explains Davis, state policies maintain a "racist fixation on people of color as the primary perpetrators of violence." She and other feminist scholars who study intersecting sources of inequality have asked white feminist allies to resist dominant constructions of criminality "as a black or Latino" and to maintain a nuanced and racially inclusive approach to solving problems of gender violence.[27]

MODEL MUGGING AND MANDATORY ARREST: THE RACIAL POLITICS OF FEMINIST SELF-DEFENSE

Some solutions to gender violence have played into racial stereotypes of criminality by assuming that most perpetrators are unknown to their victims. The 1970s saw the growth of self-defense and violence prevention programs aimed at empowering individual women to fight sexual violence. While the feminist self-defense movement emanated from efforts to illuminate so-called "private" as well as public gender violence, these efforts often focused primarily on dangers outside of the home, to the neglect of those perpetrated by intimate partners.

In 1972, a white, male martial arts specialist created a program called Model Mugging, which provided enrollees several weeks of intensive self-defense training, testing them along the way with simulated attacks from heavily padded "model muggers."[28] Model Mugging and the Women's Self-Defense Council, formed in 1975, sought to help women overcome their socialized passivity so that they might defend themselves from male attackers. These and similar efforts to empower individual women have enjoyed significant success; they appear to provide women an equal opportunity to take control over their own safety in a perilous world.

Yet the composition of these and other feminist self-defense classes that proliferated through the 1970s and '80s tended to be predominantly white and middle-class.[29] While the organizations did not explicitly exclude poor women and women of color, many offered subtly coded messages about which women most urgently need self-defense training. Some white proponents of women's self-defense echoed prevailing stereotypes by suggesting that Black women, naturally more "street-wise" and "assertive," had less need for self-defense training.[30] And the white male instructors posing as model muggers often mimicked the speech patterns of working-class or Black men when addressing their model-mugging targets.[31] While these self-defense innovations were grounded in an effort to counteract women's gender socialization, many ended up perpetuating white supremacist and classist assumptions about the likely identity of perpetrators of violence against women.[32]

Law enforcement protections for abuse survivors have been similarly tone-deaf to the racial and class implications of increased policing. In addition to their intensified surveillance of men of color, state responses were built, according to Jennifer Nash, "on the architecture of a particular kind of privacy" that has remained elusive to poor women and women of color.[33] Law enforcement's intervention into African American homes has historically been less a gesture of protection than a strategy to control and dominate.[34] Nash explains how mandatory arrest policies—in spite of their origins in an effort to protect domestic violence survivors—actually intensify "the cultural and legal hyper-surveillance of the Black body."[35] Certain policies, like "no-drop" rules that prevent victims from dropping charges if a prosecutor wishes to pursue a criminal case, further disempower women for whom the home may be their last and only vestige of privacy.[36] Since communities of color attract more intensive police scrutiny, policies designed to protect battered women have ironically added another link in a long chain of state intrusions that threaten both the autonomy and safety of women of color.[37]

Women of color and poor women face a double bind in their historic unequal protection by, and justifiable suspicion of, the US legal system. Their historic exclusion from protection and increased surveillance by law enforcement conspire to exclude them from the vindicating logic of self-defense. According to sociologist Beth Richie, women of color are often criminalized when they "take the law into their own hands" to protect themselves and their children from abusive partners.[38] Further, some states' mandatory arrest laws require the arrest of both partners if it appears that both used violence, which places women who fight back against their abusers in danger of criminal prosecution.[39]

This logic hearkens back to Sir Matthew Hale's eighteenth-century *Pleas of the Crown*, that a woman might use lethal force, without retreating, against a stranger who attempts to rape her, but she was *not* allowed to use similar force against her spouse.[40] The residues of legal coverture, which had placed women under the control of their fathers or husbands, continue to haunt the state's antiviolence interventions. While the law might protect white women who are threatened by strangers, particularly if their attackers are nonwhite, it often fails to protect these same women from violence from their own intimate partners.[41] This practice runs counter to evidence indicating that rape and domestic violence are usually perpetrated by a known individual, most often an intimate partner.[42] Indeed, marital rape was not criminalized in all states until the 1990s.[43] In the popular imagination, rape and other forms of violence against women continue to be imagined as crimes perpetrated by criminal "strangers" rather than by husbands, boyfriends, and acquaintances. Indeed, many of the most visible advocates of women's self-defense, like Paxton Quigley, author of the canonical *Armed and Female* (1989), promote the idea that the greatest threats to women are strangers.[44] In the dominant American cultural imagination, the figure of the criminal "stranger" remains a person of color.

SEEING THREAT: SEX, RACE, AND THE "AVERAGE REASONABLE PERSON"

In *Murder and the Reasonable Man,* legal scholar Cynthia Lee explores the impact of racism, sexism, and homophobia on perceptions of "reasonableness" in the courtroom. Designed to help adjudicate criminal cases in ways that acknowledge the complexity of human behavior, the reasonableness standard asks juries to consider whether a "reasonable person" might behave as the defendant did in the particular circumstances of the case. While they appear to be based on considerations of universal human nature, presumptions of reasonableness do not exist in an ideological vacuum. Legal scholar Aaron Goldstein writes, "The fictional 'average reasonable person,' who is the touchstone of all judgments of reasonableness, is thus born in the courtroom carrying all the prejudices of the twelve people who gave that person life."[45] While the reasonableness requirement allows for greater community input and flexibility to help maximize fairness, it can also be used to excuse some criminal behaviors perpetrated by "majority culture" or socially privileged defendants.[46] Lee explains how social norms shape assumptions about gender and sexuality, such as the belief that heterosexual men are justified in responding violently to unfaithful wives or girlfriends. These assumptions influence legal decisions when courts excuse certain instances of violent male behavior as "reasonable," rather than criminal.[47]

According to legal scholar Jody Armour, "The concept of reasonableness drives self-defense doctrine" because defendants must convince juries that their perception of a threat was reasonable in the moment when they claim to have acted in self-defense.[48] Inevitably, the biases of individual jurors—shaped by the prejudices of our wider social and cultural terrain—can and do disadvantage socially vulnerable individuals, including racially minoritized people, women, and gender-nonconforming people, as well as the socioeconomically disadvantaged (to name a few), when members of such groups claim to have acted in self-defense against relatively dominant social actors.[49]

In practice, says legal scholar Gayle Strommen, women who kill or maim their abusive male partners encounter an uphill battle in proving that they acted in self-defense, because they must convince the court that they acted out of reasonable fear of their abusers. Often, it is difficult for jurors to imagine that a defendant believed her attacker posed an imminent threat in the moment he was killed, and many question why the defendant did not leave her abusive partner long before the deadly encounter.[50] Since most jurors are drawn from the general population, many of whom perceive domestic violence through the lens of prevailing racial, gender, and class assumptions, it is difficult for them to imagine how a battered woman's self-defensive actions might constitute a reasonable response to a violent spouse.

Survivors of intimate-partner violence, such as Carol Stonehouse, a white police officer who was convicted of murder for killing her ex-boyfriend in 1983, often find themselves excluded from the exculpatory claims of self-defense when their fears seem unreasonable to the members of the jury. Thirty-eight when she joined the Pittsburgh police force, the twice-divorced mother of two pursued law enforcement as a path to economic and personal security. Shortly after joining the force, she met and started dating William Walsh, an older, married white man with twenty years of police experience. Soon thereafter, Walsh's behavior turned threatening. He was possessive and jealous, often coming over uninvited and banging on her door late at night. On one such occasion, Stonehouse called the police. The officers who responded to the call knew Walsh, and they dismissed the incident and did not file a report. Stonehouse, who attributed the incident to Walsh's excessive drinking, continued seeing him.[51]

Walsh's behavior steadily became more aggressive, and he took to breaking into Stonehouse's home and destroying clothing and furniture. After one argument, Walsh placed flowers by her door, later explaining that they were for her funeral.[52] The threatening behavior escalated, and Stonehouse's efforts to end the relationship were met by more frequent break-ins, destruction of property, and death threats.[53] Over the course of three years, multiple relocations, and several unsuccessful attempts to secure police protection, Stonehouse was unable to end Walsh's abuse. Her repeated appeals to the police for protection resulted in casual suggestions that she arrest him herself.[54] The details of the case were so alarming that Justice Rolf Larsen, who oversaw Stonehouse's appeal in 1989, described them as "the stuff of pulp fiction."[55]

Late on the evening of March 16, 1983, Stonehouse called the police after Walsh broke into her home in a drunken rage, but they did not arrive until it was too late. Stonehouse forced him outside, where his agitation escalated as he paced her yard. He waved his gun while shouting that she was "done now." Stonehouse fired twice from her balcony two stories up. Walsh collapsed while retreating toward his van, dying in the yard.[56] Stonehouse was charged with criminal homicide, and, in spite of her plea of self-defense, the jury found her guilty of third-degree murder.[57] On July 25, 1984, she was sentenced to seven to fourteen years in prison.

Five months later, a thirty-seven-year-old white New Yorker named Bernhard Goetz became a celebrated figure of vigilante justice for shooting four Black teens in a subway car. His victims were Barry Allen, Troy Canty, Darrell Cabey, all nineteen years old, and James Ramseur, age eighteen. Goetz pulled out his unlicensed pistol and shot each one after Canty approached him and said, "Give me five dollars." After shooting the boys, Goetz noticed that Cabey remained conscious and cowering in a corner. Goetz said, "You seem to be all right. Here's another," and fired the shot that severed Cabey's spinal cord.[58] Goetz fled north to avoid arrest but turned himself in nine days later. Charged with attempted murder, assault, reckless endangerment, and several firearm-possession offenses, Goetz pleaded self-defense. He was acquitted of all charges except for carrying an unlicensed gun, for which he served eight months in jail.[59]

Although both Stonehouse and Goetz claimed to have acted in self-defense, the outcomes of their cases rested on divergent assessments of each defendant's "reasonable" fear. In the eyes of their juries, Goetz's fear of the four unarmed Black youths was reasonable, while Stonehouse's fear of her armed white ex-boyfriend was not. Race and gender assumptions simultaneously influenced the juries' understandings of "reasonableness" in the defendants' use of self-defense. The exclusionary implications of lethal self-defense exemptions come into focus only when we follow Jennifer Nash's call to place "multiplicity . . . at the center of the inquiry," and resist tendencies to compartmentalize privileges and harms generated by racism, classism, and sexism.[60]

Carol Stonehouse's femininity, her experience of intimate partner abuse, and her professional police training undermined her ability to appear reasonable in her fear of her armed ex-boyfriend. Even though Walsh had invaded her "castle" and threatened her with a gun, Stonehouse was obliged to retreat rather than to "meet force with force." In spite of her testimony of her years of abuse, the court could not picture Walsh, a retired white police officer, as a true threat. Perhaps most damning to her case was the fact that the danger Walsh presented on March 17 did not appear "imminent" under traditional understandings of justifiable homicide. The court reasoned that Stonehouse could have retreated into the safety of her home while Walsh was in her yard shouting and waving his gun.

While Stonehouse's jury could not comprehend the urgency of the danger Walsh posed, Goetz's jury imagined *only* imminent threat from the four unarmed Black teens who approached the defendant on the subway. In both cases, armed white masculinity proved vindicating, and the floating parameters of the white man's castle haunted each. Goetz was master of his castle, which in this case extended into New York City's public transportation system; Stonehouse was not entitled to protect herself, even within her own home, against her abusive ex-boyfriend.

Carol Stonehouse's case pitted dominant perceptions of domestic violence survivors—and limitations on their capacity for "reasonableness"—against expansive legal interpretations of justifiable homicide. During an unsuccessful appeal in 1986, the prosecutor asked Stonehouse if she had been "a willing participant in the activities that went on between [her] and William Walsh."[61] In this case, as in many others, the numerous assaults made by the deceased rendered the defendant's actions untenable. After all, asked the prosecution, since Walsh treated Stonehouse so violently, why hadn't she left him earlier?

Many domestic violence experts—psychologists, social workers, and researchers—maintain that the experience of being battered lies far outside the comprehension of most people. Since, in the popular imagination, "families are supposed to provide a tranquil refuge from the strains and stresses of the outside world," writes psychologist Lenore Walker, many people are blind to the prevalence of domestic violence.[62] Widespread denial of intimate violence, in turn, makes it difficult for many to empathize with women who kill their partners in self-defense if they don't appear to be in imminent danger.[63] It is difficult for many to imagine how a woman who has spent years living under the same roof as her abuser might suddenly perceive him as an urgent threat. Consequently, we can surmise that it would be difficult for many jurors—regardless of gender—to view a domestic violence survivor's self-defensive behavior as reasonable.

Furthermore, our laws do not recognize how the cumulative effects of violence may influence a person's sense of danger and threat. Jody Armour explains how asking judge and jury to consider the battered woman's decision from "the perspective of someone in her position" contradicts the "objective" test, where one considers the defendant as an average person, not as someone who experienced exceptional trauma and violence.[64] The concept of battered-woman syndrome (BWS) emerged as a response to these legal inconsistencies. BWS developed out of a 1979 study published by Lenore Walker, who described domestic violence as a three-stage cycle resulting in deep psychological trauma and leading to acts of desperation. Among the effects of the cyclical violence was learned helplessness, which convinced the abused woman that she was powerless to leave the relationship and that she was at fault for her predicament.[65] Under this logic, abuse survivors should not be held to objective standards of reasonableness.

Claiming to be a victim of BWS in court is comparable to claiming temporary insanity; the accused maintains that he or she was incapable of rationality and reason at the time the crime was committed and therefore cannot be held responsible for his or her actions. Like Daniel Sickles, the first man who successfully claimed temporary insanity after killing his wife's lover in a fit of jealous rage in 1859, a woman claiming BWS gave up the right to be seen as a typical "reasonable" person in exchange for leniency. Yet Carol Stonehouse's attorneys did not invoke the BWS defense, nor did they request expert testimony to provide the jury with insights into the psychological effects of battering.[66] For one thing, women who successfully claim BWS must appear helpless and frail, and this remains true today.[67] Carol Stonehouse did not fit this image, as evidenced in the prosecution's suggestion that Stonehouse, as a police officer trained in lethal combat, was not capable of being abused.[68]

By contrast, Bernhard Goetz's claims of self-defense were seen as reasonable based on an unacknowledged but shared belief in Black criminality. At the time, it seemed that the judge, jury, and mainstream press were aligned in their belief that Black men were inherently threatening.[69] Thus, the majority white jury could imagine the four young men who approached Goetz in the subway as imminent threats. During the trial, Goetz's defense attorney referred to Darrell Cabey, James Ramseur, Troy Canty, and Barry Allen as "savages," "thugs," and "predators." He depicted them as fundamentally dangerous, a "gang" in search of an easy target to rob.[70] While Goetz did not personally know the four young men who approached him, his jury deemed "reasonable" his assumption that they posed an imminent threat to his safety.

Ironically, the adjudication of reasonable self-defense in the two cases also evinced a lopsided understanding of the defendants' prior knowledge of their victims. Even though Stonehouse intimately knew Walsh's violent tendencies, and had sustained actual physical injuries at his hands, her jury could not identify with her fears. Yet Goetz's experience of having been robbed before, combined with his prejudiced assumption of young Black men's fundamentally violent nature, was sufficient for the jurors to find his fears reasonable.

Responses to the trial's outcome ranged from supporters congratulating Goetz for "winning one for the good guys" to detractors who characterized him as a racist vigilante and a Nazi.[71] Supporters denied that race had anything to do with the final decision, even though some admitted that seeing James Ramseur—whom one commentator described as an "obscene thug"—take the stand caused them to identify with Goetz as a man who simply refused to be a victim.[72]

Although there was an abundance of documented evidence of Walsh's ongoing abuse and harassment, Carol Stonehouse's jury could not imagine her actions as reasonable. She was forty-eight when she was finally released from jail in 1989, her murder conviction overturned. The appellate court faulted her defense attorneys for failing to provide expert testimony on the psychological effects of domestic violence, and stated that her jury based its decision on "erroneous myths concerning the victims of such abuse."[73] Her exoneration marked the beginning of a trend: in 1990 the governor of Ohio granted clemency to twenty-five women who were imprisoned for having killed or harmed their abusers, and other governors followed suit shortly thereafter.[74]

By 2000, in a majority of states, expert testimony on BWS was admissible as evidence in cases in which defendants asserted self-defense in crimes against their attackers. But although BWS allows *some* domestic violence victims to avoid criminal penalties, as a legal tactic, it was built on the faulty logic of a battered woman's incapacity for reasonable thought. Rather than allow abused women entitlement to justifiable self-defense, BWS reinforces traditional associations of femininity with hysteria and irrationality. Legal scholar Bess Rothenberg explains how BWS rests on notions of the violence survivor as "helpless," a "passive victim," which excludes many women who appear capable or strong.[75] Given widespread stereotypes of Black women as "strong," "angry," and "emasculating," women of color have been disproportionately excluded from the exonerating possibilities of BWS.[76] Ultimately, BWS is an inadequate shield for battered women seeking refuge from criminal prosecution, just as the state's intervention into the once-private space of the home has also proved to be a double-edged sword.

FROM PUBLIC FAILURES TO PRIVATE OPPORTUNITIES:
GUNS AGAINST GENDER VIOLENCE

In the 1970s and '80s, feminists worked urgently to illuminate the harms done by domestic violence and rape, and to frame them as profound public health and social justice issues. Despite some progress, these problems have proved quite tenacious. Between 1976 and 1996, on average four women each day were killed in episodes of domestic violence.[77] And while homicide rates decreased by nearly half from 1992 to 2011, falling to their lowest levels since 1963, the incidence of domestic violence remains intractably high.[78] The Centers for Disease Control and Prevention's National Intimate Partner and Sexual Violence Survey for 2014 indicates that nearly one in four women have been subjected to serious violence by an intimate partner.[79] In 2008, 45.3 percent of female homicide victims (compared to 4.9 percent of male victims) were killed by an intimate partner.[80] Similarly, three out of four sexual assaults are committed by someone known to the victims, which is in large part why rape remains vastly underreported.[81]

Given the stubborn resistance of gender violence to law enforcement and policy solutions, it is no surprise that many have turned to lethal self-defense as a solution. Beginning in the 1970s, around the same time that women's self-defense classes were gaining popularity, the National Rifle Association began a special effort to reach out to women with messages of empowerment and personal safety. The group Women in the NRA (WINRA) emerged in the 1970s with the promise of "new programs, new approaches, new opportunities" designed specifically for female gun enthusiasts. The group also offered a booklet, *WINRA—On Personal Safety*, to educate women on "effective self-defense techniques." An ad for the booklet in July 1977 depicts a white woman walking outdoors, looking furtively over her shoulder at an approaching stranger.[82] Like many of the self-defense courses based on martial arts, the NRA frames women's primary threat as the criminal stranger, not the abusive spouse or partner. And the logical solution is a lethal one.

The NRA's focus on women's self-defense accompanied the organization's radical political shift to the right. While the NRA originally supported the 1968 Gun Control Act, in large part to subdue the perceived threat of armed Black militancy, it soon thereafter became a reactionary social movement against all forms of gun regulation.[83] By the late 1970s, the NRA had become a champion of unrestricted gun access, invoking the Second Amendment as a call for armed citizenship.

Reinventing itself as an advocate for individual gun rights, the NRA adopted a new motto in 1977: "The Right of the People to Keep and Bear Arms Shall Not Be Infringed." Mimicking the language of civil rights, encrypted into federal legislation that prohibited discrimination, gun rights centered on the individual's right to own and carry firearms. Robert J. Spitzer, author of *Guns Across America*, traces how this interpretation marked an extreme departure from earlier interpretations of the Second Amendment as upholding a right to bear arms *collectively* in state militias. Spitzer argues that contemporary claims about the unconstitutionality of gun regulation are based on a mythological past, when, lobbyists assert, access to firearms guaranteed safety in the "wild west" and other locations of insecurity and danger.[84]

At the heart of the NRA's ideological shift were deepening concerns about big government, violent crime, and perceived threats to white lives and white property. Journalist Dave Gilson has tracked how NRA advertisements signaled the organization's political transformation. The advertisements increasingly gave vent to suspicion of the government's infringement on individual gun possession. For example, a 1970 ad warned readers of "powerful forces—possibly well-intentioned, but ill-informed—working eagerly and relentlessly to curb and eventually to abolish the hunting rights, privileges and freedoms that you enjoy today!"[85]

The ads became more overt in their appeals to white anxiety and antigovernment sentiment, especially in the wake of the 1975 establishment of the NRA's lobbying arm, the Institute for Legislative Action, which focused on building a political advocacy machine to support gun ownership.[86] The NRA's new propaganda machine deployed images of urban crime and home invasion to cultivate a fear-driven need for armed self-defense among whites who felt threatened by the social justice movements and civil rights legislation of the 1960s. The organization seized the opportunity to build on the momentum of a growing reactionary right-wing movement whose Republican "Southern strategy" appealed to racism and status anxiety to court Southern white voters beginning in the 1960s.

By the mid- to late 1980s, the organization's scare tactics had intensified. It was then that NRA ads, appearing in *Guns and Ammo,* *American Rifleman,* and *Guns* magazine, began to reflect the reactionary, antigovernment tone that would characterize the organization in the twenty-first century. Print ads highlighted dangerous streets, and armed criminals breaking into middle-class households at night. Gilson explains that "fears about violent crime fueled these ads promoting concealed-carry laws and individual self-protection," while urging "law-abiding" citizens to take their personal safety into their own hands.[87] The racial implications of the imagery were implicit in invocations of "urban violence" and dangerous city streets. The ads also targeted the federal government as a threat to gun ownership and public safety. By the 1990s, the ads condemned the government's hostility to citizen's rights to self-protection, comparing the FBI to a totalitarian regime. Ads urged readers to "take back your government and save your guns." Even in the face of decreasing crime rates, the NRA portrayed a law-abiding, white citizen at risk for violent crime, and armed self-defense as an urgent need.

An appeal to (white) women's safety was a significant part of the NRA's transformation. Ads increasingly capitalized on fears of women's vulnerability to rape, some featuring dark alleyways crosscut with shadows, and white women walking alone. Headlines shrieked "Should You Shoot a Rapist Before He Cuts Your Throat?" and "Why Can't a Policeman Be There When You Need Him?"[88] These ads suggested that the vulnerability of white women was a consequence of state incompetence and law enforcement failures. For the gun rights lobby, the vulnerable *white* woman became a convenient symbol, and the tortured logic held that if more women had weapons, fewer of them would be raped, battered, or killed. Yet the NRA's appeals to women effaced the realities of family violence, even as the number of women killed by intimate partners peaked in the late 1980s.[89] By underscoring the potential danger and criminality of strangers, the organization drew on implicitly racist fears while ignoring the actual dangers women faced in their own homes.

The gun rights lobby continues its aggressive outreach to women, and the numbers of women who own firearms has grown significantly. Between 2005 and 2013, gun ownership among women grew from 13 to 23 percent.[90] The online presence of the gun rights lobby is substantial, with websites and informational videos designed to appeal to female gun enthusiasts. The gun manufacturer Smith and Wesson maintains a website called NRA Women, offering information about women's safety and training programs, links to product information and reviews, and web-based programming. The videos balance empowering messages about the joy of learning to shoot with the fear-based urgency of individual self-defense.[91] An advertisement for the National Association for Gun Rights, a one-issue nonprofit that "believes in absolutely 100% NO COMPROMISE on gun rights issues," depicts a young woman aiming a pistol with the caption "Mama didn't raise a victim."[92] Notably, almost all the women depicted in these images are white, and they cite their reliance on guns for personal protection. They also utilize the language of consumer "choice" and personal "empowerment" in their pleas to "protect our fundamental Constitutional right to choose to defend ourselves."[93]

In early 2015, Governor Scott Walker of Wisconsin eliminated the forty-eight-hour waiting period for gun purchases in his state. He publicly supported the law by suggesting that women will be better able to protect themselves from abusers if they have easier access to firearms.[94] State Representative Jesse Kremer, who coauthored the bill, similarly promoted the legislation as offering "another option for those who may find themselves in harmful situations, such as victims of domestic violence."[95] Representative Samantha Kerkman joined the chorus of support for removing the waiting period, because easier access to firearms "would curb domestic violence against women."[96] The bill's supporters capitalize on anxiety about gender violence, while expressing a paternalistic interest in women's protection. In this way the reactionary right can portray itself as concerned about "women's health and safety," even as they curtail women's access to basic human rights and health services.[97]

Gun rights activists' and policymakers' support for women's safety rings hollow in light of their vocal opposition to any limitations on gun ownership. Recent studies show that an abused woman is five times more likely to be killed if her partner owns a gun.[98] The vast majority of women killed by firearms are killed by intimate partners and ex-partners.[99] In spite of this data, many states continue to allow perpetrators of domestic violence to purchase or retain firearms even after being convicted of abuse.[100] A recent investigation of all fifty states that tracked the impact of lax or unenforced gun laws on domestic violence victims and survivors concluded that "the most dangerous place for a woman in the developed world is America."[101]

Moreover, the prevailing gun rights security narrative represents the violent criminal stranger as the greatest threat to (white) women, rather than the angry spouse or ex-spouse whose ownership of the "castle" legitimates his domination. By focusing on threats lurking outside the supposedly protective confines of the home, gun rights advocates capitalize on images of female vulnerability, without compromising the strength of their appeal to a predominately white male base. For the NRA and its supporters on the reactionary right, the castle remains a white man's space of refuge, and acknowledging its danger to women would compromise its sanctity. Ultimately, the denizens of armed citizenship have never intended for women to use firearms in self-defense against male heads of households.

Jody Armour emphasizes the common political concerns at stake for survivors of intimate violence and people of color: "At bottom, advocates for battered women and advocates for disadvantaged minorities must overcome the same entrenched conservative assumptions to successfully defend their respective clients. These assumptions bolster the subordination of women and impoverished Blacks by making their plight seem natural and just."[102] The power of DIY-security citizenship rests on its ability to make armed citizenship appear necessary and natural for all law-abiding citizens while ensuring that—in practice—"law-abiding" applies only to a select few.

Ongoing struggles against gender violence have shown that racialized assumptions about masculinity and femininity constitute the scaffolding for our contemporary ideals of armed citizenship. Gun rights activists' appeals to personal protection raise the specter of the white woman in perpetual danger, the damsel in distress fleeing criminal strangers lurking in the bushes. Calls for women's protection hark back to a long tradition of criminalizing men of color as a threat to white women, while denying the ways in which women of color have been subject to racist sexual violence. Indeed, until recently, Black women have been notably scarce in the NRA's targeted appeals to citizens to find empowerment and safety in firearms.

Although feminist organizing and advocacy called public attention to the scourge of gender violence occurring in the supposedly safe space of the home, the wider systemic and historic factors that contribute to domestic violence remain misunderstood and stubbornly resistant to legal interventions. In the words of feminist legal scholar Reva Siegel, the "law would appear to be a double-edged weapon of social change, repeatedly demonstrating the capacity to legitimate privileges it seems at first to challenge."[103] Today, the vulnerable position of intimate-violence survivors and continued criminalization of people of color reveal the stark exclusionary cracks in the armor of armed self-defense.

SEVEN

AVOIDING A "FATE WORSE THAN DEATH"

How We Learned to Stand Our Ground

*"WARNING: Armed citizen, nothing
in my house is worth your life."*

—STICKER PROVIDED BY THE ARMED CITIZEN PROJECT

*Where was the NRA on Trayvon Martin's right to stand
his ground? What happened to their principled position?
The Trayvon Martins of the world never had that right because
the "ground" was never considered theirs to stand on.*

—ROBIN D. G. KELLEY, 2013

As part of a complex web of legal innovations in response to perceived security anxieties, particularly fears of violent crime and home invasion, the nation's first stand-your-ground law was passed in Florida in 2005. The laws vary across the thirty-three states in which they have been passed, but most expand the boundaries of the "castle" by allowing lethal self-defense without retreat in response to "reasonable" threats. Many also grant criminal or civil immunity for defendants who "reasonably" claim to have killed in self-defense. In addition to their powerful legal implications, the laws have had a profound effect on the nation's culture, reinforcing the belief that a good, law-abiding citizen is an armed citizen.

The ethos of individualized, lethal self-defense as the solution for multiple, and sometimes conflicting, safety concerns has become pervasive. Now, more than ever, a man's castle—the sanctuary of white, property-owning heteromasculinity—seems under siege by forces within as well as beyond the nation's boundaries.[1] Today's DIY-security impulse emerges at the intersection of multiple intensifying fear factors: panic in the wake of the September 11, 2001, terrorist attacks, and more recently in response to the influence of the extremist Islamic State of Iraq and the Levant; suspicion of undocumented immigrants; and a perceived onslaught of criminality, barely contained by a growing and corporatized prison industrial complex. Each threat summons an image of the criminal stranger, who haunts our boundaries and threatens the safety—and *sanctity*—of our nation's most treasured castles. Alongside the fear of multiplying threats to the nation's security grows a generalized suspicion of the federal government's intrusion into our private affairs. The proliferation of SYG laws and the culture that has made them possible reassure us that the boundaries of a man's castle will remain unassailable.

THE BIRTH OF A STAND-YOUR-GROUND NATION

The passage of the nation's first stand-your-ground law originated with a deadly encounter in Pensacola, Florida. In the early morning hours of November 2, 2004, fifty-six-year-old Kathy Workman and her seventy-seven-year-old husband, James, were awakened by a noise outside. The white retirees were staying in a FEMA trailer after Hurricane Ivan had wrecked their home, and they looked out the window to see a stranger wandering through their yard. After the stranger failed to respond when the couple hailed him from their window, James grabbed his .38 caliber handgun and headed outside.[2] Kathy called 911.

It is not clear why thirty-five-year old Rodney Cox, a white contractor working temporarily for FEMA, was on the Workmans' property in the middle of the night. He had called 911 earlier in the evening, disoriented and confused, claiming to have witnessed a domestic disturbance a few miles away. No one knows what brought him to the Workmans' yard or what provoked him to enter the couple's trailer after James confronted him. The 911 dispatcher's recording captured Kathy's panicked voice pleading for police assistance, then her screams in response to a scuffle between her husband and Cox, then gunshots. At the hospital,

Cox was pronounced dead on arrival. He was also found to have a mysterious skull fracture, which may explain his erratic behavior.[3]

James Workman was never arrested, but he and Kathy waited anxiously for the state to decide whether he was culpable in the killing of an unarmed man. Had the case gone to court, a jury would likely have perceived Workman's fear of Cox as reasonable. The shooting took place inside the couple's FEMA trailer, an extension of their castle, at night and following reports of multiple home break-ins. Yet Cox had not been armed, and it was unclear whether his behavior was considered immediately threatening. Ultimately, the attorney general's office concluded, on January 30, 2005, that the killing had been justifiable, exonerating James of any guilt.

James Workman, an elderly white man defending his provisional castle and his wife from a nighttime intruder, became a poster child for advocates of DIY-security citizenship. Although he was neither incarcerated nor charged with any crime, many could not countenance his having to wait almost three months as the attorney general's office deliberated. It was this "legal limbo," the agonizing delay as the state decided whether James would be charged for homicide, that prompted lawmakers to push for a change to the state's self-defense laws.[4] After all, reasoned proponents, a law-abiding citizen should not be penalized for defending his castle and his wife from an intruder. With the support of the NRA, Republican state representative Dennis Baxley and Republican state senator Durell Peaden drafted a bill providing immunity from criminal prosecution and civil action for a person using lethal violence in self-defense. The bill also eliminated the duty to retreat and expanded the terms of the castle doctrine beyond the home to any place a person may legally be.[5]

The politicians who promoted SB 436, the bill that would become the nation's first stand-your-ground law, emphasized the Workmans' terror and confusion. They implicitly referenced James's vulnerability as an elderly homeowner who had defended his property from a younger, presumably stronger man. Inaccurate depictions of the matter and of preexisting self-defense laws fueled the debate over proposals to expand the terms of the castle doctrine. Dennis Baxley described Cox as a

"perpetrator" who "broke into" the Workmans' trailer.[6] Mischacteriz-
ing the Workmans' ages and the circumstances under which Workman
shot Cox, Republican state senator Greg Evers told lawmakers, "One of
the major reasons I support this bill is for a seventy-two-year-old man
lying in bed at night with his sixty-eight-year-old wife, trying to sleep,
when an intruder came in on them." He continued, inaccurately, "The
man shot the intruder, wounded him, did not fatally kill him. But yet
for six months, he wondered if he was going to be charged with shooting the man. Folks, that's not right."[7] Few of Evers's "facts" were right.
He exaggerated the circumstances of the encounter—the Workmans
asleep in their bed when Cox burst into their home at night—downplayed the harm done to Cox, and doubled the length of time James had
to await exoneration.

Similar misrepresentations, which minimize the harm done by the
person claiming self-defense and exaggerate the threat posed by the
person who has been killed, have long been common among advocates
of lethal self-defense. Since its introduction as a regular feature of the
NRA's *American Rifleman* in 1926, the Armed Citizen column has provided readers with predictable, heroic bedtime stories, crafted from the
content of actual news items, in which a clearheaded citizen defends
him- or herself from a criminal perpetrator.[8] Little about these stories
has changed over the decades: faced with a threat, often a nighttime
home intruder, a would-be victim emerges triumphant thanks to quick
thinking and armed preparedness. Similarly, in the Armed Citizen column, the description of Workman's case offers no gray area wherein
James might have remained in his provisional home and called the
police, instead of approaching the trespasser. The column characterized Cox as having "forced his way" into the Workmans' trailer, leaving
James no choice but to kill.[9]

Just as issues of race seem absent or irrelevant in the Armed Citizen
column, Workman's case appeared to turn on straightforward issues
of universal home security and personal safety. Yet home security itself
is haunted by the nation's historic exclusions based on property rights
and racialized notions of criminality. When State Senator Peaden told
the legislature, "You're entitled to protect your castle," he meant that

people like James and Kathy Workman, white homeowners, were entitled to protect their lives and property.[10] Repeated references to James Workman's age and property ownership echoed the 1870s homicide trials of James Erwin and John Runyan, where *white* men's defensive violence was excused in the name of a "true man's" right to protect himself against an attacker. James Workman's whiteness, masculinity, age, and property ownership made him the ideal poster child for new legislation ensuring that *some* people might lethally stand their ground without risking criminal prosecution.

While Workman's situation was compelling and useful to advocates of SB 436 because it placed the sanctity of the white man's castle front and center, the passage of the Florida law also hinged on concerns for white women's sexual vulnerability. Former NRA president Marion Hammer contributed a unique twist to the lobbying effort. Born in Columbia, South Carolina, in the 1940s, Hammer became an NRA lobbyist in 1978, around the time the organization made its radical turn from hunting, gun safety, and education to gun rights. As she lobbied against gun regulations and in support of more substantive self-defense laws, including SB 436, Hammer repeatedly recounted the story of her own terrifying encounter with violent strangers, and how a firearm saved her from "a fate worse than death."

Hammer told of being pursued on a parking deck in the 1980s by a carload of rowdy men, describing to the predominantly white male members of the Florida legislature how "the men, who were either drunk or on drugs, screamed obscenities" while following her in their car as she tried to escape to safety. "They made it very clear what they intended to do," she explained. "I felt sure I was going to die, or be left in a condition where I would have wished I had died."[11] Although she did not indicate the race of her perpetrators, Hammer's invocation of the "fate worse than death" echoed historical associations of nonwhite men with sexual violence, such as Thomas Dixon's early-twentieth-century literary portrayal, in *The Clansman*, of the Southern white woman who chooses to commit suicide rather than live with the stain of her "disgrace" by a Black rapist.

But Hammer's was not the typical story of white feminine vulnerability, as hers featured an upbeat, empowering ending. Instead of fleeing from her pursuers, Hammer retrieved her six-shot .38-caliber revolver from her purse and "stepped up to the car, between the headlights." The heroic tale ends with "the driver slamm[ing] the car in reverse and careen[ing] wildly backward through the parking deck and into the street."[12] Hammer's quick thinking and readily accessible handgun saved the day.

Marion Hammer's capacity to be her own protector—an armed citizen—and her refusal to retreat in the face of danger saved her from the inevitable violence of drunken criminal strangers. Prior to the vote on the SYG law, stories like hers capitalized on paranoia about pervasive criminality perpetrated by "thugs," the inadequacy of law enforcement, and the vulnerability of white women in public spaces. Gun ownership held out the promise of safety and independence for women who "refused to be victims." Yet in the minds of Hammer and other supporters, the laws needed serious adjustment to allow law-abiding citizens to use lethal violence without retreating. Hammer urged lawmakers, "You can't expect a victim to wait before taking action to protect herself, and say: 'Excuse me, Mr. Criminal, did you drag me into this alley to rape and kill me or do you just want to beat me up and steal my purse?'"[13]

Hammer's dramatic testimony was powerful, but it was also inaccurate. Existing laws in Florida did *not* require a woman to discern the motive of her attacker, or to try to retreat before fighting back, as long as she was in reasonable fear for her life—*and as long as the attacker was not her spouse*. Hammer's inspired lobbying efforts conjured the chilling threat of stranger rape, emphasizing unarmed women's vulnerability to criminal strangers, while ignoring the realities of gender violence perpetrated by spouses and acquaintances. Traditional self-defense laws held that one who was attacked and who was not the aggressor could "meet force with force" if she reasonably believed she was in great danger. The new stand-your-ground laws did little to enhance this already robust provision for women to fight back against would-be rapists, and they did nothing to address the danger of attackers who were not strangers.

Opposing the SYG bill may have "seemed like political suicide in Florida," yet some expressed vocal opposition.[14] Miami's former police chief, John Timoney, forecasted that the law would encourage the use of deadly force among civilians. Gun control groups similarly warned that expanding the boundaries of lethal self-defense would actually contribute to, rather than reduce, violent crime.[15] Those resisting the bill emphasized its likely effects on public safety, but those in favor enjoyed the support of the NRA and the American Legislative Exchange Council (ALEC), a conservative political action organization funded primarily by corporations.[16] Against this powerful and well-funded consortium, the voices of reason and general safety had little chance.

The Florida House of Representatives voted in favor of SB 436, 92–20, before the Senate voted for the bill unanimously. On October 1, 2005, Governor Jeb Bush signed Florida's stand-your-ground law, the nation's first, praising it as "a good, common-sense, anticrime issue."[17] The law, composed in gender- and race-neutral language, stipulates that

> a person is justified in using or threatening to use deadly force if he or she reasonably believes that using or threatening to use such force is necessary to prevent imminent death or great bodily harm to himself or herself or another or to prevent the imminent commission of a forcible felony. A person who uses or threatens to use deadly force in accordance with this subsection does not have a duty to retreat and has the right to stand his or her ground if the person using or threatening to use the deadly force is not engaged in a criminal activity and is in a place where he or she has a right to be.[18]

Legal scholar Mary Ann Franks neatly summarizes the Florida law's three main innovations. First, it justifies lethal force against someone found in "commission of a forcible felony," which could mean a nonviolent robbery. Allowing one person to kill another for attempted robbery represents a significant departure from the law's traditional claims to protect human life above property. Second, the law expands the castle-doctrine exemption to spaces beyond a person's home; Florida's law stipulates that people are not obliged to retreat in any place where they may legally be. Finally, the law offers criminal and civil immunity from prosecution to those who reasonably claim self-defense.[19]

With Marion Hammer in command of its vast propaganda machine, the NRA continued aggressively promoting these laws in other states with support from ALEC, using the Florida law as a template and starting with red states before canvassing blue ones. Within a year, similar laws were passed in Alabama, Georgia, Kansas, Oklahoma, and Louisiana. As of spring 2016, thirty-three states had adopted some version of an SYG law, some alternatively called Make My Day laws and Castle laws.

The names and terms of the legislation vary from state to state, but most SYG laws contain allowances for law enforcement to bypass criminal proceedings in cases where defendants reasonably believed they were in imminent danger, and most laws extend immunity to spaces beyond one's castle. According to Franks, someone claiming to have killed in self-defense may be able to avoid criminal prosecution as long as law enforcement agents or a judge believe that their fear for their life was reasonable. Another major departure from traditional self-defense law is the automatic presumption of "reasonable fear" in cases where someone breaks into another's home or car. According to journalist Elizabeth Chuck, "A person is presumed to have reasonable fear of imminent death or great bodily harm when using defensive force if an intruder has broken into his or her home or vehicle and is justified in using force."[20]

"A LOW-COST LICENSE TO KILL": VIOLENT CONSEQUENCES

While proponents such as economist John Lott insist that SYG laws save lives by "mak[ing] it easier for would-be victims to protect themselves when the police can't arrive fast enough," evidence suggests that the laws increase the incidence of lethal violence.[21] Research on SYG states reveals a 7 to 9 percent increase in homicides since the laws' passage.[22] The American Bar Association published a report in 2015 recommending the repeal of SYG laws because they "provide a low-cost license to kill."[23] Data collected since the first law's passage also reveals a correlation between increased racial violence and SYG laws. According to legal scholar David A. Harris, SYG laws have not only "increased deadly violence," they also have had "a distinct racial impact."[24] In his study of racial disparities in the adjudication of homicide cases in SYG states, John K. Roman, a senior fellow at the Urban Institute, concluded that "the odds a white on black homicide is found justified is 281 percent greater than the odds a Black on white homicide is found justified."[25] Implicit bias—the unconscious snap judgments we make about strangers in a persistently racist, and (hetero)sexist society—have a profound effect on the ways lethal self-defense plays out. And SYG laws serve to accentuate our nation's already unequal distribution of protection and security.

Together with more liberal firearm ownership and carry laws, SYG laws expand the boundaries of a man's castle by encouraging *some* people to use lethal force to defend themselves from perceived threats, without an obligation to retreat. Starting in the 1980s, most states passed lenient, "shall-issue" gun permit policies, which on their surface provide concealed-carry permits to all who meet minimal requirements.[26] While the percentage of gun owners in the nation has decreased since 1977, in large part due to declining interest in hunting, the number of guns acquired for self-defense has grown steadily.[27] Firearms are increasingly concentrated in the hands of a smaller population; approximately a third of Americans own guns, and 20 percent of these gun owners possess about two-thirds of the nation's guns.[28] As a nation, we own 40 to 50 percent of the world's guns, and the number of registered firearms now outnumbers people.[29]

As of 2015, approximately thirteen million concealed-carry licenses have been issued in the United States.[30] Yet American gun ownership is a distinctly racialized and gendered phenomenon. The vast majority of firearms are owned by whites, specifically white men. While African Americans are less than half as likely as whites to have a firearm in their homes, they are significantly more likely to die from gun violence.[31] Moreover, some states' procedures for issuing concealed-carry permits favor people living in middle- and upper-class suburbs, while demonstrating bias against nonwhites and people living in underserved areas.[32]

After its ban on concealed carry was overturned in 2013, Illinois became the final state to permit citizens who pass certain requirements to carry firearms outside their homes.[33] Since the state began licensing concealed carry, most permits have been issued to whites living in relatively well-off, low-crime suburbs, rather than to the people who—according to many gun rights activists' rhetoric—most need weapons for self-defense.[34] A study conducted by the *Washington Times* discovered that approximately 90 percent of concealed-carry permits in Chicago were being issued to residents of affluent suburbs, such as Palos Park, whose populations are disproportionately white. Journalist Kelly Riddell explained that the high cost of permits, combined with the relative inaccessibility of shooting ranges, makes a permit practically inaccessible to residents of socioeconomically disadvantaged neighborhoods. As a result, these communities have the fewest concealed-carry permits in the state. According to Riddell, 90 percent of the state's concealed-carry licenses have been issues to white residents.[35] The distribution of concealed-carry permits to residents in wealthy, low-crime areas helps support the gun lobby's overly simplistic assertion that "more guns = less crime."[36]

There is also evidence that the state's review process is skewed against African American applicants. The board, which keeps its selection process a secret and refuses to answer requests to explain its decisions, has turned down more than eight hundred requests for licenses, including from qualified African American applicants who fulfilled all licensing criteria, while issuing permits more liberally to whites.[37] More than one hundred Black applicants have sued the state to obtain reconsideration. The review board may deny licenses to anyone it perceives as less than "law-abiding." Also, because African Americans are more frequently subject to police scrutiny for spurious infractions, such as "driving while Black," the review board can find more ways to deny licenses to nonwhite applicants. Such prohibitions prove the lie of the universal claims of armed citizenship. Legal structures conspire with classist and racist exclusionary principles to ensure that armed citizens remain predominantly white, male, and economically privileged.

The selective logic of armed citizenship exists interdependently with larger assumptions about criminality and threat in a world of shrinking resources to provide for citizens' safety and welfare. Select law-abiding civilians take on the responsibilities of law enforcement, protecting themselves while policing others, sometimes as participants in the National Neighborhood Watch community-policing initiative. According to the institute's website, "National Neighborhood Watch empowers citizens to become active in homeland security efforts through participation in Neighborhood Watch groups."[38] The call for ordinary citizens to serve as quasi-police protectors for their communities assumes that citizens patrolling their neighborhoods are able to differentiate between dangerous criminals and the law-abiding citizens they are tasked to protect, yet the grim reality is that they often make this distinction through the prism of widespread social biases.

This was the case in February 2012, when twenty-nine-year-old George Zimmerman, leader of his Neighborhood Watch program in Sanford, Florida, encountered seventeen-year-old Trayvon Martin, walking home after purchasing snacks at a nearby convenience mart. Zimmerman, a white-appearing man of multiracial heritage, was on high alert after hearing of recent break-ins in his middle-class gated community. Trayvon Martin was an African American high school student from Miami-Dade, visiting the home of his father's fiancée. As a young Black man in a hooded sweatshirt, Martin seemed unfamiliar and suspicious to Zimmerman, who pursued Martin even after police instructed him not to. Accounts are mixed as to what happened next, but Zimmerman admitted to shooting and killing the unarmed teen.[39]

Florida's stand-your-ground law ensured that Zimmerman would not be arrested after convincing law enforcement agents that he shot Martin in self-defense. Since the only other eyewitness to the case was dead, there was no evidence to counter his claim. Six weeks after Martin's death, amid much public protest of Zimmerman's racial profiling and the state's failure to investigate the shooting, Zimmerman was charged with second-degree murder. In July 2013, a jury of six women—all white except for one of mixed Latina heritage—acquitted Zimmerman of murder, after deliberating for two days. The jury reasoned that the prosecution had failed to prove beyond a reasonable doubt that Zimmerman had not acted in self-defense. In the eyes of the court, he had stood his ground and shot Martin in "reasonable" fear for his life. Martin's mere presence as a young Black man in the predominantly white middle-class gated community had constituted a threat to the sanctity of Zimmerman's expansive castle.

In the wake of Zimmerman's acquittal, the nation witnessed a wave of public outrage in response to what many recognized as a flagrant miscarriage of justice. People protested the tragic, willful murder of an unarmed Black teen in the name of racially coded appeals to "public safety." Martin's death and Zimmerman's exoneration exemplified the clash between the violent protection of white property and the nation's professed commitment to equal protection under the law. The tragedy became the catalyst for the Black Lives Matter movement, cofounded by Patrisse Cullors, Opal Tometi, and Alicia Garza. The three African American activists have used social media, originally through the Twitter hashtag #BlackLivesMatter, to build an online community to call attention to the nation's shameful disregard for the rights and safety of Black citizens. Martin's death is not unique in a nation that has historically perceived Black masculinity as a threat to white privilege and security, but it proved especially illuminating as a moment in which an unarmed Black youth was seen as *the* threat against which the "law-abiding citizen" must defend himself. Trayvon Martin's untimely death clearly illuminated the unholy alliance between lethal self-defense and white supremacist power.

OPERATION HERO GUARD: ARMED WHITE MASCULINITY AND THE OBAMA EFFECT

And yet, heroic, seemingly color-blind invocations of patriotic duty continue to frame the armed citizen as the nation's only hope for security in desperate times. On a scorching July afternoon in Cleburne, Texas, a small group of armed white men stood purposefully outside the US Army recruiting office. The men were part of Operation Hero

Guard, a spontaneous response to the July 16, 2015, shooting of five military personnel in Chattanooga, Tennessee, by twenty-four-year-old Muhammad Youssef Abdulazeez.[40] Inspired to violence by extremist propaganda and armed with a semiautomatic rifle and a .9mm handgun, Abdulazeez had opened fire in the recruiting office, killing four people immediately and fatally wounding one.[41]

Days after the shooting, Operation Hero Guard responders rallied in Cleburne and other Texas towns, and in cities in Alabama, Ohio, Virginia, and Wisconsin with the goal of guarding the local military recruitment center. Each responder brought a rifle or semiautomatic gun. Under federal law, military personnel may not carry weapons in recruitment centers, so civilian guards sought to "do what Obama won't do for recruiting offices" by protecting servicemen and -women from future attacks.[42] Members expressed frustration at the federal government's failure to protect military personnel, whom they described as "sitting ducks," vulnerable to terrorist violence.[43] These armed citizens disparage the failures of the liberal government, as personified by President Obama, to protect those who have served their country. For them, self-defense against "terrorists" is a matter of patriotism and honor.

For many advocates of armed citizenship, the election of the first Black president inspired tremendous fear and suspicion, as well as the deepening perception that the federal government was becoming increasingly inimical to Second Amendment rights.[44] Among fellow Democratic contenders for the presidency, Obama's stance on gun control was moderate. While on the campaign trail, he reassured voters of his "support for the Second Amendment" and for hunting rights. In keeping with others in the Democratic Party, he expressed support for expanding the reach of criminal background checks and limiting sales of semiautomatic weapons.[45]

In spite of his support for modest, "common-sense" gun control and safety laws, a record 60 percent spike in gun sales accompanied his election in 2008.[46] Among gun rights supporters and lobbyists, President Obama's liberalism—but perhaps more important, his blackness—reinforced an impression that the federal government was soft on crime, ineffectual against terrorism, and threatening to white property. The reactionary responses are often comically ironic, as in an image of the president's face Photoshopped into a photo of a firearm-wielding member of the Black Panther Party that has circulated widely on conservative blogs and Twitter feeds.[47] This imaginative effort to stoke white fears of the president's Black radicalism undermined claims that he is antigun. Stanley Kurtz dubbed President Obama the "radical in chief" in his 2012 book of that title. For detractors of what they imagine to be the president's radical, socialist, "antiwhite" agenda, the need for DIY-security citizenship, particularly in protection of the white man's castle, has grown more urgent than ever.[48]

The misguided call to arms is seductive in its promise of individual empowerment and safety through lethal self-defense. Appeals to American ideals of equality, heroism, and individualism mask the racial, class, and gender exclusions of the DIY-security-citizenship ideal. Predominantly male-dominated paramilitary organizations, such as Arizona sheriff Joe Arpaio's border and school-patrolling posse and Operation Hero Guard recruit average citizens to take up arms as a civic duty. Increasingly, new marketing campaigns by gun manufacturers and advocates of gun rights try to persuade women to join the call of armed heroism by purchasing guns and related accessories. These ads promise that only the "Well-Armed" women who "Refuse to Be a Victim" (another registered phrase of the NRA, as is "Armed Citizen") will find safety in the treacherous waters of post-9/11 America. And for those without the resources to purchase weapons and accessories, campaigns for "gun welfare" promise to democratize participation in the effort to keep terrorists and criminals at bay.[49]

THE WELL-ARMED WOMAN: WHERE GIRL POWER MEETS DIY-SECURITY CITIZENSHIP

In spite of the disproportionate number of men traditionally engaged in armed citizenship, our contemporary embrace of a universal right to self-defense holds out the promise that women can and should join the call. According to Sergeant Betsy Brantner Smith, a former police officer in Naperville, Illinois, "The more law abiding citizens who train and arm themselves, the less victims we have."[50] Smith's idealized armed citizen is the antidote to what she calls the "war on cops" and "increased workplace violence." She reasons that if victims of serial killers such as Ted Bundy and John Wayne Gacy had been armed, they might have saved themselves and countless other victims. After all, says Sergeant Smith, "You don't have to have a badge to wear a white hat and be one of the good guys."

And you don't have to be a guy. Indeed, the new millennium has ushered in a proliferation of products and websites designed for female gun enthusiasts, and since 2005, gun ownership among women has increased by almost 77 percent.[51] Although the NRA began to use fears of stranger violence to promote gun ownership starting in the 1970s, the organization was relatively slow to reach out to women as gun users and consumers. Today, the NRA's website maintains a page specifically for women, which includes links to training information, the NRA Women's Network, and "Women on Target" instructional clinics.[52] They also sponsor a variety of resources and informational blogs designed specifically to prepare women to protect themselves and their children from criminal threats.

Armed citizens such as Arizonan Carrie Lightfoot, author of *The Well Armed Woman's Concise Guide to Concealed Carry*, have helped bolster the NRA's appeal to women. In response to her disappointment at finding scant information tailored to her specific needs as a "woman gun owner," she started *The Well Armed Woman* (*TWAW*) website in 2012 with the motto "Where the Feminine and Firearms Meet." *TWAW* has launched shooting chapters to provide gun instruction to women nationwide and boasts a mission of "Educating, equipping and empowering woman shooters."[53] The website celebrates consumer choice in a growing marketplace of woman-centered shooting products and works to link women with up-to-date information about advances in firearm technology and accessories.

TWAW links to advertisements by gun companies marketing specifically to women. An ad for "GLOCK Pistols for Women" insists: "You have every right to defend yourself! . . . But you won't find a 'Woman's' model here. If someone crosses that line, you require equal stopping power. You might first look at our Sub-Compact and Slimline models, but with our Modular Back Strap System, any GLOCK is within your reach."[54] The advertisement's ambivalent appeal to the woman customer's right to defend herself weighs her particular need for safety with the necessity for "equal stopping power." The promise for equal-opportunity purchasing power is nevertheless couched in a special plea for enhanced safety in a smaller package. In spite of the empowering, self-help language of contemporary advertising copy, the SYG culture feeds upon fear, insecurity, and the suspicion that criminals are always lurking in spaces that should be safe. The good citizen is one who takes her own safety seriously and, like Marion Hammer, does not back down in the face of danger.

Invocations of women's special need for protection appear in the NRA's "Refuse to Be a Victim" training, which involves a four-hour seminar for $45. The five-minute promotional video states: "Experts agree that the single most important step toward ensuring your personal safety is making the decision to refuse to be a victim. That means that you must have an overall personal safety strategy in place before you need it."[55] It features vignettes overlaid with commentary from white male personal-safety experts and white female customers discussing the pressing need for training. In one of the opening scenes, a blond woman walks through a parking lot as a dark, faceless figure looms behind her.

Echoing Marion Hammer's personal narrative of terror thwarted by pluck and bravery, Refuse to Be a Victim is based on the assumption that the dangers women face are from criminal strangers lurking in dark alleyways or seeking to enter their homes at night. Furthermore, the campaign imagines that the only way to refuse victimhood is to carry a weapon designed purely for the efficient destruction of human life. There is no space for other personal-safety measures that are less lethal.

Proponents of DIY security continue to frame sexualized stranger-danger as urgent justification for enhanced armed citizenship. The Students for Concealed Carry movement, established by college students after the deadly 2007 shooting at Virginia Tech, has been lobbying states to pass legislation allowing concealed carry on college campuses.[56] Lawmakers and gun rights activists have seized on this opportunity to promote concealed carry as a solution to the stubborn problem of campus sexual assault. Michele Fiore, a Nevada assemblywoman, remarked in 2015, "If these young, hot little girls on campus have a firearm, I wonder how many men will want to assault them. The sexual assaults that are occurring would go down once these sexual predators get a bullet in their head."[57]

Fiore and other proponents of concealed carry on campus misleadingly overemphasize the threat of stranger rape, perpetrated by sexual predators lurking in bushes, parking lots, or outside dormitories. This narrative is consistent with the party line of the NRA's armed citizen, which emphasizes individual gun ownership as the remedy for larger societal problems—in this case, sexual assault—while ignoring the actual complexities of systemic gender violence. The logic of the armed co-ed shooting a stranger she imagines might be about to rape her blithely ignores the reality of sexual assault, which is that the majority of rape victims know their attackers.[58] The uncomfortable truth is that women's acquaintances, *not* predatory strangers, are most frequently implicated in sexual assault.

The command to "refuse victimhood" obscures the grim reality of women's historical and contemporary endangerment by male spouses and acquaintances.[59] The movement's focus on criminal strangers ignores the dangers that women face in their own homes and personal lives. Furthermore, like survivors of domestic violence, rape survivors are routinely challenged about the legitimacy of their claims, questioned about whether they somehow "asked for it"—by drinking too much, wearing provocative clothing, or behaving outside the boundaries of acceptable femininity. Given these conditions, how likely would it be for a jury to acquit a college student who killed an ex-boyfriend to prevent an assault? Would her word—her allegation that he was raping or threatening to rape her—appear reasonable to the jury?

Armed citizenship constitutes a dangerous and wrong-headed response to violence against women. It enhances racial profiling by disseminating mythological portrayals of predatory strangers who are usually assumed to be men of color as the ultimate threat to women's safety and security. Furthermore, recent research by community-health experts Emily Rothman and Michael Siegel reveals that higher rates of gun ownership correlate to higher rates of women's gun deaths. Rothman and Siegel undertook a landmark study in which they analyzed more than thirty years' worth of data on gun deaths collected from all fifty states. The data offered empirical proof that, contrary to the assertions of gun rights activists, gun ownership actually makes women significantly less safe.[60]

Statistical evidence showing the correlation of gun ownership and gun deaths continues to fall on deaf ears. Many echo the assertion of legal scholar David Kopel that "the security of a free state requires that the entire people be armed."[61] In this view, the individual investment in self-defense becomes nothing less than a civic virtue. The most seductive promise of DIY-security citizenship is that each and every one of us can and *should* participate in making ourselves, and our society, more secure. This impulse is made to seem especially urgent for those people most in need of protection, when in reality the concentration of weaponry and the legal expansion of lethal self-defense make the most vulnerable citizens less safe.

Gun Welfare and the Privatized Answer to Insecurity

In answer to the state's presumed persistent failure to protect its citizens from danger, the armed citizen steps into the void. Launched in 2013 and funded by private donations, the Armed Citizen Project (ACP), whose motto is "Deterring Crime by Empowering Neighborhoods," offers free shotguns and gun training to people living in presumably high-crime areas. Kyle Coplen, the project's founder, explains the roots of the initiative: "Criminals have no desire to die in your hallway. We want to use that fear."[62]

Private donations are used to provide defensive weapons and licenses to people who do not have the means to purchase weapons themselves. The group is "dedicated to facilitating the arming of law abiding citizens" so that they are empowered to defend their own property from criminals. A banner on the ACP website reads: "WARNING: Armed citizen, nothing in my house is worth your life." (The warning is also available as a sticker.) The project focuses on what members describe as mid- to high-crime areas in order to develop "gun-rich" areas. It is not clear how they determine which neighborhoods to target or how many weapons they've donated, but there seems to be an effort to promote their services to single women and mothers, who, lacking male partners, need guns to protect themselves and their children.

In addition to providing gun welfare to under-resourced citizens, ACP leaders anticipate an enriching research and data-collection goal as well. As they distribute weapons, they plan to document the connection between crime rates and gun ownership, proving once and for all that gun ownership thwarts crime. Coplen explains the hypothesis: "The goal is to find if there exists a causal link between an increase in the presence of firearms and the level of crime." Poor citizens are the guinea pigs on whom these theories are to be tested.[63] According to the project leaders, the success of the initiative will prove that armed citizens can solve the problems of economic insecurity and social inequality.

In December 2015, a former Colorado congressman, Tom Tancredo, wrote, "Congress should consider buying firearms for low-income people so 100 million Americans could be part of state-based militias to fight 'Islamists.'"[64] In February 2016, Arizona lawmakers proposed HB 2494, which would provide gun owners a tax credit of up to eighty dollars for firearms training.[65] The bill's creator, House Majority Leader Steve Montenegro, insists that the effort to make concealed-carry permits more affordable "promotes safety."[66] Montenegro, Tancredo, and other advocates of gun welfare are convinced that providing people with the means to purchase and carry firearms will help prevent crime. Personal firearms help "urban citizens" fight "terrorists and criminals," thus serving the larger national security agenda.[67]

At its core, the ideology of lethal self-defense emphasizes the vulnerability of the law-abiding citizen and the menace of the criminal stranger. It promotes the belief that good citizens must empower themselves against widespread danger and insecurity. This ideology ostensibly encourages all people, not just the wealthy, to use lethal violence in defense of their expanded castles. Recently, the NRA has updated the images of feminine vulnerability in its promotional materials. A 2015 video features an elderly Black woman who "marched behind Martin Luther King at Selma" describing how her inability to keep a firearm in her "government high-rise" subjected her to the threat of "gang bangers and drug dealers." Only by "knowing her rights" and "having a gun" could she find safety.[68] The ad capitalizes on recent activist efforts to illuminate the precariousness of Black lives, but it does so through racially coded invocations of threat in the form of "thugs" and "gang bangers." The NRA's patronizing depiction of Black civil rights activism also ignores the way the reactionary gun rights movement emerged in response to fears of militant Black struggles for the basic rights of citizenship. If gun rights are among our most vital civil rights, as the NRA claims, they are rights that, in practice, are reserved only for the select few.

Recent efforts to universalize DIY-security citizenship appear to entreat us all to take up arms, but in fact they are based on and help to perpetuate deep-seated exclusionary principles. Proponents make believe that any and all citizens may answer the call of armed citizenship, that everyone receives an equal shot at the American Dream of self-protection and safety. Yet pervasive and implicit biases such as widespread perceptions that people of color, particularly men and gender-nonconforming individuals, are criminal threats belie the egalitarian promises of armed citizenship. When we legalize lethal self-defense in the name of personal security and the preservation of property, we place at greater risk people already subject to white supremacist and misogynist bias.

Our selective call to armed citizenship boasts a steadily growing body count. Its tragic exclusionary effects were illuminated in the police shootings of Alton Sterling and Philando Castile, within one day of each other in July 2016. Each man was carrying, but not brandishing, a firearm at the time of his death. We might ask why the Second Amendment's right to bear arms failed to protect the two men and why the NRA did not come forward to defend their right to carry firearms for personal self-defense. Journalist David Graham contends that these episodes offer further proof that "the Second Amendment does not apply to Black Americans the same way it does to white Americans."[69] Indeed, our nation's history has proved this statement true time and time again. Armed citizenship was always intended for the powerful few, at the expense of the many.

Legal scholar Kathryn Russell-Brown argues, "Self-defense law that consistently works to the disadvantage of African Americans operates as a kind of legal macroaggression."[70] It is clear that our expanding culture of lethal self-defense has contributed to, rather than ameliorated, the disparate treatment of whites and people of color under the law, and that they simultaneously undermine all women's ability to defend themselves against abusive partners, even as they pretend to protect them. However, there is a larger frame for this portrait of inequity: our laws are not just innocent by-products of injustice—they are vital elements of a vast ideological matrix built upon racist, heteropatriarchal, and capitalist privilege, intended to protect the white castle, at all costs.

KILL OR BE KILLED—
AN AMERICAN MANTRA

The pathological detritus of the past
does not necessarily stay in the past.

—KARLA HOLLOWAY, 2014

As history has shown, it is no accident that armed citizenship—and the treacherous ideological foundations that made it possible—enhance the precarity of our nation's most vulnerable citizens. Our embrace of lethal self-defense has always been selective and partial, upholding a selective right to kill for some, while posing others as legitimate targets. In spite of the democratic rhetoric used to promote SYG laws, "gun welfare," and "refuse to be a victim" propaganda, standing one's ground remains a privilege of the very few. But it is not the laws alone that need to change; we must rethink our fundamental understandings of criminality and insecurity themselves. The roots of our collective implicit biases run deep, and they are tapped into the nation's original understandings of safety and threat, and of an unambiguous boundary separating law-abiding citizenship from criminality. The task at hand is to penetrate the veneer of equality and empowerment promised by DIY-security citizenship and expose the violent exclusions that have become second nature.

In spite of the spread of SYG laws to a majority of states and the widespread celebration of defensively armed citizenship, the duty to retreat lives on for many, and the supposed protections of lethal self-defense remain elusive for those most vulnerable to racist, sexist, and transphobic violence. Many domestic violence survivors who "stand their ground" against abusive partners fall prey to faulty perceptions of vulnerability and threat. Marissa Alexander's case exemplifies how a law-abiding citizen can be perceived as a criminal when she defends herself from patriarchal violence.

On August 1, 2010, twenty-nine-year-old Alexander was retrieving items from the Jacksonville, Florida, home she had once shared with her estranged husband. She had prematurely given birth to the couple's daughter only nine days earlier and was eager to start a new life without the stress of an abusive marriage. But before she could finish packing, her husband arrived with his children from a prior relationship. After reading some text messages on her phone, he flew into a jealous rage, threatening to kill her and exclaiming, "If I can't have you, nobody will." He tried to prevent her from leaving, blocking her way out, so Alexander fired a warning shot into the wall. After fleeing the premises, her husband called the police, who arrested Alexander and charged her with assault with a deadly weapon.[1]

State attorney Angela Corey, who later oversaw George Zimmerman's trial for the murder of Trayvon Martin, refused to grant Alexander criminal immunity under SYG. According to Corey, Alexander "was angry" when she fired her weapon; "she was not in fear."[2] In May 2012, a jury that deliberated for less than fifteen minutes convicted Alexander of aggravated assault with a deadly weapon.[3] She received Florida's mandatory minimum sentence of twenty years in prison, which Corey then increased to sixty years because Alexander had earlier refused a three-year plea deal. In January 2015, after serving three years of her sentence, and in response to persistent pressure from advocacy groups and political leaders, Alexander was released and placed on house arrest.[4]

Among those critical of Alexander's conviction was Florida congresswoman Corrine Brown, who observed, "If women who are victims of domestic violence try to protect themselves, the Stand Your Ground law will not apply to them."[5] Rita Smith, a psychologist who directs the National Coalition Against Domestic Violence similarly asserted, "Most battered women who kill in self-defense end up in prison. There is a well-documented bias against women."[6] Congresswoman Brown underscored the inconsistent application of the state's SYG law by comparing the outcome of Alexander's case with that of George Zimmerman's: "If you are Black, the system will treat you differently. A mere fifty miles away in Sanford, Florida, a white man who shot a Black teenager and claimed self-defense was not even arrested until community leaders and people around the world expressed their outrage."[7]

Comparison of the two cases reveals the starkly unequal ideological ground on which self-defense laws have taken shape, exposing the tight connection of racism and sexism to our nation's distribution of justice. Pervasive stereotypes of Black women as "angry" rather than fearful exclude African American domestic violence survivors from the sheltering claims of self-defense, and those who try to stand their ground against violent male partners are often seen as "unreasonable" in their perception of an imminent threat.

Alexander's case bears many similarities to that of Callie Adams, another African American mother incarcerated for defending herself against an abusive spouse. On July 22, 2011, in Jacksonville, Adams, forty-three, and her husband, Rodney, had a fight in a local bar. The argument escalated in the parking lot, and when Callie attempted to drive away, Rodney got into the back seat and attacked her. She pulled a gun out of the glove compartment and shot him twice, killing him.[8]

In the SYG hearing to determine whether her case would go to trial, Adams's defense attorneys provided evidence of years of abuse and battered-woman syndrome, arguing that her actions were justified under Florida's SYG law. Judge Adrian G. Soud rejected Adams's SYG motion, arguing that Adams could not prove beyond a reasonable doubt that she was in fear for her life. Soud cited inconsistencies in Adams's testimony, and also asked why she never contacted police during her alleged twenty years of abuse. Prosecutors also asked why she had not simply left the vehicle when her husband started beating her. Perhaps they assumed that Adams, an African American ex-Marine, was immune to violence and too "strong" or "competent" to be afraid. Adams was charged with second-degree murder. As of spring 2016, Adams is out on bail, while her lawyers work to appeal this decision.

Whitlee Jones is another African American woman who fought back against her violent male partner and claimed self-defense in South

Carolina, another SYG state. On November 21, 2012, Jones, twenty-three, had an altercation with her boyfriend, Eric Lee, at the home they shared in North Charleston. When Lee pushed her and then dragged her down the street by her hair, Jones tried unsuccessfully to call 911 for help. After escaping from Lee, Jones fled to the house to pack up her belongings. Lee blocked her access to the door and shook her violently, at which point Jones stabbed him with a knife that she had hidden in her bra. He died shortly thereafter.[9]

In a departure from Alexander's and Adams's cases, the judge who presided over Jones's initial hearing deemed the homicide justified under the state's SYG law, and Jones did not face criminal prosecution. However, state prosecutors disagreed with the decision to exempt her and worked for years to appeal it. According to Assistant Solicitor Culver Kidd, SYG laws were *not* created with battered women in mind. Kidd explained, "A woman's right to stand her ground in a domestic dispute is less than a man's right to stand his ground with some stranger he's gotten into a fight with."[10] Rather, said Kidd, SYG laws were intended to "provide law-abiding citizens greater protections from external threats in the form of intruders and attackers."[11]

This candid statement about the law's original intent—to protect "law-abiding citizens" from home "intruders," but *not* to protect women from abusive partners—runs counter to the rhetoric of many of the law's original proponents, who promised that stronger self-defense laws would help women protect themselves from all forms of violence.[12] Kidd's logic implicitly casts doubt on whether abused women like Jones, Alexander, and Adams can ever qualify as law-abiding citizens. Kidd's claim that SYG laws were not designed to "reach into our homes and personal relationships" echoes past ideals of family privacy that justified the law's hands-off approach to domestic violence.[13]

The selective application and enforcement of SYG laws evince the racist and misogynist assumptions that have long haunted the castle doctrine. When they defended themselves from abusive male partners, none of these women could access the larger society's interest in protecting (white) femininity from criminal strangers. Yet their attackers, all Black men, benefited from patriarchal power to justify their expansive territorial claim on the castle in question. The law's interest in defending a man's castle—which in many jurisdictions denotes his right to stand his ground wherever he may legally be—would appear to transcend its efforts to protect women from their abusers.

Moreover, the women's claims to reasonable fear of their attackers, and their vulnerability as victims of violence, were undermined by enduring stereotypes of Black women as powerful and emasculating—or "angry," as Angela Corey characterized Marissa Alexander—rather than vulnerable to patriarchal and white supremacist aggression.[14] Sociologist Beth Richie describes how Black women's victimization gets downplayed in the criminal justice system: "the angry Black woman [and] the crazed Black woman out of her mind" are common tropes that inhibit their access to equal protection. According to Richie, "It is almost as if Black women in the court system are seen to not have a full range of emotions and only act out of anger, aggression, vindictiveness—not fear, pain, or terror."[15]

The convictions of Alexander and Adams echo Carol Stonehouse's case decades before, when the victim, a police officer, was not considered "weak" or "vulnerable" enough to be seen as a victim of domestic violence. Indeed, even our seemingly race- and gender-neutral invocations of the castle doctrine continue to rest on biased understandings of vulnerability, criminality, and our nation's corresponding commitment to separate "good" or "law-abiding" citizens from criminal strangers.

Black women's historic criminalization and exclusion from dominant perceptions of vulnerability continue to influence how violence against women is treated in criminal law, even in cases where perpetrators are held accountable. Daniel Holtzclaw, a white police officer in Oklahoma City, stalked and raped at least thirteen Black women while on duty. He targeted women with police records—women he perceived as criminals rather than as law-abiding citizens—with the expectation that they would be less likely to fight back or to report his assaults. One victim, who was seventeen when Holtzclaw assaulted her, explained why she didn't immediately report the attack: "What kind of police do you call on the police?"[16] Coming forward as victims of crime was especially difficult for women caught in a pernicious matrix of presumed criminality. Even as an all-white jury convicted Holtzclaw on eighteen charges in December 2015, sentencing him to prison, his victims were subjected to invasive questioning about their own past misconduct, as if they were on trial themselves.[17]

"On Trial for Surviving a Hate Crime": Gender, Race, and Reverse Victimization

Victims of transphobic hate crimes find themselves similarly placed on trial when they attempt to protect themselves. Late on June 5, 2011, CeCe McDonald, a twenty-three-year-old Black transgender woman, was attacked by a group of white people yelling racist and sexist obscenities. A white woman slashed McDonald's face with a glass bottle, creating a wound that would require stitches. In the fight that ensued, forty-seven-year-old Dean Schmitz, a white man with a long criminal history, attacked McDonald as she was trying to flee the scene. McDonald stabbed him with a pair of scissors she kept in her purse. Schmitz died from loss of blood, and McDonald was arrested and charged with second-degree murder.[18]

While McDonald maintained that she acted in self-defense, the prosecuting attorney, Michael Freeman, insisted that she had had every opportunity to retreat to safety. Since Minnesota is not an SYG state, Freeman cited each individual's duty to retreat from danger when attacked outside the home. McDonald's failure to retreat therefore made her a murderer. Insisting that "the scales of justice have got a blindfold on them for a reason," Freeman signaled the blindness of the law to human differences such as race and sex.[19] Thus he could dismiss the racist and transphobic origins of the attack against which McDonald defended herself, insisting that the deadly encounter was no different from an ordinary bar brawl with both sides being equal. In the end, McDonald pled guilty to second-degree manslaughter. She was sentenced to forty-one months, and served nineteen, in an all-male prison.[20]

According to Katie Burgess, executive director of the Trans Youth Support Network, McDonald was placed "on trial for surviving a hate crime."[21] The prosecution refused to consider the nature of the threats made against McDonald when they deliberated on whether she reasonably feared that her life was in danger. Claims of legal neutrality therefore allowed the court to ignore McDonald's social vulnerability as a Black transgender woman, shifting the blame for the attack onto the shoulders of the victim.

But if CeCe McDonald had been attacked in an SYG state, would the outcome have been any different? Widespread transphobia and homophobia construct gender-nonconforming people of color as *perpetrators* of crime, rather than potential victims. Ky Peterson, an African American trans man, was twenty years old when he was attacked in Georgia, an SYG state. On October 28, 2011, Peterson was walking home when he was hit on the head, dragged into an abandoned trailer, and raped. Eventually assisted by his brothers, who followed the sounds of his screams, Ky threw off his attacker, seized his gun from his backpack, and fired. Samuel Chavez, a twenty-nine-year-old Honduran immigrant with a history of assault, lay dead on the ground.[22]

In their panic, Ky and his brothers attempted to hide Chavez's body. They eventually confessed to police, but law enforcement concluded that the shooting resulted from a botched robbery. In spite of positive rape-kit results, which confirmed the assault on Peterson, police concluded that he and his brothers had lured Chavez with the promise of sex. Peterson was charged with armed robbery, aggravated assault, malice murder, two counts of felony murder, and three counts of possession of a firearm during the commission of a felony.

Peterson had purchased his gun after a prior rape, and after the police had been unresponsive when he reported the assault. As an African American, gender-nonconforming individual in the South, Peterson felt that his safety was in his own hands. His decision to arm himself conformed to the principles of DIY-security citizenship, but he ultimately suffered the consequences of the law's intrinsic biases. Journalists Mitch Kellaway and Sunnivie Brydum asked, "Could Georgia's police even fathom a Black, masculine person being a victim of sexual assault, being the target of a violent attack that was unprovoked, killing in self-defense?" In spite of the evidence, and the fact that Peterson had been raped before, the answer was an unequivocal no.

Peterson's public defender failed to invoke SYG laws at his trial, nor did he inform Peterson of the state's SYG provision. In August 2012, Peterson was sentenced to twenty years for involuntary manslaughter. He remains imprisoned at Pulaski State Prison, a medium-security women's prison in Hawkinsville, Georgia. As of spring 2016, Peterson is trying to find a new defense team to appeal his case. As a young, gender-nonconforming person of color with limited means, Peterson faces an uphill battle in his quest for justice.

Taken together, these cases highlight how DIY-security citizenship contributes to the exclusion and criminalization of people who occupy non-dominant subject positions. Joey Mogul, Kay Whitlock, and Andrea Ritchie call these exclusionary frames the "queer injustice" of criminal law. Gender-nonconforming and nonwhite individuals' demands for inclusion and equal treatment are threatening to the sanctity of cherished social boundaries separating white from nonwhite, male from female, safe from unsafe. For these reasons, their access to the law's equal protection remains elusive.[23]

People whose gender presentation does not readily conform to tidy delineations of masculinity or femininity often trigger terror and rage in an intensely transphobic nation. The National Coalition of Anti-Violence Program found that 72 percent of the victims of hate-crime homicides in 2013 were transgender women, 67 percent of them people of color. The report also found that transgender people of color were six times as likely to experience violence at the hands of police as gender-conforming whites.[24] Not surprisingly, as evidenced in Ky Peterson's decision to arm himself after his rape and the police failure to investigate it, LGBT people of color are less likely to seek out state support or protection when they most need it. In our culture, gender-nonconforming individuals, particularly people of color, are seen as threatening to our most deeply ingrained conventions of social belonging. Thus, homophobia and transphobia undermine victims' claims of being threatened, preventing most law enforcement officials and civilians alike from seeing their fears as "reasonable."

Because they rely on the existence of reasonable threat—or what an "average person" would find threatening or dangerous—contemporary

SYG laws are inherently biased. "Average people" are coded as race and gender neutral, which in practice is assumed to mean white, gender-conforming, and typically male. Thus, it's not surprising that SYG laws make it easier for straight, cisgender people to kill queer people, for white people to kill people of color, and for men to kill women, while preventing targeted minorities from defending themselves.

Similarly, contemporary appeals to DIY-security citizenship presume clear and distinct boundaries between "law-abiding citizens" and "criminals." And the heroic armed citizen is intuitively able to differentiate good from evil at first sight. According to the sociologist Jennifer Carlson, "citizen-protectors" follow a neat and linear "moral script" that endorses and supports the heroism and judgment of those who carry weapons for protection.[25] But armed citizens such as George Zimmerman see criminality through the prism of race and gender bias. For a literal example of how beliefs in Black male criminality play out, gun ranges designed both for police and civilian target practice have used photographs of Black men as targets.[26] Is it any wonder, then, that both civilian and police "protectors" often mistake unarmed Black men as appropriate targets of suspicion and violence?

Responding to statistics on the numbers of unarmed Black men and boys killed at the hands of police, journalist Jelani Cobb wrote, "Skin is a uniform, too."[27] According to recent studies, 1,134 people died at the hands of police officers in 2015.[28] The majority fell into one or more of three categories: they were armed; they were mentally unstable; or they ran away when police commanded them to halt.[29] Although Black men make up 6 percent of the population, they accounted for 40 percent of the unarmed people killed. Three out of five unarmed victims who were killed after exhibiting nonthreatening behavior were Black or Latino.[30] When the police shot and killed someone who was armed and behaving threateningly, in most cases the victim was white. Very few officers are convicted for wrongdoing in lethal confrontations. During the past decade, only eleven of the sixty-five police who were charged in lethal shootings were convicted.[31]

Against the moral absolutism of police violence and DIY-security citizenship, the Black Lives Matter and #SayHerName movements have emerged to call out the deadly consequences of racist, classist, and (het-ero)sexist violence. Beyond critiquing police violence, these movements challenge the larger structures that serve white supremacist, patriarchal power. Black Lives Matter, a network founded by three queer-identified women of color, "affirms the lives of Black queer and trans folks, dis-abled folks, Black-undocumented folks, folks with records, women and all Black lives along the gender spectrum."[32] This "intersectional" ap-proach to systemic violence considers the simultaneity of identity threat for vulnerable populations, and it is profoundly threatening to the DIY-security citizenship ideal. Black Lives Matter and #SayHerName challenge the epistemic roots of inequality, as well as its maliciously an-tidemocratic effects.

Today, we witness multiple instances that illuminate the collision course between the armed citizen impulse and intersectional calls for justice. In the summer of 2015, members of an armed group that calls it-self Oath Keepers patrolled the Ferguson, Missouri, protests where Black Lives Matter protesters and others marked the one-year anniversary of the shooting death of eighteen-year-old Michael Brown by a white police officer, Darren Wilson. Founded in 2004 by a former US Army paratrooper, Stewart Rhodes, Oath Keepers is a group of former mili-tary and first responders claiming to "defend the Constitution against all enemies, foreign and domestic."[33] Most members are white males. Members of the group began appearing in Ferguson, armed with assault rifles and wearing bulletproof vests and camouflage clothing.[34] Missouri laws allow people with concealed-weapon permits to carry their guns openly, unless they demonstrate an "angry or threatening manner."[35] Oath Keepers' media director, Jason Van Tatenhove, explained the pur-pose of the group: "to protect not only businesses and homes, but the citizens themselves." According to Van Tatenhove, the presence of this quasi-military organization was vital to maintaining order and safety "during the riots last November and December" that took place in the wake of Michael Brown's death.[36]

Notably, the group boasted of its protection of good citizens, busi-nesses, and homes, while characterizing the protests for racial justice as riots. This description conflates protesters demanding racial justice with riot-like assaults on public safety, order, and property. Using racially coded language associating Black protest with criminality, the Oath Keepers emphasized the need for armed white militants to defend white property. When counter-protesters at Black Lives Matter demonstrations insist that "blue lives matter," they highlight police vulnerability while denying the susceptibility of people of color to police violence. Similar characterizations of protests against police violence as examples of reverse racism proliferate on social media. For example, some gun rights activists have circulated a cartoon, created by George Trosley, featuring a violent Black criminal—whose features are drawn to appear almost simian—protesting his rough treatment by two serene, nonviolent, white policemen trying to handcuff him in the wake of his murderous rampage through a liquor store. This image was among those posted on the Facebook page of Jamie Gilt, the white Florida gun rights activist who achieved notoriety after being shot in the back by her four-year-old.[37]

Urgent cries for armed self-defense in the United States seem to have peaked in the wake of the November 13, 2015, terrorist attacks in Paris. Posts to news blogs confirm the widespread support for armed citizenship. One *Yahoo News* blog post captures the spirit of many: "If law abiding people in this world were allowed to carry a weapon this wouldn't happen. If one third of the people in the movie theater had a gun there would have been a lot less innocent people killed."[38] Campus-wide concealed carry was recently approved for eligible students at Liberty University, a Christian college in Lynchburg, Virginia. On December 2, 2015, there was a mass shooting in San Bernardino, California. After the incident, Jerry Falwell Jr., the president of Liberty University, made explicit the usually implicit biases and perceptions of "stranger danger" that fortify the DIY-security citizenship ideal when he stated: "If more good people had concealed-carry permits, then we could end those Muslims before they walked in."[39] The appeal to "good" and "law-abiding" people to serve as their own armed protectors against terrorism not only promises an easy, homegrown solution to our deepest insecurities; it reinforces the idea that a criminal stranger who is a religious and ideological extremist can be immediately recognized on sight.

Fears of terrorism and rampant criminality fuel what historian Jill Lepore foretells will be "an end to civilian life," when we are all engaged in panic-induced DIY security and "the only good citizen is an armed one."[40] The United States has experienced close to a thousand mass shootings since the Sandy Hook massacre of December 2012, and many believe that the solution to these acts of mass violence is to continue to build our arsenal.[41] Although the United States accounts for just 4.4 percent of the world's population, we possess 40 to 50 percent of the world's civilian-owned guns, and the stockpiling of weapons continues.[42] We have indeed become a nation of *selectively* armed citizens.

But as the Black Lives Matter and #SayHerName movements are teaching us now, our current insecurities will not be mitigated by endowing more citizens with the right to shoot first, and ask questions later. Indeed, eliminating gun restrictions and the duty to retreat has only intensified the violence against our nation's most vulnerable citizens. It should not surprise us that SYG laws and more liberal gun-carry laws—in spite of their ostensibly race neutral framing—continue to place people of color outside of our nation's protective boundaries. The deliberate misidentification of criminality and vulnerability is embedded in our very ideals of citizenship.

A look to the past exposes what literary and legal scholar Karla Holloway calls this nation's "pathological detritus," the legal and representational residues that remain from our nation's founding in white supremacist settler colonialism.[43] The stark fissures in the legal and cultural foundations of self-defense continue to separate those with privileges and immunities from those excluded from the rights and protections of full citizenship. And they continue to shape our "reasonable" perceptions of the boundaries separating belonging from exclusion, vulnerability from criminality, and citizen from stranger.

DIY-security citizenship allows the powerful to dominate and control the vulnerable without the explicitly racist emblems of nooses and burning crosses. Indeed, contemporary appeals to armed citizenship are based on the disavowal of the ways in which our violent past continues to shape our present. The contemporary liberalization of gun rights and the expansion of the castle doctrine do not stop at legalizing deadly self-defense in public spaces beyond the home. SYG laws, and the broader exclusionary ideals of DIY-security citizenship that made such laws possible, generate a reverberating ideological force.

And it is an ideology with a growing body count. What has become second nature—the morality politics of "kill or be killed"—continues to excuse mass violence in the name of security for the few. Our seemingly gender- and race-neutral structures of protection will continue to exclude and criminalize those whom legal scholars Lani Guinier and Gerald Torres have called the "miner's canaries," the people most susceptible to our nation's destructive and antidemocratic exclusions.[44] Ultimately, the terror-induced carnage places us all at risk.

Acknowledgments

Although my name appears alone on the cover, this book owes its existence to the support and fellowship of an immense network of allies, friends, mentors, students, colleagues, and family, who all contributed to the project from start to finish. I owe this book's strengths to that community's exceptional generosity, and all mistakes and omissions are my own. Early conversations with Chiwen Bao, Kimberly Juanita Brown, Jeanne Follansbee, Claire Houston, Stephanie May, Jennifer Pettit, and Linda Schlossberg helped inspire the idea for the book. I wish to thank them all for helping me think through the historical implications of today's recurring expressions of power and injustice, and for reminding me that answers will not be found in strict adherence to the rules of any one discipline.

I am grateful to Jennifer C. Nash and Paul C. Taylor, who each read an early draft of the manuscript, offering encouragement and indispensable guidance on key elements of the project. Both helped me tighten my argument in the interest of reaching a wider audience. Ashley Farmer and Emily Owens each shared vital insights from their forthcoming books, both of which will be required reading on historical intersections of race, gender, and sexuality. Federal defender Heather E. Williams kindly shared her research on the case of Alexander Allen.

Thanks to those who provided advice and guidance at multiple stages of writing: to Susanna Siegel and the brilliant students in her spring 2016 graduate seminar, Violence and Democracy; to Joy Ladin for encouraging writerly vulnerability; to Vincent Harris for reminding me to "Say Her Name"; to Meredith Reiches for close readings and unflagging camaraderie; to Rachel Meyer and Aubry Threlkeld for necessary doses of sanity; to Ted Roese and Katie Connelly Steffelbach for their vital perspectives from law enforcement; to Amy Parker, Robert Berlin, and Matthew Murphy for keeping me up-to-date on SYG in the news. Thanks to Bill Churchill, Mitch Kellaway, and Bill Norrett for reading multiple drafts and for editorial direction and advice far above and beyond the call of friendship. I am grateful to all my colleagues in Harvard's Program in Studies of Women, Gender, and Sexuality Studies.

I could not have completed this project without the support of Harvard University librarians Sue Gilroy, Laureen Esser, and Terri Saint-Amour. I was also fortunate to work with a group of outstanding research assistants, thanks to funding from Harvard's Institute of Politics and the Program in Studies of Women, Gender, and Sexuality. Amy Howe, Laura Lane-Steele, and Corinne Bain helped me gather and sift through mountains of historical and contemporary data in the book's early stages. Josh Stallings and Angela Lee served as astute readers and developmental editors, in addition to helping me locate and analyze sources. Their thoughtful contributions have shaped my arguments as well as the data I've used to support them. Thanks to Bradley Craig, who contributed his excellent insights on the introduction and helped assemble the index.

I received guidance on decoding legal terminologies and procedure from Anne Stephens Lloyd, Steve Klionsky, Terry Aladjem, Karen Bauerle, Maritza Karmely, and Melissa Nasson, Beacon Press's in-house counsel. Victoria Tarasova, intern at Beacon, carefully combed through an early draft, providing detailed legal notes while guiding me on the finer points of our nation's legal process. I am grateful to Judge Charles Spurlock, who read chapter drafts and generously shared his insights on criminal (in)justice.

I owe a tremendous debt to the magnificent editorial staff at Beacon Press and to Michael Bronski, for supporting my book proposal and for introducing me to Beacon's editorial director, Gayatri Patnaik. Gayatri helped me transform my nascent, academic ideas into something more broadly relevant. Heartfelt thanks to senior editor Jill Petty, whose critical insights, wit, and patience have been essential throughout this process. This book has benefited tremendously from the painstaking copyediting of Susan Lumenello and Katherine Scott. Thanks also to Ayla Zuraw-Friedland and Marcy Barnes, who patiently led me through the book's final production.

I am grateful to Matt Cubstead for sharing my rage at our nation's continued injustices and for reading draft after draft while shouldering many neglected household duties. Thanks to Jocelyn, Miriam, and Andrew for their patience and for eschewing peaceful dinnertime conversations for discussions about race, gender, and violence. Thank you for giving me hope for a more humane future.

Thanks to my parents for providing an endless reservoir of support and love. Henry and Angelica Light also shared their legal knowledge while uncomplainingly engaging in discussions of legalized injustice. And to Sandy Light, thank you for raising me to ask *why*, for being my most encouraging reader, and for helping me get the story straight. Mom, this one's for you.

Notes

AUTHOR'S NOTE

1. See Linton Weeks, "Are Shooting Ranges the New Bowling Alleys?" NPR.org, January 31, 2013.
2. See 2013 Pew Research Center (website), "Why Own a Gun? Protection Is Now Top Reason," March 12, 2013, http://www.people-press.org/2013/03/12/why-own -a-gun-protection-is-now-top-reason/#gunowners
3. Jonathan Masters, "US Gun Policy: Global Comparisons," Council of Foreign Relations—CFR Backgrounders (website), June 24, 2015, http://www.cfr.org /society-and-culture/us-gun-policy-global-comparisons/p29735.
4. See Dan Griffin, "Gun Ownership by the Numbers," *Daily Caller*, November 4, 2014; Christopher Ingraham, "There Are Now More Guns Than People in the United States," *Washington Post*, November 5, 2015; A Factual Look at Guns in America (a gun advocacy website), http://americangunfacts.com/; and Sripal Bangalore and Franz Messerli, "Gun Ownership and Firearm-Related Deaths," *American Journal of Medicine* 126, no. 10 (October 2013): 873–76.
5. Robert Spitzer, *Guns Across America: Reconciling Gun Rules and Rights* (New York: Oxford University Press, 2015), 4.
6. See the Gun Violence Tracker, maintained by the Gun Violence Archive, http:// www.gunviolencearchive.org/.
7. Michael Kimmel, "Masculinity, Mental Illness and Guns: A Lethal Equation?," CNN.com, December 19, 2012.
8. The NRA has registered the phrase "Armed Citizen" for its online stories about citizens who defended themselves against attackers or home intruders.
9. Roxanne Dunbar-Ortiz, *An Indigenous Peoples' History of the United States* (Boston: Beacon Press, 2014), 8.
10. Similarly heroic collective memories surface when armed white men occupied the Malheur Wildlife Refuge in eastern Oregon in the winter of 2015–16. They protested the federal government's "tyrannical" control of public lands, never mind that they received low-cost grazing rights to property maintained by federal taxes.
11. María Carla Sánchez, "Stars, Bars, and Unspoken Languages," *Huffington Post*, June 22, 2015.
12. Brittany Newsome, interview with Amy Goodman, *Democracy Now*, July 2, 2015, http://www.democracynow.org/.

13. Sandy Light, "Mass Shootings Are Symptomatic of America's 'Historical Lunacy,'" *Roanoke Times*, July 25, 2015.
14. German Lopez, "Gun Violence in America, in 17 Maps and Charts," Vox.com, August 26, 2015; "Guns in the U.S.: The Statistics Behind the Violence," *BBC News*, January 5, 2016.

INTRODUCTION

Epigraph sources: Sabrina Strings, "Protecting What's White: A New Look at Stand Your Ground Laws," *Feminist Wire*, January 30, 2014, http://www .thefeministwire.com/2014/01/protecting-whats-white-a-new-look-at-stand -your-ground-laws/; Ta-Nehisi Coates, "Stand Your Ground and Vigilante Justice," *Atlantic*, March 22, 2012.
1. Stephen Kinzer, "The United States of Fear and Panic," *Boston Globe*, December 20, 2015.
2. Susan Faludi, *The Terror Dream: Myth and Misogyny in an Insecure America* (New York: Metropolitan Books, 2007).
3. Matt Apuzzo, "War Gear Flows to Police Departments," *New York Times*, June 8, 2014.
4. Jennifer Carlson, *Citizen-Protectors: The Everyday Politics of Guns in an Age of Decline* (Oxford, UK: Oxford University Press, 2015).
5. Dave Grossman and Loren W. Christensen, "On Sheep, Wolves, and Sheepdogs," in *Warriors: On Living with Courage, Discipline and Honor*, ed. Loren W. Christensen (Boulder, CO: Paladin Press, 2004).
6. Ta-Nehisi Coates, "Fear of a Black President," *Atlantic*, September 2012.
7. Lindsay Cook, "The NRA Should Send Obama a 'Thank-You' Card," *US News and World Report*, June 23, 2015.
8. Emilio Depetris-Chauvin, "Fear of Obama: An Empirical Study of the Demand for Guns and the US 2008 Presidential Election," *Journal of Public Economics* 130 (October 2015): 66–79.
9. Dinesh D'Souza, *The Roots of Obama's Rage* (Washington, DC: Regnery, 2010), characterizes the president as a "dangerous man" determined to dismantle American democracy. See also interview of Dinesh D'Souza by talk-show host Glenn Beck, September 15, 2010, http://www.glennbeck.com/.
10. Coates, "Fear of a Black President."
11. National African American Gun Association website, naaga.com.
12. Jews for the Preservation of Firearms Ownership website, jpfo.org.
13. Zach Carter, "Gun Sales Exploded in the Year After Newtown Shooting," *Huffington Post*, December 6, 2013.
14. Tyler Kingkade, "Rand Paul: Sandy Hook Shooting Could Have Been Prevented If Teachers Had Guns," *Huffington Post*, April 3, 2013. See also Forrest Wickman, "Do Armed Citizens Stop Mass Shootings?," *Slate*, December 18, 2012.
15. *National School Shield: Safeguarding Our Children*, https://www.nationalschool shield.org/media/1857/national-school-shield-safeguarding-our-children.pdf), March 2013. The report was funded by the NRA.
16. Abbey Oldham, "2015: The Year of Mass Shootings," *PBS News Hour*, January 1, 2016.

17. Gregor Aisch and Josh Keller, "What Happens After Calls for New Gun Restrictions? Sales Go Up," *New York Times*, June 13, 2016.
18. Philip Smith, interview with Atane Ofiaji, "The Rise of Gun Ownership and Gun Clubs Among African Americans," *This Is Africa*, July 2, 2015, http://thisisafrica.me/.
19. Donald Trump, quoted in Cameron Joseph, "Trump Says More Guns Would Have Prevented the Orlando Massacre," *New York Daily News*, June 13, 2016.
20. Nicki Stallard, "The LGBT Case for Guns," *New York Times*, June 22, 2016.
21. "Pink Pistols Utility Manual," October 2013, pinkpistols.org.
22. Wayne LaPierre, quoted in Mark Memmott, "Only 'A Good Guy with a Gun' Can Stop School Shootings, NRA Says," NPR, December 21, 2012.
23. District of Columbia v. Heller, 554 U.S. 570 (2008).
24. Jonathan Meltzer, "Open Carry for All: Heller and Our Nineteenth-Century Second Amendment," *Yale Law Journal* 123, no. 5 (March 2014): 1495, 1518–22.
25. See Crime Prevention Research Center, *Concealed Carry Permit Holders Across the United States*, July 9, 2014.
26. Florida Code § 776.013 (2005).
27. Robin D. G. Kelley, "The U.S. v. Trayvon Martin: How the System Worked," *Huffington Post*, July 15, 2013.
28. On the impact of right-to-carry laws, see John J. Donahue, Abhay Aneja, and Alexandria Zhang, "The Impact of Right to Carry Laws and the NRC Report: The Latest Lessons for the Empirical Evaluation of Law and Policy," Stanford Law and Economics Olin Working Paper No. 461, September 4, 2014; Cheng Cheng and Mark Hoekstra, "Does Strengthening Self-Defense Law Deter Crime or Escalate Violence? Evidence from Expansions to Castle Doctrine," *Journal of Human Resources* (December 2013).
29. John Roman, "'Stand Your Ground' Laws: Civil Rights and Public Safety Implications of the Expanded Use of Deadly Force," testimony before the Senate Committee on Judiciary Subcommittee on Constitution, Civil Rights and Human Rights, October 29, 2013. Researchers studying the disparate racial impact of SYG laws have difficulty tracking their impact for nonwhites other than African Americans because police and arrest data tend not to record defendants' or victims' race or ethnicity other than "white" or "black."
30. Coates, "Stand Your Ground and Vigilante Justice."
31. Mary Ann Franks, "Real Men Advance, Real Women Retreat: Stand Your Ground, Battered Women's Syndrome, and Violence as Male Privilege," *University of Miami Law Review* 68, no. 1099 (September 9, 2014): 1099–1128.
32. "An Act to Establish a Uniform Rule of Naturalization," US Congress, March 26, 1790.
33. Kelley, "The U.S. v. Trayvon Martin: How the System Worked."
34. Cheryl Harris, "Whiteness as Property," in *Critical Race Theory: The Key Writings That Formed the Movement*, ed. Kimberlé Crenshaw, Neil Gotanda, Gary Peller, and Kendall Thomas (New York: New Press, 1995), 280.
35. Jeannie Suk, *At Home in the Law: How the Domestic Violence Revolution Is Transforming Privacy* (New Haven, CT: Yale University Press, 2009), 58.

36. Lord William Blackstone, *Commentaries on the Laws of England*, vol. 4 (repr. Worcester, MA, by Isaiah Thomas, 1790) (hereafter Blackstone 4).

37. For a discussion of Semayne's Case (1604), see Sir Edward Coke, *The Institutes of the Laws of England*, 1628; Suk, *At Home in the Law*, 2.

38. Beard v. United States, 158 U.S. 550 (1895).

39. Martha Hodes, *White Women, Black Men: Illicit Sex in the Nineteenth-Century South* (New Haven, CT: Yale University Press, 2011); Rebecca Traister, "When Michael Dunn Compared Himself to a Rape Victim, He Was Following an Old, Racist Script," *New Republic*, February 23, 2014.

40. See, for example, the cases of Ky Peterson and CeCe McDonald, discussed in the conclusion.

41. Harris, "Whiteness as Property."

42. Evan Osnos, "Making a Killing: The Business and Politics of Selling Guns," *New Yorker*, June 27, 2016, 37–38.

CHAPTER ONE: "THAT GREAT LAW OF NATURE"

Epigraph sources: Sir Edward Coke, *Semayne's Case* (1604), printed in *An Exact Abridgement in English, of the Eleven Books of Reports of the Learned Sir Edward Cook* [sic], *Knight, Late Lord Chief Justice of England, and of the Council of Estate to His Majesty, King James* (London: Chancery Lane, ca. 1666); John Locke, *An Essay Concerning the True Original, Extent, and End of Civil Government*, 1690, para. 11.

1. Blackstone 4, 184–85.

2. Ibid., 177. On *vindices injuriarum*, see Sir Matthew Hale, *The History of the Pleas of the Crown*, 1736; available at archive.org.

3. Blackstone 4, 177.

4. Thomas Hobbes, *Leviathan or the Matter, Forme and Power of a Common Wealth Ecclesiasticall and Civil* (London: Printed for Andrew Crooke, at the Green Dragon in St. Paul's Churchyard, 1651).

5. Locke, *An Essay Concerning the True Original, Extent, and End of Civil Government*.

6. Coke, *Semayne's Case* (1604).

7. Lord William Blackstone, *Commentaries on the Laws of England*, vol. 1 (repr. Worcester, MA, by Isaiah Thomas, 1790) (hereafter Blackstone 1), 442.

8. Henry William De Saussure, *Reports of Cases Argued and Determined in the Court of Chancery of the State* (Columbia, SC: Cline & Hines, 1817), 33–44.

9. Blackstone 1, 444.

10. Ibid., 445.

11. See, for example, the tort of seduction, which allowed fathers to sue their daughters' "seducers" for their property interests in their daughters' chastity. See Martha Bailey, "Girls and Masters: The Tort of Seduction and the Support of Bastards," *Canadian Journal of Family Law* 10 (1991): 137–62.

12. Blackstone 4, 180–81.

13. Daniel Davis quoting Blackstone, quoted in George Caines and T. Lloyd, *Trial*

of Thomas O. Selfridge, Attorney at Law, Before the Hon. Isaac Parker, Esquire. For Killing Charles Austin, on the Public Exchange, in Boston, August 4th, 1806 (Boston, c. 1806), 11.

14. Hale, *The History of the Pleas of the Crown.*

15. For a detailed inventory of early gun control laws that applied specifically to free and enslaved African Americans, see Clayton E. Cramer, "The Racist Roots of Gun Control," *Kansas Journal of Law & Public Policy* 4, no. 2 (Winter 1995): 17–25.

16. Randall Kennedy, *Race, Crime, and the Law* (New York: Pantheon, 1997), 30–34.

17. Ibid., 35.

18. Jennifer Morgan, "'Partus Sequitur Ventrem': Law and Reproduction for Slave Women," keynote address for Pregnancy, Childbearing and Infant Care: Historical Perspectives from Slave and Non-Slave Societies, New York University, April 8, 2015. See also Kathleen Brown, *Good Wives, Nasty Wenches, and Anxious Patriarchs: Gender, Race, and Power in Colonial Virginia* (Chapel Hill: University of North Carolina Press, 1996), chapters 4 and 6.

19. Emily A. Owens, "Fantasies of Consent: Black Women's Sexual Labor in 19th-Century New Orleans," PhD diss., Harvard University, 2015.

20. Melton McLaurin, ed., *Celia, A Slave* (New York: Avon, 1993).

21. Peter Bardaglio, *Reconstructing the Household: Families, Sex, and the Law in the Nineteenth-Century South* (Chapel Hill: University of North Carolina Press, 1995), xi.

22. Thomas Selfridge, public statement in the Boston *Gazette*, August 4, 1806. For the full text of Selfridge's ad, see Jack Tager, "Politics, Honor, and Self-Defense in Post-Revolutionary Boston: The 1806 Manslaughter Trial of Thomas Selfridge," *Historical Journal of Massachusetts* 37, no. 2 (Fall 2009): 87.

23. The following quotes from the trial transcript are from the testimony of James Richardson, quoted in Caines and Lloyd, *Trial of Thomas O. Selfridge.*

24. Theophilus Parsons, quoted in ibid., 5–6.

25. Davis, quoted in ibid., 10.

26. Richardson, quoted in ibid., 10–14.

27. *Evening Post* (New York, NY), January 30, 1807.

28. Gore, quoted in Caines and Lloyd, *Trial of Thomas O. Selfridge*, 39–40.

29. Ibid., 129.

30. Ibid., 127, 128.

31. See Robert Baldick, *The Duel: A History of Dueling* (London: Chapman & Hall, 1965).

32. Mika LaVaque-Manty, "Dueling for Equality: Masculine Honor and the Modern Politics of Dignity," *Political Theory* 34, no. 6 (December 2006): 719.

33. C. A. Harwell Wells, "The End of an Affair? Anti-Dueling Laws and Social Norms in Antebellum America," *Vanderbilt Law Review* 54, no. 4 (2001): 1820.

34. Judge Parsons, quoted in Caines and Lloyd, *Trial of Thomas O. Selfridge*, 6.

35. Attorney General Sullivan, quoted in ibid., 138.

36. Ibid., 136–37.

37. Ibid., 38.

38. Ibid., 52.

39. Ibid., 166.

40. Article 1, Section 9, Clause 1 of the Constitution had prevented the termination of the slave trade before January 1, 1808, to appease delegates from slave-holding states.

41. Act Prohibiting Importation of Slaves, Ninth Congress (2 Stat. 426), enacted March 2, 1807.

42. Sojourner Truth, speech before Women's Rights Convention in Akron, Ohio, June 21, 1851, from an account published on that date in the *Anti-Slavery Bugle*, Salem, OH. See http://sojournertruthmemorial.org/sojourner-truth/her-words/.

43. Stowe, 1869, quoted in *American Women Authors and Literary Property, 1822–1869*, ed. Melissa Homestead (New York: Cambridge University Press, 2005), 29.

44. Harriet Jacobs, under the pseudonym Linda Brent, ed. by Lydia Maria Child, *Incidents in the Life of a Slave Girl* (Boston: Published for the Author, 1861), 55.

45. Some Southern and Western state constitutions originally recognized limited women's property rights, which reflected the influence of French and Spanish colonial law codes.

46. The Texas law was influenced by Spanish civil law, which allowed married women some individual property rights.

47. Jacobs, *Incidents in the Life of a Slave Girl*, 55.

48. E. C. Stanton, "Declaration of Sentiments," September 1848.

49. New York Married Women's Property Act, Section 1, April 7, 1848.

50. Wells, "End of an Affair?"

51. Jack K. Williams, *Dueling in the Old South: Vignettes of Social History* (College Station: Texas A&M University Press, 2000), 6.

52. John Lyde Wilson, *The Code of Honor; or Rules for the Government of Principals and Seconds in Dueling* (1838).

53. Ibid.

54. Saul Cornell and Eric M. Rubin, "The Slave-State Origins of Modern Gun Rights," *Atlantic*, September 30, 2015.

55. Clayton Cramer, *Concealed Weapon Laws of the Early Republic: Dueling, Southern Violence, and Moral Reform* (Westport, CT: Praeger, 1999), 2–3.

56. *Acts Passed at the Annual Session of the General Assembly of the State of Alabama* (Tuscaloosa and Eaton, 1839), chapter 77.

57. Decision in *State v. Reid* quoted in Meltzer, "Open Carry for All," 1514.

58. *Gallagher v. State*, 3 Minn. 270, 272 (1859).

59. The following account of the Sickles trial is based on Felix G. Fontaine, *Trial of the Hon. Daniel E. Sickles for Shooting Philip Barton Key, Esq., U.S. District Attorney, of Washington, D.C. February 27th, 1859* (New York: R. M. De Witt, 1859).

60. Robert Ould, quoted in ibid., 15.

61. Ibid., 101.

62. Graham, quoted in ibid., 27.

63. Ibid., 26.

64. Ibid.

65. Ibid., 31.

66. Frederick Douglass, "West India Emancipation," speech given at Canandaigua, NY, August 3, 1857.

CHAPTER TWO: DEFENSIVE VIOLENCE AND THE "TRUE MAN"

Epigraph sources: Abraham Lincoln, "The Emancipation Proclamation," 1863; Niblack in Runyan v. State, 57 Ind. 80 (1877); David Blight, *Race and Reunion: The Civil War in American Memory* (Cambridge, MA: Harvard University Press, 2001), 57.

1. Some states, including South Carolina and Virginia, still did not confer independent legal status on married women even into the 1870s. Marital rape was not outlawed until the late twentieth century. To this day, most hetero-married women continue to take their husband's last name, their family name legally subsumed into their husband's.

2. Questionnaire distributed by commission leaders Robert Dale Owen, James McKaye, and Samuel G. Howe, 1863, American Freedman's Inquiry Commission, 702, box 1, Houghton Library, Harvard University.

3. Kennedy, *Race, Crime, and the Law*, 29.

4. Ibid., 38.

5. Ibid., 37.

6. "Mass Meeting of the Colored Citizens of Charleston," *Charleston Daily News*, March 22, 1867.

7. *Report of the Select Committee on the New Orleans Riots*, 39th Congress, 2nd session, 1867, 18. See https://archive.org/stream/reportofselectc003unit#page/n7/mode/2up.

8. Charles Lane, *The Day Freedom Died: The Colfax Massacre, the Supreme Court, and the Betrayal of Reconstruction* (New York: Henry Holt, 2008), 18.

9. The armed aggressors were known citizens and members of the New Orleans police force, but they were not prosecuted in the riot's aftermath. In fact, the state government tried to prosecute surviving convention participants under the Crimes Act of 1805.

10. This amendment was created to bolster the citizenship and equal protection clauses of the Civil Rights Act of 1866.

11. Native people would not receive formal citizenship rights until passage of the 1924 Indian Citizenship Act.

12. Elizabeth Cady Stanton, "Address to the National Woman Suffrage Convention, Washington, D.C.," January 19, 1869.

13. Frederick Douglass, speech before the Equal Rights Association, May 12, 1869. Quoted in Philip S. Foner, *Frederick Douglass on Women's Rights* (Boston: De Capo Press, 1992), 87.

14. *Daily Journal* (Wilmington, NC), November 14, 1867.

15. "Southern Exchanges on the Reconstruction Plan!," *Charleston Daily News*, March 22, 1867.

16. Sen. James R. Doolittle, "A Plea for the Life of the Republic" (response to the Wisconsin legislature), US Senate, February 16, 1866. Doolittle's speech was printed in the *Daily Milwaukee News*, March 2, 1867.

17. "From Washington: The Practical Overthrow of the Government—Progress of Radicalism—A General Democratic Convention Called For," *Raleigh Sentinel*, January 16, 1867.

18. "From the Boston Pioneer, a Leading German Radical Organ," *Wilmington (NC) Journal*, May 8, 1868.

19. Hazel Carby, *Reconstructing Womanhood: The Emergence of the Afro American Woman Novelist* (New York: Oxford University Press, 1987), 39.

20. Bardaglio, *Reconstructing the Household*, 196–97; Jennifer Wriggins, "Rape, Racism, and the Law," *Harvard Women's Law Journal* 6 (1983): 119–23.

21. In 1866, President Johnson offered amnesty to former Confederate landowners, ordering all confiscated land returned to them. In the process, many thousands of freedmen were dispossessed of land they had been given after the war. See Claude F. Oubre, *Forty Acres and a Mule: The Freedmen's Bureau and Black Land Ownership* (Baton Rouge: Louisiana State University Press, 1978).

22. South Carolina's "Act to Establish and Regulate the Domestic Relations of Persons of Colour, and to Amend the Law in Relation to Paupers and Vagrancy," Section XCVI, *Acts of the General Assembly of the State of South Carolina Passed at the Sessions of 1864–65* (Columbia: 1865), 291–304.

23. Mississippi Black Codes, 1866, part 3 (Mississippi Vagrant Laws), Section 2.

24. Ibid.

25. Black men were fined fifty dollars, while whites were fined two hundred; terms of imprisonment for "the free negro [were] not exceeding ten days, and the white man not exceeding six months."

26. Keri Leigh Merritt, "'One Continuous Graveyard': Emancipation and the Birth of the Professional Police Force," *African American Intellectual History Society*, July 11, 2016. http://www.aaihs.org/emancipation-and-the-birth-of-the -professional-police-force/.

27. See Theodore B. Wilson, *The Black Codes of the South* (Tuscaloosa: University of Alabama Press, 1965), and Alexander DeConde, *Gun Violence in America: The Struggle for Control* (Boston: Northeastern University Press, 2001), 72.

28. Mississippi Black Codes, 1866, part 4 (Penal Laws), section 1.

29. See Meltzer, "Open Carry for All," 1516–17, and Akhil Reed Amar, *The Bill of Rights: Creation and Reconstruction* (New Haven, CT: Yale University Press, 1998).

30. Rep. Clarke's testimony to the 39th Congress 1st Session, April 7, 1866. Quoted in Stephen P. Halbrook, "The Fourteenth Amendment and the Right to Keep and Bear Arms: The Intent of the Framers," *Report of the Subcommittee on the Constitution of the Committee on the Judiciary, US Senate*, 97th Congress, February 1982, 68–82, http://www.guncite.com/journals/senrpt/.

31. Enforcement Act of 1870.

32. The lack of precision is due to the fact that many bodies were rumored to have been dumped in the river, never to be recovered. See Lane, *Day Freedom Died*, 265–66, and Henry Louis Gates, "What Was the Colfax Massacre?" *The Root*, July 29, 2013.

33. Cited in Lane, *Day Freedom Died*, 84.

34. United States v. Cruikshank, 92 U.S. 542 (1875).

35. Gates, "What Was the Colfax Massacre?"

36. United States v. Cruikshank, 92 U.S. 553 (1875).

37. Merritt, "One Continuous Graveyard."

38. Richard Franklin Bensel, *The American Ballot Box in the Mid-Nineteenth Century* (New York: Cambridge University Press, 2004), 21.

39. Richard M. Brown, *No Duty to Retreat: Violence and Values in American History and Society* (Norman: University of Oklahoma Press, 1994), 11; George Hazzard, *History of Henry County, Indiana, 1822–1906*, vol. 1 (New Castle, IN: G. Hazzard, 1906), 227, 234; Home for Disabled Veterans, 1905 death and intake records; see census records at Indiana Civil War Soldier Database Index, 1861–1865, and the Historical Register of National Homes for Disabled Volunteer Soldiers, 1866–1938 (National Archives Microfilm Publication M1749, 282 rolls), Records of the Department of Veterans Affairs, Record Group 15, National Archives, Washington, DC.

40. Brown, *No Duty to Retreat*, 12–13.

41. *Runyan v. State.*

42. Brown, *No Duty to Retreat*, 12.

43. "Murder at New Castle—Fears of Lynching," *Cambridge City (IN) Tribune*, November 11, 1876.

44. Ibid.

45. See, for example, the column titled "Telegraphic Notes," *Coffeyville (KS) Weekly*, November 18, 1876. The story is a report of a riot between Black and white voters in Charleston, South Carolina.

46. *Runyan v. State.*

47. The number of Civil War casualties is a subject of debate. See J. David Hacker, who estimates between 620,000 and 850,000 total (including civilian) casualties, "A Census-Based Count of the Civil War Dead," *Civil War History* 57, no. 4 (December 2011).

48. Herbert G. Gutman, "The Tompkins Square 'Riot' in New York City on January 13, 1874: A Re-examination of Its Causes and Its Aftermath," *Labor History* 6, no. 1 (1965).

49. Blight, *Race and Reunion*, 2, 138–39.

50. "The Result," *Alexandria Gazette*, November 8, 1876.

51. Blight, *Race and Reunion*, 91, 138.

52. Erwin v. State, 29 Ohio St. 186 (1876).

53. Brown, *No Duty to Retreat*, 9.

54. *Erwin v. State.*

55. This principle of allowing "the lives of would-be robbers, murders, and ravishers" to be "in the hands of their intended victims" recurs with regularity in the language of the NRA and its lobbyists.

56. "Eight Years Imprisonment," *Chicago Inter Ocean*, February 21, 1877.

57. *Runyan v. State.*

58. Ibid.

59. Blight, *Race and Reunion*, 3.

60. Suk, *At Home in the Law*, 56–62.

61. Texas Penal Code, Article 567.

62. Carole Marks, *Farewell—We're Good and Gone: The Great Black Migration* (Bloomington: Indiana University Press, 1989); James N. Gregory, *The Southern Diaspora: How the Great Migrations of Black and White Southerners Transformed America* (Chapel Hill: University of North Carolina Press, 2007).

63. US Department of Commerce, Bureau of the Census, *Library, Bicentennial Edition: Historical Statistics of the United States, Colonial Times to 1970*, http://www.census.gov/library/publications/1975/compendia/hist_stats_colonial-1970.html; *Current Population Reports, Series P-23, Ancestry and Language in the United States: November 1979*, http://eric.ed.gov/?id=ED227680.

64. Horace V. Redfield, *Homicide, North and South: Being a Comparative View of Crime Against the Person in Several Parts of the United States* (Philadelphia: Lippincott, 1880); Steven Messner, Robert Baller, and Matthew Zevenbergen, "The Legacy of Lynching and Southern Homicide," *American Sociological Review* 70, no. 4 (August 2005).

65. Hodes, *White Women, Black Men*, 176.

66. William F. Brundage, *Lynching in the New South: Georgia and Virginia, 1880–1930* (Urbana: University of Illinois Press, 1993), 8.

67. Equal Justice Initiative, *Lynching in America: Confronting the Legacy of Racial Terror* (2015), http://eji.org/reports/lynching-in-america.

CHAPTER THREE: "A MIGHTY POWER IN THE HANDS OF THE CITIZEN"

Epigraph sources: Frederick Jackson Turner, "The Significance of the Frontier in American History," paper presented to the American Historical Association, Chicago, 1893, https://www.learner.org/workshops/primarysources/corporations/docs/turner.html; *Gourko v. United States*, 153 US 183 (1894).

1. Joseph Beale Jr., "Retreat from a Murderous Assault," *Harvard Law Review* 16 (1903): 567, 581.

2. Brown, *No Duty to Retreat*, 22–24.

3. Pamela Haag, *The Gunning of America: Business and the Making of American Gun Culture* (New York: Basic Books, 2016).

4. See Brenda Buchanan, *Gunpowder, Explosives and the State: A Technological History* (Aldershot, UK: Ashgate, 2006).

5. Figures from the US Census Bureau: "Population of the United States in 1860," Bureau of the Census, Washington, DC, 1864; "Population of the United States in 1900," Bureau of the Census, Washington, DC, 1901. Note that Native people were not often included in the census before 1900 unless they were living among the general population and had renounced their tribal affiliation. Census data available at http://www.census.gov/.

6. See Rodolfo Acuna, *Occupied America: The Chicano's Struggle Toward Liberation* (New York: Harper & Row, 1972); Benjamin H. Johnson, *Revolution in Texas: How a Forgotten Rebellion and Its Bloody Suppression Turned Mexicans into Americans* (New Haven, CT: Yale University Press, 2003); William D. Carrigan, "The Lynching of Persons of Mexican Origin or Descent in the United States, 1848 to 1928," *Journal of Social History* 37, no. 2 (2003): 411–38.

7. Michael Carrigan and Clive Webb, "When Americans Lynched Mexicans," *New York Times*, February 20, 2015.

8. Ronald Takaki, *Strangers from a Different Shore: A History of Asian Americans* (New York: Penguin Books, 1990), 79–92.

9. For more information about the exclusion of Chinese from the basic rights and privileges of US citizenship, see Charles J. McClain, *In Search of Equality: The Chinese Struggle Against Discrimination in Nineteenth-Century America* (Berkeley: University of California Press, 1994).

10. See Peggy Pascoe, *What Comes Naturally: Miscegenation Law and the Making of Race in America* (New York: Oxford University Press, 2010).

11. The original law, passed in 1850, excluded only African Americans from marriage with whites. Leti Volpp, "American Mestizo: Filipinos and Anti-Miscegenation Law in California," in *Mixed Race American and the Law: A Reader*, ed. Kevin R. Johnson (New York: New York University Press, 2003), reveals how state marriage exclusions reflected concerns about predominantly male, immigrant populations as threats to white femininity.

12. Native Americans were excluded from marriage with whites in Georgia, Idaho, Nevada, North Carolina, Oregon, South Carolina, Tennessee, and Virginia. In Virginia, the law was qualified in 1924 by the "Pocahontas Exception," which allowed whites with no more than one-sixteenth Native heritage to marry other whites.

13. Dunbar-Ortiz, *An Indigenous Peoples' History of the United States*, 103–4.

14. In 1909, Wisconsin's Supreme Court declared self-defense a divine right. Quoted in Brown, *No Duty to Retreat*, 20.

15. Texas Penal Code, Art. 573 (1879).

16. State v. Reed, 37 Pac.174, 179 (Kan. 1894). See also State v. Hatch, 46 Pac. 708, 709 (Kan. 1896): "The doctrine that a party unlawfully attacked must 'retreat to the wall' before he can be justified in taking the life of his assailant in self-defense does not obtain in this State."

17. State v. Bartlett, 71 S.W. 148, 151 (Mo. 1902); Miller v. State, 119 N.W. 850, 857 (Wis. 1909).

18. No relation to Judge Isaac Parker, who tried the Thomas Selfridge case, discussed in chapter 1.

19. S. W. Harman, *Hell on the Border: He Hanged Eighty-Eight Men* (Fort Smith, AZ: Phoenix Publishing Co., ca. 1898), 53.

20. Harry P. Daily, "Judge Isaac C. Parker," *Chronicles of Oklahoma* 11, no. 1 (March 1933): 680–81.

21. Harman, *Hell on the Border*, 699.

22. Ibid.

23. Ibid., 691.

24. Ibid., 692.

25. Ibid. Italics in original.

26. James S. Davenport, Plaintiff in Error, v. The United States, No. 747 October 1895.

27. Davenport v. United States, 163 U.S. 682, 683 (1896).

28. "J. S. Davenport Acquitted," *Fort Gibson (OK) Post*, October 21, 1897.

29. Carolyn G. Hanneman, "Davenport, James Sanford (1864–1940)," *Oklahoma Historical Society Encyclopedia*, http://www.okhistory.org/publications/enc/entry.php?entry=DA013.

30. Harman, *Hell on the Border*, 15.

31. See Nell Irvin Painter, *Exodusters: Black Migration to Kansas After Reconstruction* (New York: W. W. Norton, 1976).

32. Census data suggests that Alexander was able to read and write, while Henson and the Erne boys could not. See Allen v. United States, 150 U.S. 551, 553 (1893); Heather E. Williams, "Letter from the Defender," *Federal Defender Newsletter*, Eastern District of California, September 2015.

33. Allen v. United States, 15 S.Ct. 720 (1895).

34. Allen v. United States, 164 U.S. 492, 501–2 (1896).

35. David B. Kopel, "The Self-Defense Cases: How the United States Supreme Court Confronted a Hanging Judge in the Nineteenth Century and Taught Some Lessons for Jurisprudence in the Twenty-First," *American Journal of Criminal Law* 27, no. 293 (2000): 307.

36. J. Gladston Emery, *Court of the Damned: The Story of Judge Isaac C. Parker* (New York: Comet Press, 1959), 174.

37. Allen v. United States, 150 U.S. 551, 555 (1893).

38. Ibid.

39. Ibid., 555–56.

40. Ibid.

41. Allen v. United States, 15 S.Ct. 720 (1895).

42. An 1877 act allowed the right of appeal to the Supreme Court to all capital cases occurring in the Indian Territory under the circuit court's jurisdiction.

43. Allen v. United States, 150 U.S. 551, 561 (1893); Thompson v. United States, 155 U.S. 271, 281 (1894).

44. *Thompson v. United States.*

45. Chief Justice Fuller, *Allen v. United States.*

46. *Thompson v. United States.*

47. Kopel, "Self-Defense Cases," 304. See also Harman, *Hell on the Border*, 179n12.

48. Allen v. United States, 164 U.S. 492, 501–2 (1896).

49. Ibid.

50. Jerome Michael, "Recent Decisions," *Columbia Law Review* 11, no. 7 (November 1911): 677.

51. Francis Wharton, *The Law of Homicide* (Rochester, NY: Lawyers' Co-operative Publishing Company, 1907), 316–62.

52. *Gourko v. United States.*

53. Judge Isaac Parker's instructions to the jury quoted in Gourko v. United States, 153 U.S. 183 (1894).

54. Ibid.

55. *Thompson v. United States.*

56. Harman, *Hell on the Border*, 343.

57. Ibid., 354.

58. Ibid., 690.

59. *Gourko v. United States.*

60. "Pardon for Alexander Allen," *Washington Post*, February 18, 1897.

61. Beard v. United States, No. 542, 158 U.S. 550, May 1895.

62. See Kopel, "Self-Defense Cases."

63. *Allen v. United States* (1896).

64. Kopel, "Self-Defense Cases," 295.

65. Brown v. United States, 256 U.S. 335 (1921).

CHAPTER FOUR: "QUEER JUSTICE" AND
THE SEXUAL POLITICS OF LYNCHING

Epigraph sources: Ida B. Wells, *New York Age*, 1891; Thomas Dixon Jr.,
The Clansman: An Historical Romance of the Ku Klux Klan (New York:
Grosset & Dunlap, 1905).

1. Bryan Stevenson, introduction to Equal Justice Initiative, *Lynching in America*, 5.
2. Ibid., 5–6.
3. See Sherrilyn A. Ifill, *On the Courthouse Lawn: Confronting the Legacy of Lynching in the Twenty-First Century* (Boston: Beacon Press, 2007).
4. W. E. B. Du Bois, *Black Reconstruction* (1935), 711.
5. See also Myrta L. Avary, *Dixie After the War* (1906).
6. Jefferson Davis, *The Rise and Fall of the Confederate Government*, vol. 2 (1881), 192.
7. Ibid., 192–93.
8. Jefferson Davis, *The Rise and Fall of the Confederate Government*, vol. 1 (1881), viii.
9. Davis, *The Rise and Fall of the Confederate Government*, vol. 2, 171.
10. Claude Bowers, *The Tragic Era: The Revolution After Lincoln* (1929), vi.
11. William A. Dunning, *Essays on the Civil War and Reconstruction and Related Topics* (1897, 2nd ed. 1904); William A. Dunning, *Reconstruction, Political and Economic, 1865–1877* (1907).
12. United Daughters of the Confederacy website, http://www.hqudc.org/history-of -the-united-daughters-of-the-confederacy, accessed August 25, 2015.
13. Sponsored by the Phil Cook Chapter of the UDC. See David N. Wiggins, *Georgia's Confederate Monuments and Cemeteries* (Charleston, SC: Arcadia Publishing, 2006), 95.
14. See Historical Marker Project, www.historicalmarkerproject.com/markers /HM1AQ9_arizona-confederate-veterans-memorial_Sierra-Vista-AZ.html; accessed June 1, 2016.
15. Bryan Stevenson, interview with Alex Carp, "Walking with the Wind," *Guernica*, March 17, 2014, http://www.guernicamag.com/interviews /walking-with-the-wind/.
16. Blight, *Race and Reunion*, 2, 138–39.
17. Crystal Feimster, *Southern Horrors: Women and the Politics of Rape and Lynching* (Cambridge, MA: Harvard University Press, 2009), 6; Nell Irvin Painter, *Southern History Across the Color Line* (Chapel Hill: University of North Carolina Press, 2002), 118.
18. Painter, *Southern History Across the Color Line*.
19. See Hodes, *White Women, Black Men*.
20. Wriggins, "Rape, Racism, and the Law," 106.
21. Affidavit of Rhoda Ann Childs, cited in Bardaglio, *Reconstructing the Household*, 195.
22. Hodes, *White Women, Black Men*, chapter 8.
23. See, for example, "Coroners and Freedmen," *CSI: Dixie*, https://csidixie.org /exodus/coroners-freedmen.
24. See Bardaglio, *Reconstructing the Household*, chapter 2.

25. Feimster, *Southern Horrors*, 4–5. See also Hodes, *White Women, Black Men.*

26. Bardaglio, *Reconstructing the Household*, 190.

27. Wriggins, "Rape, Racism, and the Law," 105–7.

28. Ibid., 112–13.

29. Rebecca Latimer Felton, "Women on the Farm," speech to the Georgia Agricultural Society, August 11, 1897. See http://history.house.gov/People/Listing/F/FELTON,-Rebecca-Latimer-(F000069)/.

30. See the description of a Boston journalist who criticized Felton's speech, "Fired at Mrs. Felton," *Macon Telegraph*, August 18, 1897.

31. Examples include "They Stormed the Jail," *Ashville Citizen-Times*, August 11, 1897; "Rapist Lynched," *Daily Arkansas Gazette*, August 16, 1895; "Recent Outrages," *Wilmington Messenger*, August 25, 1899.

32. Ida B. Wells [as "Iola"], "Our Women," *New York Freeman*, January 1, 1887.

33. Ida B. Wells, entry April 11, 1887, unpublished diary. Quoted in Wells, *Crusade for Justice: The Autobiography of Ida B. Wells*, ed. Alfreda M. Duster (Chicago: University of Chicago Press, 1970), xvii.

34. Ida B. Wells, "The Lynchers Wince," editorial, *New York Age*, September 19, 1891, in Wells, *Crusade for Justice*, 33–34.

35. "Memphis Mob: Facts About the Recent Lynching at Memphis," *Appeal* (St. Paul, MN), March 26, 1892.

36. White newspapers, such as the *Piqua (OH) Daily Call*, March 8, 1892, characterized Moss and his allies as a "mob."

37. "Disarmed and Disbanded," *St. Paul Globe*, March 26, 1892.

38. Wells, *The Light of Truth.*

39. Ida B. Wells, editorial, *Free Speech and Headlight*, May 21, 1892. See http://iip digital.usembassy.gov/st/english/publication/2009/11/20091117101358amgnowo .2483942.html#axzz4EQHowwRl.

40. "A Southern Protest Against Lynch Law," *Chicago Daily Tribune*, June 15, 1892, 12.

41. Wells, *Southern Horrors: Lynch Law in All Its Phases.*

42. Frederick Douglass, "Lynch Law in the South," *North American Review* (July 1892).

43. Gail Bederman, *Manliness and Civilization: A Cultural History of Gender and Race in the United States, 1880–1917* (Chicago: University of Chicago Press, 1995), 57–60.

44. Wells, *Southern Horrors.*

45. Ibid., 8.

46. Ibid., 42.

47. Ibid.

48. Bederman, *Manliness and Civilization*, 46.

49. Ibid., 60–62, 67–70.

50. President William McKinley, inaugural address, March 4, 1897.

51. Isaac C. Parker, "How to Arrest the Increase of Homicides in America," *North American Review* (1896): 667–73.

52. From the *Times-Picayune*, October 24, 1911.

53. Maria de Longoria, "Stranger Fruit: The Lynching of Black Women—the Cases of Rosa Richardson and Marie Scott," PhD diss., University of Missouri–Columbia, December 2006, 116–17.

54. Governor Lee Cruce, letter to the *Crisis,* August 1911, 153.
55. "Along the Color Line—Crime," *Crisis,* July 1911, 99–100.
56. Ibid., 100.
57. Cruce, letter to the *Crisis.*
58. De Longoria, "Stranger Fruit," 74.
59. "Murderess of Lemuel Peace . . . ," *Muskogee Times-Democrat,* March 31, 1914.
60. *Standard* (Anaconda, MT), March 31, 1914.
61. *Hobart (OK) Daily Republican,* April 1, 1914.
62. "Oklahoma Chivalry: Colored Woman Taken from Jail by Mob of One Hundred Men," *Emporia (KS) Gazette,* March 31, 1914.
63. "One Hundred Men Lynched Negro Woman at Wagoner," *Tulsa Star,* April 4, 1914.
64. Associated Press, April 1, 1914.
65. "This Woman, a Martyr!" *Cleveland Gazette,* April 4, 1914.
66. "Afro-American Woman Lynched by Americans," *Appeal* (St. Paul, MN), April 18, 1914.
67. "Chivalry of No-Man's-Land," *New York Age,* April 9, 1914.
68. Hodes, *White Women, Black Men,* 10.
69. Feimster, *Southern Horrors,* 5–6; Painter, *Southern History,* 112–13.
70. "Their Wrath Felt," *Daily Democrat* (Huntington, IN), March 16, 1892.
71. Roosevelt and *New York Times* editorial (March 16, 1891) quoted in Ed Falco, "When Italian Immigrants Were 'the Other,'" special to CNN.com, July 10, 2012, http://www.cnn.com/2012/07/10/opinion/falco-italian-immigrants/.
72. Richard Gambino, *Vendetta: A True Story of the Worst Lynching in America; the Mass Murder of Italian-Americans in New Orleans in 1891* (Garden City, NY: Doubleday, 1977), 93, 126. See also Heather Hartley, dir., *Linciati: Lynchings of Italians in America,* documentary film (2004).
73. Cristogianni Borsella, *On Persecution, Identity, and Activism: Aspects of the Italian-American Experience from the Late 19th Century to Today* (Boston: Dante Press, 2010), 48.
74. David Pacchioli, "Dark Legacy," *Penn State News,* May 1, 2004.
75. Woodrow Wilson, Proclamation of July 26, 1918.
76. *Congressional Record,* House, 65th Congress, 2nd session (May 7, 1918): 6177; "Anti-Lynching Bill," 1918, Senate Reports (7951), 67th Congress: 2nd Session, 1921–22, vol. 2, 33–34.
77. Anti-Lynching Crusaders, "The Shame of America," November 1922, http://www.digitalhistory.uh.edu/active_learning/explorations/lynching/shame.cfm; Tiffany A. Player, "The Anti-Lynching Crusaders: A Study of Black Women's Activism," master's thesis, University of Georgia, 2008.
78. C. M. Ledbetter, "Lynching—Its Cause and Cure," *Atlanta Constitution,* April 4, 1922.
79. Harvard Sitkoff, interview with Robert Siegel, "Anti-Lynching Law in U.S. History," NPR, June 13, 2005.
80. Harry Farrell, *Swift Justice: Murder and Vengeance in a California Town* (New York: St. Martin's Press, 1993).
81. George C. Rable, "The South and the Politics of Antilynching Legislation, 1920–1940," *Journal of Southern History* 51, no. 2 (1985): 201–20.
82. "South Fights Lynching Bill," *New York Amsterdam News,* April 20, 1935.

83. Sitkoff, "Anti-Lynching Law in U.S. History."
84. Stevenson, *Lynching in America*, 6.
85. See Angela Davis, *Violence Against Women and the Ongoing Challenge to Racism*, vol. 5, Freedom Organizing Series (Latham, NY: Kitchen Table/Women of Color Press, 1985); Angela Davis, *Women, Race, and Class* (New York: Vintage, 1981); Patricia Hill Collins, *Black Sexual Politics: African Americans, Gender, and the New Racism* (New York: Routledge, 2004).

CHAPTER FIVE: "AN AMERICAN TRADITION"

Epigraph sources: Robert F. Williams, *Negroes with Guns* (New York: Marzani and Mansell, 1962), 72; Ann Coulter, "Negroes with Guns," April 18, 2012, AnnCoulter.com, http://www.anncoulter.com/columns/2012-04-18.html; Randall Kennedy, "The Civil Rights Movement and the Politics of Memory," *American Prospect* (Spring 2015).
1. See, for example, Timothy Tyson, *Radio Free Dixie: Robert F. Williams and the Roots of Black Power* (Chapel Hill: University of North Carolina Press, 1999); Nicholas Johnson, *Negroes and the Gun: The Black Tradition of Arms* (Amherst, NY: Prometheus, 2014); Charles Cobb, *This Nonviolent Stuff'll Get You Killed: How Guns Made the Civil Rights Movement Possible* (Durham, NC: Duke University Press, 2014); Christopher Strain, *Pure Fire: Self-Defense as Activism in the Civil Rights Era* (Athens: University of Georgia Press, 2005); Akinyele Umoja, *We Will Shoot Back: Armed Resistance in the Mississippi Freedom Movement* (New York: New York University Press, 2013); Lance E. Hill, *The Deacons for Defense: Armed Resistance and the Civil Rights Movement* (Chapel Hill: University of North Carolina Press, 2004).
2. Cobb, *This Nonviolent Stuff'll Get You Killed*, 7.
3. Tyson, *Radio Free Dixie*, 21.
4. Ibid., 55–56.
5. See Devon Douglas-Bowers, "Debt Slavery: The Forgotten History of Sharecropping," *The Hampton Institute* (online journal) (November 7, 2013), http://www.hamptoninstitution.org/sharecropping.html#.V1BQBFJUFpk; accessed June 2, 2016; Roger L. Ransom and Richard Sutch, "Debt Peonage in the Cotton South After the Civil War," *Journal of Economic History* 32 (1972): 3; Pete Daniel, *The Shadow of Slavery: Peonage in the South, 1901–1969* (Urbana: University of Illinois Press, 1972); Michelle Alexander, *The New Jim Crow: Mass Incarceration in the Age of Colorblindness* (New York: New Press, 2010).
6. Douglas A. Blackmon, *Slavery by Another Name: The Re-Enslavement of Black People in America from the Civil War to World War II* (New York: Doubleday, 2008). See also Alex Lichtenstein, *Twice the Work of Free Labor: The Political Economy of Convict Labor in the New South* (New York: Verso, 1996).
7. Angela Davis, *Are Prisons Obsolete?* (New York: Seven Stories Press, 2005), 32. See also David Oshinsky, *Worse Than Slavery: Parchman Farm and the Ordeal of Jim Crow Justice* (New York: Free Press, 1997); Mary Ann Curtin, *Black Prisoners and Their World, Alabama, 1865–1900* (Charlottesville: University of Virginia Press, 2000); Matthew Mancini, *One Dies, Get Another: Convict Leasing in the American South, 1866–1928* (Charleston: University of South Carolina Press, 1996).

8. John Walker, "Before Kelly Gissendaner, the Last Woman Georgia Executed Was Falsely Convicted and Black," Fusion.net, September 30, 2015; "To Be the First Woman to Die in Georgia Chair," *Kansas City Plaindealer*, January 26, 1945.

9. Danielle McGuire, *At the Dark End of the Street: Black Women, Rape, and Resistance* (New York: Vintage, 2010), xvii.

10. See "Memorial Day Remembrance: Lynching of Black Veterans After World War II," *Rhapsody in Books* (blog), May 25, 2009; Vincent P. Mikkelsen, "Coming from Battle to Face a War: The Lynching of Black Soldiers in the World War I Era," PhD diss., Florida State University, April 24, 2007.

11. Rachel Williams, "Run Home If You Don't Want to Be Killed: The Detroit Race Riot of 1943," *The Red Magpie* (blog), April 7, 2014, http://rachelwilliams .squarespace.com/magpie-musings; Marilynn S. Johnson, "Gender, Race, and Rumours: Re-Examining the 1943 Race Riots," *Gender and History* 10, no. 2 (1998): 252–77.

12. See Hugh Whitaker, "A Case Study in Southern Justice: The Emmett Till Case," master's thesis, Florida State University, 1963, 103–5.

13. Simeon Wright, *Simeon's Story: An Eyewitness Account of the Kidnapping of Emmett Till* (Chicago: Lawrence Hill, 2010), 50–51.

14. Kennedy, *Race, Crime, and the Law*, 61–62.

15. William Bradford Huie, "The Shocking Story of Approved Killing in Mississippi," *Look*, January 1956.

16. Ibid., quoting J. W. Milam.

17. Jeanne Theoharis, *The Rebellious Life of Mrs. Rosa Parks* (Boston: Beacon Press, 2014), ix–x; McGuire, *At the Dark End of the Street*, xvii.

18. Roland Sheppard, "On Its 50th Anniversary: The Lessons of the Montgomery Bus Boycott," *Labor Studies and Radical History* (November 2005).

19. Kennedy, *Race, Crime, and the Law*, 60–66.

20. Tyson, *Radio Free Dixie*, 148; Johnson, *Negroes and the Gun*, 25.

21. Quoted in Tyson, *Radio Free Dixie*, 149.

22. Martin Luther King Jr., "The Social Organization of Non-Violence," *Liberation*, October 1959, quoted in Williams, *Negroes with Guns*, 14. Although Robert's name appears alone on the publication, I acknowledge the authorship of his wife, Mabel, since the couple collaborated on most of their published work.

23. Ibid., 14.

24. Williams, *Negroes with Guns*; Tyson, *Radio Free Dixie*, 91–92.

25. King, 1959, quoted in Williams, *Negroes with Guns*, 13.

26. Tyson, *Radio Free Dixie*, 86–88; Johnson, *Negroes and the Gun*, 21–22.

27. Williams, *Negroes with Guns*, 39.

28. Ibid., 41.

29. Mabel Williams, "On Armed Self-Defense and the Klan," presentation to the Freedom Archives, San Francisco, 2005. See http://www.freedomarchives.org /Mabel.html.

30. Ibid.

31. Mabel Williams, interviewed by David Cecelski, August 20, 1999, interview K-0266, Southern Oral History Program Collection (#4007), University of North Carolina, Chapel Hill.

32. Williams, "On Armed Self-Defense and the Klan."
33. Jill Lepore, "Battleground America: One Nation, Under the Gun," *New Yorker*, April 23, 2012.
34. Williams, interview with Cecelski, 1999.
35. Ibid.
36. Daisy Bates, *The Long Shadow of Little Rock, a Memoir* (New York: David McKay, 1986), 168–72.
37. Johnson, *Negroes and the Gun*, 13.
38. See Hill, *Deacons for Defense.*
39. Akinyele O. Umoja, "'We Will Shoot Back': The Natchez Model and Paramilitary Organization in the Mississippi Freedom Movement," *Journal of Black Studies* 32, no. 3 (January 2002): 288.
40. Elizabeth Hinton, "Creating Crime: The Rise and Impact of National Juvenile Delinquency Programs in Black Urban Neighborhoods," *Journal of Urban History* 41, no. 5 (2015): 1–17.
41. *The Black Panther*, October 7, 1972, 10.
42. See Ashley D. Farmer, "What You've Got Is a Revolution: Black Women's Movements for Black Power," PhD diss., Harvard University, 2013.
43. Tressie McMillan Cottom, "When You Are the Demographic You Study: Interrogation of Self Versus Going Native," *Some of Us Are Brave*, March 10, 2013, https://tressiemc.com/.
44. For example, in 1969, twenty-one-year-old Fred Hampton was gunned down while asleep in his bed. Joshua Bloom and Waldo Martin, *Black Against Empire: The History and Politics of the Black Panther Party* (Berkeley: University of California Press, 2014), 6.
45. Edward W. Williams, "Fear of a Black Gun Owner: Ironically, the NRA Used to Support Gun Control—When the Black Panthers Started Packing," *The Root*, January 23, 2013.
46. Adam Winkler, *Gunfight: The Battle over the Right to Bear Arms in America* (New York: W. W. Norton, 2011), 231.
47. David Hilliard, *This Side of Glory: The Autobiography of David Hilliard and the Story of the Black Panther Party* (Chicago: Lawrence Hill, 2001); Bloom and Martin, *Black Against Empire.*
48. Ashley Halsey Jr., "Black Panthers and Blind Kittens," *American Rifleman*, September 1970, 20.
49. Ronald Reagan, address to the NRA annual meeting, *American Rifleman*, May 1984, 40.
50. Elizabeth Hinton, "A War Within Our Own Boundaries," *Journal of American History* 102 (2015): 1, 100.
51. Ibid.
52. Robert C. Maynard, "Black Revolutionaries Feed on Ghetto Anger," *San Antonio Express*, October 8, 1967. This article was part of a six-part series, "The Black Revolt in the United States."
53. Ibid.
54. Ibid.
55. Ibid.
56. See Elizabeth Hinton, *From the War on Poverty to the War on Crime: The Making*

of Mass Incarceration in America (Cambridge, MA: Harvard University Press, 2016).

57. Rachel Manning, Mark Levine, and Alan Collins, "The Kitty Genovese Murder and the Social Psychology of Helping: The Parable of the 38 Witnesses," *American Psychologist* 62, no. 6 (2007): 555.

58. Stephen Tuck, " 'We Are Taking Up Where the Movement of the 1960s Left Off': The Proliferation and Power of African American Protest During the 1970s," *Journal of Contemporary History* 43, no. 4 (October 2008): 637.

59. Andrew Marx and Tom Tuthill, "Resisting the Klan: Mississippi Organizes," *Southern Exposure* 8, no. 2 (Summer 1980): 73–76.

60. Ibid.

61. James Baldwin, "Stranger in the Village," *Notes of a Native Son* (orig. 1955; Boston: Beacon Press, 1984), 160.

62. See Kennedy, "The Civil Rights Movement and the Politics of Memory."

63. Lepore, "Battleground America," cites Mark Tushnet's work on the "rights revolution." See Mark Tushnet, "The Rights Revolution in the Twentieth Century," *The Cambridge History of Law in America*, vol. 3, *The Twentieth Century and After*, ed. Michael Grossberg and Christopher Tomlins (New York: Cambridge University Press, 2008).

64. Williams, "Fear of a Black Gun Owner."

65. Williams, interview with Cecelski, 1999.

66. John Bender, "Gun Control: Racist and Elitist," *Federal Observer*, December 10, 2002.

67. John Bender, "Black History and the Second Amendment," *Ether Zone*, February 5, 2003, available at www.freerepublic.com/focus/news/805202/posts.

68. Benjamin Carson, *A More Perfect Union: What We the People Can Do to Protect Our Constitutional Liberties* (New York: Sentinel Press, 2015), 61.

69. Coulter, "Negroes with Guns."

70. Johnson, *Negroes and the Gun*, 13.

71. See Theoharis, *Rebellious Life of Mrs. Rosa Parks*; Peter Dreier, "Rosa Parks: Angry, Not Tired," *Dissent* 53, no. 1 (2006): 88–92; McGuire, *At the Dark End of the Street*, xvii; Nikki Giovanni, *Rosa Parks* (New York: Macmillan/Hyperion, 2004).

72. Recent examples include Don McDougall, "Do All Lives Matter? 5 Questions for the Anti-Gun Left," Ammoland.com, March 15, 2016, and the KKK-sponsored "White Lives Matter" demonstration in Anaheim, CA, February 27, 2016.

CHAPTER SIX: "THE STUFF OF PULP FICTION"

Epigraph sources: Jody David Armour, *Negrophobia and Reasonable Racism: The Hidden Costs of Being Black in America* (New York: New York University Press, 2000), 57; Wayne LaPierre, quoted in Aaron Blake, "NRA Head: A 'Violent Rapist Deserves to Face . . . a Good Woman with a Gun,' " *Washington Post*, March 15, 2013, https://www.washingtonpost.com/news/post-politics/wp/2013/03/15/nra-head-a-violent-rapist-deserves-to-face-a-good-woman-with-a-gun/.

1. Claire Houston, "How Feminist Theory Became (Criminal) Law: Tracing the

Path to Mandatory Criminal Intervention," *Michigan Journal of Gender and Law* 21, no. 2 (2014): 217–72.

2. For a discussion of the shifting implications of home in criminal law, see Suk, *At Home in the Law.*

3. McGuire, *At the Dark End of the Street,* xvii, 13–14.

4. Suk, *At Home in the Law,* 13; Reva Siegel, "'The Rule of Love': Wife Beating as Prerogative and Privacy," *Yale Law Journal* 105, no. 8 (1996): 2122–27.

5. Siegel, "'The Rule of Love,'" 2141; Linda Gordon, *Heroes of Their Own Lives: The Politics and History of Family Violence, Boston, 1880–1960* (Urbana: University of Illinois Press, 2002), 272.

6. Louis Brandeis and Samuel Warren, "A Right to Privacy," *Harvard Law Review* 4, no. 5 (1890).

7. Gordon, *Heroes of Their Own Lives*; Houston, "How Feminist Theory Became (Criminal) Law," 225; Siegel, "'The Rule of Love,'" 2142.

8. Houston, "How Feminist Theory Became (Criminal) Law," 223–24.

9. Siegel, "'The Rule of Love,'" 2170.

10. See Kate Millett, *Sexual Politics* (New York: Doubleday, 1969); Del Martin, *Battered Wives* (San Francisco: Volcano, 1976); Houston, "How Feminist Theory Became (Criminal) Law," 233. See also Les Moran and Beverly Skeggs, *Sexuality and the Politics of Violence* (New York: Routledge, 2004), 91; and Diana Russell, *Rape in Marriage* (New York: Macmillan, 1982).

11. McGuire, *At the Dark End of the Street,* xix.

12. Beth Richie, *Compelled to Crime: The Gender Entrapment of Battered Black Women* (New York: Routledge, 1996), 145.

13. See Third World Women's Alliance, *Triple Jeopardy* 2, no. 1 (1972) on the exclusionary mechanisms of welfare.

14. Combahee River Collective, "Combahee River Collective Statement," 1977, http://circuitous.org/scraps/combahee.html.

15. Nancy A. Matthews, *Confronting Rape: The Feminist Anti-Rape Movement and the State* (London: Routledge, 1994), 8.

16. Susan Brownmiller, *Against Our Will: Men, Women, and Rape* (New York: Simon & Schuster, 1975).

17. Angela Davis, "The Color of Violence Against Women," keynote address, "Color of Violence" conference, Santa Cruz, CA, October 10, 2000.

18. Mending the Sacred Hoop continues to provide support to survivors and to generate research on indigenous women's experience of domestic violence. See, for example, Thomas Peacock et al., *Community-Based Analysis of the US Legal System's Intervention in Domestic Abuse Cases Involving Indigenous Women,* report prepared for the US Department of Justice, December 2002, www.ncjrs .gov/pdffiles1/nij/grants/199358.pdf.

19. Chicana Service Action Center, *Chicana Feminist Thought: The Basic Historical Writings* (New York: Routledge, 1997), 149.

20. Houston, "How Feminist Theory Became (Criminal) Law," 267; Suk, *At Home in the Law,* 10.

21. Marie Gottschalk, *The Prison and the Gallows: The Politics of Mass Incarceration in America* (New York: Cambridge University Press, 2006), 130.

22. Houston, "How Feminist Theory Became (Criminal) Law," 261.

23. Jennifer C. Nash, "From Lavender to Purple: Privacy, Black Women, and Feminist Legal Theory," *Cardozo Women's Law Journal* 11 (2004): 314.

24. Davis, *Women, Race, and Class*; Kimberlé Crenshaw, "Mapping the Margins," in Crenshaw et al., *Critical Race Theory*; Gloria Anzaldúa, *Borderlands/La Frontera: The New Mestiza* (San Francisco: Aunt Lute Books, 1987); Nellie Wong, "When I Was Growing Up," in *This Bridge Called My Back: Writings by Radical Women of Color*, ed. Cherríe Moraga and Gloria Anzaldúa (Watertown, MA: Persephone, 1981); Dorothy Roberts, *Killing the Black Body: Race, Reproduction, and the Meaning of Liberty* (New York: Pantheon, 1997); bell hooks, *Ain't I a Woman: Black Women and Feminism* (Boston: South End Press, 1981); bell hooks, "Understanding Patriarchy," *Louisville Anarchist Federation, Louisville Lending Library* (2013), http://imaginenoborders.org/pdf/zines/Understanding Patriarchy.pdf.

25. Davis, "Color of Violence Against Women."

26. Gottschalk, *Prison and the Gallows*, 131.

27. Davis, "Color of Violence Against Women." See also Davis, *Women, Race, and Class*, for her critique of Susan Brownmiller (178–79).

28. Shannon Jackson, "Representing Rape: Model Mugging's Discursive and Embodied Performances," *Drama Review* 37, no. 3 (Autumn 1993): 111.

29. See Patricia Searles and Ronald Berger, "The Feminist Self-Defense Movement: A Case Study," *Gender and Society* 1, no. 1 (March 1987). Shannon Jackson's own Model Mugging class was all white except for one Asian American woman, and all were college-educated. Jackson also mentions the high cost of tuition. Jackson, "Representing Rape," 119–20.

30. Searles and Berger, "Feminist Self-Defense Movement," 72.

31. Jackson, "Representing Rape," 126.

32. Ibid., 127.

33. Nash, "From Lavender to Purple," 329.

34. Richie, *Compelled to Crime*, 152–53.

35. Nash, "From Lavender to Purple," 319.

36. Richie, *Compelled to Crime*, 39, 83.

37. Miriam H. Ruttenberg, "A Feminist Critique of Mandatory Arrest: An Analysis of Race and Gender in Domestic Violence Policy," *American University Journal of Gender, Social Policy & the Law* 2 (1994): 172; Suk, *At Home in the Law*, 7.

38. Richie, *Compelled to Crime*, 152–53.

39. Ibid., 181.

40. Hale, *The History of the Pleas of the Crown*.

41. Ruttenberg, "Feminist Critique of Mandatory Arrest," 179; Richie, *Compelled to Crime*, 100.

42. Ruttenberg, "Feminist Critique of Mandatory Arrest," 187–88n81; Shannan Catalano et al., "Female Victims of Violence," Bureau of Justice Statistics, Selected Findings, NCJ228356 (Washington, DC: US Department of Justice, Office of Justice Programs, October 23, 2009), www.bjs.gov/content/pub/pdf/fvv.pdf.

43. See, for example, "Laura X," letter to the editor, *Off Our Backs*, January 1985, 24, detailing the criminalization of marital rape in twenty-two states, and "dar's" discussion of state laws that exempted husbands from criminal prosecution in "Marital Rape," *Off Our Backs*, April 1989, 5.

44. Paxton Quigley, letter to the editor, *Los Angeles Times*, January 14, 1992.
45. Aaron Goldstein, "Race, Reasonableness, and the Rule of Law," *Southern California Law Review* 76 (2003): 1191–93, 1199.
46. Cynthia Lee, *Murder and the Reasonable Man: Passion and Fear in the Criminal Courtroom* (New York: New York University Press, 2007), 3.
47. Ibid., 17–22.
48. Armour, *Negrophobia and Reasonable Racism*, 4.
49. Gayle Strommen, "Criminal Law–Battered Women and Self-Defense," *Temple Law Review* 63 (1990): 375.
50. Ibid.
51. Ibid., 376.
52. Commonwealth of Pennsylvania v. Stonehouse, 555 A.2d 772, 212 (Pa. 1989), 813.
53. *Commonwealth of Pennsylvania v. Stonehouse*, 941–42; Strommen, "Criminal Law," 376–77.
54. "Carol Stonehouse," National Registry of Exonerations, University of Michigan, posted March 11, 2013, https://www.law.umich.edu/special/exoneration/Pages/casedetail.aspx?caseid=4117.
55. *Commonwealth of Pennsylvania v. Stonehouse*.
56. Ibid. Forensic specialists would discover that Walsh's blood alcohol content was .14.
57. "Police Woman Found Guilty in Ex-Cop's Killing," *Pittsburgh Press*, September 14, 1983.
58. See Max Kutner, "30 Years After Bernhard Goetz, a Subway Shooting Evokes Comparisons," *Newsweek*, March 13, 2015; Patricia Williams, *Alchemy of Race and Rights* (Cambridge, MA: Harvard University Press, 1992), 73–74; Goldstein, "Race, Reasonableness, and the Rule of Law," 1191–93; Armour, *Negrophobia and Reasonable Racism*, 4–5.
59. Nadine Klansky, "Bernard Goetz, a 'Reasonable Man': A Look at New York's Justification Defense," *Brooklyn Law Review* 53 (Winter 1988): 1153–54.
60. Nash, "From Lavender to Purple," 328.
61. Ibid., 1186.
62. Lenore Walker, *Battered Women* (New York: Harper & Row, 1979), x.
63. Donald Alexander Downs, *More Than Victims: Battered Women, the Syndrome Society, and the Law* (Chicago: University of Chicago Press, 1996), 111; Roberta K. Thyfault, "Self-Defense: Battered Woman Syndrome on Trial," *California Western Law Review* 20 (1984): 491–92.
64. Armour, *Negrophobia and Reasonable Racism*, 83–84.
65. Walker, *Battered Women*, 13–14.
66. *Commonwealth of Pennsylvania v. Stonehouse*.
67. Ruttenberg, "Feminist Critique of Mandatory Arrest," 189; see also Sharon Angella Allard, "Rethinking Battered Woman Syndrome: A Black Feminist Perspective," *UCLA Women's Law Journal* 1 (1991): 193–94.
68. *Commonwealth of Pennsylvania v. Stonehouse*.
69. Williams, *Alchemy of Race and Rights*, 77.
70. Cynthia Lee, "Race and Self-Defense: Toward a Normative Conception of Reasonableness," *Minnesota Law Review* 81 (1996); Armour, *Negrophobia and Reasonable Racism*, 5.

71. Otto Friedrich, Roger Franklin, and Raji Samghabadi, "'Not Guilty': A Jury Acquits the Subway Gunman, but the Argument Goes On," *Time*, June 29, 1987, 10–11. The authors describe the signs that Goetz's supporters and detractors carried outside the courtroom.

72. Ibid. See also "Neither Villain Nor Hero," *Economist*, June 20, 1987, 41.

73. *Commonwealth of Pennsylvania v. Stonehouse*, Opinion of Justice Larsen, 521.

74. Alafair Burke, "Rational Actors, Self-Defense, and Duress: Making Sense, Not Syndromes, Out of the Battered Woman," *North Carolina Law Review* 81, no. 1 (December 2002): 263–64; Isabel Wilkerson, "Clemency Granted to 25 Women Convicted of Assault or Murder," *New York Times*, December 22, 1990.

75. Bess Rothenberg, "'We Don't Have Time for Social Change': Cultural Compromise and the Battered Woman Syndrome," *Gender and Society* 17, no. 5 (October 2003): 778, 782.

76. Patricia Hill Collins, *Black Feminist Thought: Knowledge, Consciousness, and the Politics of Empowerment* (New York: Routledge, 1991), 67–78; Michelle Wallace, *Black Macho and the Myth of the Superwoman* (New York: Verso, 1990), xx, 105–10.

77. Lawrence A. Greenfeld et al., *Violence by Intimates: Analysis of Data on Crimes by Current or Former Spouses, Boyfriends, and Girlfriends*, Bureau of Justice Statistics Factbook, NCJ #167237 (Washington, DC: US Department of Justice, 1998), http://bjs.gov/content/pub/pdf/vi.pdf.

78. The homicide rate fell from 9.3 per 100,000 US residents in 1992 to 4.7 in 2011. See Office of Justice Programs, Bureau of Justice Crime Statistics, "Homicide in the U.S. Known to Law Enforcement," December 30, 2013, http://www.bjs.gov/index.cfm?ty=pbdetail&iid=4863.

79. See Centers for Disease Control, National Intimate Partner and Sexual Violence Survey, "National Data on Intimate Partner Violence, Sexual Violence, and Stalking," 2014, http://www.cdc.gov/violenceprevention/pdf/nisvs-fact-sheet-2014.pdf. Also, in 2001, nearly nine times as many women were murdered by men they knew as were killed by male strangers. See Violence Policy Center, *When Men Murder Women: An Analysis of 2001 Homicide Data*, September 6, 2013, http://www.vpc.org/studies/wmmw2013.pdf.

80. In cases in which the relationship between killer and victim was known. See Bureau of Justice, "Homicide Rates Fall to Lowest Rate in Four Decades," press release, November 16, 2011, http://www.bjs.gov/content/pub/press/htus8008pr.cfm.

81. Rape, Abuse, and Incest National Network, "Statistics," https://rainn.org/statistics.

82. "WINRA—On Personal Safety," advertisement, *American Rifleman*, July 1977, 37.

83. Kevin Lewis O'Neill, "Armed Citizens and the Stories They Tell: The National Rifle Association's Achievement of Terror and Masculinity," *Men and Masculinities* 9, no. 4 (April 2007): 461.

84. Spitzer, *Guns Across America*, 2–3.

85. Dave Gilson, "This Collection of NRA Ads Reveals Its Descent into Crazy," *Mother Jones*, April 10, 2013.

86. John M. Bruce and Clyde Wilcox, *The Changing Politics of Gun Control* (Lanham, MD: Rowman & Littlefield, 1998); Kelly D. Patterson, "Political Firepower:

The National Rifle Association," in *After the Revolution: PACs, Lobbies, and the Republican Congress*, ed. Robert Biersack, Paul S. Herrnson, and Clyde Wilcox (Boston: Allyn and Bacon, 1999), 67.

87. Gilson, "This Collection of NRA Ads."

88. Ibid.

89. "Violence by Intimates," Department of Justice statistics, March 1998. See http://bjs.gov/content/pub/pdf/vi.pdf.

90. Gallup poll data, cited in Elizabeth Nolan Brown, "Percentage of Women Who Own Guns Is on the Rise," Bustle.com, October 1, 2013.

91. See NRA Women, http://www.nrawomen.tv.

92. See National Association for Gun Rights, http://www.nationalgunrights.org.

93. NRA Women, http://www.nrawomen.tv/home/video/womens-leadership -forum-retreat-self-defense/list/home-feature, accessed September 4, 2015.

94. Dana Ferguson, "Walker Ends Handgun Waiting Period," Associated Press, June 24, 2015.

95. VICE News, "Scott Walker Loosens Gun Restrictions in Wisconsin Ahead of Expected Presidential Bid," June 25, 2015.

96. Quoted in Awr Hawkins, "Scott Walker To Remove Waiting Period for Wisconsin Gun Purchases," *Breitbart*, June 10, 2015, http://www.breitbart.com/.

97. See *Chipping Away at Choice: Growing Access to Women's Health Care and Autonomy*, 2015 update, People for the American Way, a study of Republican assaults on reproductive rights, http://www.pfaw.org/rww-in-focus.

98. Jacquelyn C. Campbell et al., "Risk Factors for Femicide in Abusive Relationships: Results from a Multisite Case Control Study," *American Journal of Public Health* 93 (July 2003): 1089, 1092; Michael B. Siegel and Emily F. Rothman, "Firearm Ownership and the Murder of Women in the United States: Evidence That the State-Level Firearm Ownership Rate Is Associated with the Nonstranger Femicide Rate," *Violence and Gender* (January 2016).

99. Violence Policy Center, *When Men Murder Women*.

100. Everytown for Gun Safety, "Guns and Violence Against Women—America's Uniquely Lethal Domestic Violence Problem," June 18, 2014, http://everytown .org/article/guns-and-violence-against-women.

101. Ibid.

102. Armour, *Negrophobia and Reasonable Racism*, 7.

103. Siegel, " 'Rule of Love,' " 2183.

CHAPTER SEVEN: AVOIDING A "FATE WORSE THAN DEATH"

Epigraph sources: Armed Citizen Project, https://www.facebook.com /TheArmedCitizenProject/; Kelley, "The U.S. v. Trayvon Martin."

1. See Susan Faludi, *The Terror Dream: Myth and Misogyny in an Insecure America* (New York: Metropolitan Books, 2007).

2. Kathryn Russell-Brown, "Go Ahead and Shoot—The Law Might Not Have Your Back," in *Deadly Injustice: Trayvon Martin, Race, and the Criminal Justice System*, ed. Devon Johnson, Amy Farrell, and Patricia Warren (New York: New York

University Press, 2015); Jacki Lyden, "Examining the Foundation of 'Stand Your Ground' Laws," NPR, July 20, 2013, http://www.npr.org/templates/story/story .php?storyId=204013757; Ben Montgomery, "Florida's 'Stand Your Ground' Law Was Born of 2004 Case, but the Story Has Been Distorted," *Tampa Bay Times*, April 14, 2012.

3. Montgomery, "Florida's 'Stand Your Ground' Law."
4. Dennis Baxley, member of Florida's House of Representatives, quoted in Alex Altman, "Beyond Trayvon: How 'Stand Your Ground' Laws Spread from Florida to Half the US," *Time*, March 28, 2012.
5. Judicial Advocacy Team, National Black Law Students Association, "Stand Your Ground: History, Development, and Significance of the Trayvon Martin Case," white paper, September 20, 2012, http://nblsa.org/wp-content/uploads/2014/06 /NBLSA_Stand_Your_Ground_White_Paper.pdf; Franks, "Real Men Advance, Real Women Retreat."
6. Dennis Baxley, "The Law Is Needed, But Not in This Case," *New York Times*, March 21, 2012. Altman, "Beyond Trayvon," also refers to Cox as a burglar.
7. Greg Evers quoted in Montgomery, "Florida's 'Stand Your Ground' Law."
8. O'Neill, "Armed Citizens."
9. NRA, "The Armed Citizen Trailer Parks," February 25, 2016, cites the story in the *Tallahassee Democrat*, November 5, 2004, about the Workman incident, http:// www.americas1stfreedom.org/articles/2016/2/25/the-armed-citizen-trailer-parks.
10. Quoted in Montgomery, "Florida's 'Stand Your Ground' Law," and in Russell-Brown, "Go Ahead and Shoot," 120.
11. Quoted in Ann O'Neill, "NRA's Marion Hammer Stands Her Ground," CNN.com, April 15, 2012, http://www.cnn.com/2012/04/15/us/marion-hammer -profile/.
12. Rick Bragg, "Leader as Hard as Nails Is Taking Reins at NRA," *New York Times*, April 14, 1996.
13. Hammer quoted in Ann O'Neill, "NRA's Marion Hammer."
14. Ibid.
15. Russell-Brown, "Go Ahead and Shoot," 121.
16. John Nichols, "ALEC Exposed," *Nation*, July 12, 2011.
17. See Ben Montgomery and Coleen Jenkins, "Five Years Since Florida Enacted 'Stand Your Ground' Laws, Homicides Are Up," *Tampa Bay Times*, October 15, 2010; Bush quoted in Janie Campbell and Amanda McCorquodale, "Eight Florida Republicans Who Helped Pass 'Stand Your Ground' or Worked to Keep It On," *Huffington Post*, July 15, 2013.
18. Florida Code § 776.012, 2005.
19. Franks, "Real Men Advance, Real Women Retreat," 1107.
20. Elizabeth Chuck, "Florida Had First Stand Your Ground Law, Other States Followed in 'Rapid Succession,'" *ABC News*, July 18, 2013.
21. John Lott, "In Defense of Stand Your Ground Laws," *Chicago Tribune*, October 28, 2013.
22. Cheng and Hoekstra, "Does Strengthening Self-Defense Law Deter Crime or Escalate Violence?"; Chandler McClellan and Erdal Tekin, "Stand Your Ground Laws, Homicides, and Injuries," NBER Working Paper No. 18187 (Cambridge, MA: National Bureau of Economic Research, June 2012).

23. Mark Obbie, "American Bar Association Calls for Repeal of SYG Laws," *The Trace*, September 29, 2015, www.thetrace.org/2015/09/american-bar-association -calls-for-repeal-of-stand-your-ground-laws/.

24. David A. Harris, "Stand Your Ground Laws and Implicit Bias," *Jurist*, October 17, 2014, http://www.jurist.org/forum/2014/10/harris-stand-your-ground-laws-and -implicit-bias.php.

25. John K. Roman, *Race, Justifiable Homicide, and Stand Your Ground Laws: Analysis of FBI Supplementary Homicide Report Data* (Washington, DC: Urban Institute, 2013), 9.

26. David Yamane, "The History of Concealed Weapons Laws in the United States, Part 3: The Rise of the Shall-Issue (Right-to-Carry) Era of Concealed Carry," *Gun Culture 2.0* (blog), June 19, 2014; Brian Anse Patrick, *Rise of the Anti-Media: In-Forming America's Concealed Weapon Carry Movement* (Lanham, MD: Rowman & Littlefield/Lexington Books, 2010), ix–x.

27. Bindu Kalesan, Marcos Villarreal, Katherine Keyes, and Sandro Galea, "Gun Ownership and Social Gun Culture," *Injury Prevention* (June 29, 2015). See also Maggie Fox, "One in Three Americans Own Guns; Culture a Factor, Study Says," *ABC News*, June 29, 2015.

28. Violence Policy Center, *A Shrinking Minority: The Continuing Decline of Gun Ownership in America* (May 2015). The study claims that in 1977, 53 percent of households owned a gun, compared to 2014, when the percentage had fallen to 32 percent. They attribute the decline to waning interest in hunting.

29. Masters, "US Gun Policy"; Christopher Ingraham, "There Are Now More Guns Than People in the US," *Washington Post*, October 5, 2015.

30. A recent Pew Institute study places the number at 12.8 million in summer 2015. Kellan Howell, "Murder Rates Drop as Concealed Weapons Permits Soar: Report," *Washington Times*, July 14, 2015.

31. Rich Morin, "The Demographics and Politics of Gun-Owning Households," Fact Tank, Pew Research Center, July 15, 2014.

32. Kelly Riddell, "Data Divulges Racial Disparity in Chicago's Issuance of Gun Permits," *Washington Times*, September 29, 2014.

33. John O'Connor, "Illinois Concealed Carry Law Enacted as State Legislature Overrides Governor's Veto," *Huffpost Chicago*, September 8, 2013.

34. Kelly Riddell, "Illinois Concealed-Carry Requirements Disproportionately Impact Poor, Black Communities," *Washington Times*, September 29, 2014.

35. Ibid.

36. See John Lott, *More Guns, Less Crime: Understanding Crime and Gun Control Laws* (Chicago: University of Chicago Press, 1998).

37. Jackson Marciana and Arman B., "Lawsuits Filed As Chicago Denies Black People Concealed Carry Licenses," *Counter Current News*, July 14, 2014.

38. National Neighborhood Watch website, "Our History," http://www.nnw.org /our-history.

39. For example, Matt Gutman and Seni Tienabeso, "Trayvon Martin Shooter Told Cops Teenager Went for His Gun," *ABC News*, March 26, 2012, suggest that Martin was the aggressor in the encounter with Zimmerman.

40. Robert Cadwallader, "Update: Armed Guards Now Standing Watch at Burleson Recruiting Office," *Star-Telegram* (Fort Worth, TX), July 21, 2015.

41. See Richard Fausset, "Chattanooga Gunman Mohammod Youssuf Abdulazeez: 'Life Is Short and Bitter,'" *New York Times*, July 16, 2015; Joan Garrett McClane and Joy Lukachich Smith, "Terrorist or Extremist, Was Abdulazeez a Man with a Plan?," Timesfreepress.com, July 23, 2015.

42. "Operation Hero Guard: Do What Obama Won't Do for Recruiting Offices," *Clash with Doug Giles*, July 22, 2015, http://clashdaily.com/2015/07/operation -hero-guard-do-what-obama-wont-do-for-the-recruiting-offices.

43. Quoted in Andrew Welsh-Huggins, "After Tennessee Shootings, Armed Citizens Guard Recruiters," *Marine Corps Times*, July 23, 2015, http://www.marinecorps times.com/story/military/2015/07/22/after-tenn-shootings-armed-citizens-guard -recruiters/30510685/, accessed July 2016.

44. FBI files indicate that there were 65,376,373 background checks for firearm purchases between February 2009, the first full month of Barack Obama's presidency, and February 2013. The number of background checks in Obama's first term is 91.1 percent higher than President George W. Bush's first-term total of 34,214,066. See Gregory Gwyn-Williams Jr., "65.4 Million Gun Purchases Since Obama Took Office, 91% More Than Bush's First-Term Total," CNSNews.com, February 11, 2013.

45. See President Obama's speech on September 9, 2008, transcript, CBSnew.com, http://www.cbsnews.com/news/transcript-obamas-health-care-speech; "Hofstra Debate Transcript," second debate between Barack Obama and Mitt Romney, October 16, 2012, http://www.ontheissues.org/2012–2.htm.

46. A similar spike accompanied Obama's reelection in 2012. See Lindsay Cook, "The NRA Should Send Obama a 'Thank-You' Card," *US News and World Report*, June 23, 2015.

47. Sam Seder, "Black Panther Obama? Sam Seder Proves the Widely Circulated Photo Is a Fraud," on "Debunked," *MajorityX*, December 31, 2005.

48. Stanly Kurtz, *Radical-in-Chief: Barack Obama and the Untold Story of American Socialism* (New York: Threshold Editions, 2010).

49. Manny Schewitz, "Colorado Republican Proposes Welfare Solution: Give Everyone Guns," *Forward Progressives*, December 11, 2015; Laurie Roberts, "House Panel OKs Welfare for Arizona Gun Owners," *Arizona Republic*, February 10, 2016.

50. Betsy Brantner Smith, "Cops and Armed Citizens," *PoliceLink*, 2016, http:// policelink.monster.com/training/articles/144113-cops-and-armed-citizens.

51. Celia Bigelow, "Why Female Gun Ownership Is Up 77% Since 2005," Townhall .com, February 27, 2013.

52. "Women's Programs," http://women.nra.org.

53. The Well Armed Woman, http://thewellarmedwoman.com.

54. "Glock Women," https://us.glock.com/products/sector/women.

55. NRA Explore, "Refuse to Be a Victim," https://rtbav.nra.org.

56. Students for Concealed Carry, http://concealedcampus.org.

57. Quoted in Alan Schwarz, "A Bid for Guns on Campuses to Deter Rape," *New York Times*, February 18, 2015.

58. Mary Ann Franks, "Stand Your Ground's Woman Problem," *Huffington Post*, March 3, 2014.

59. See, for example, Catalano et al., "Female Victims of Violence," and Nancy

Thoennes and Patricia Tjaden, *Full Report of the Prevalence, Incidence, and Consequences of Violence Against Women: Findings from the National Violence Against Women Survey*, NCJ 183781 (Washington, DC: US Department of Justice, National Institute of Justice, November 2000).

60. Siegel and Rothman, "Firearm Ownership and the Murder of Women."

61. David Kopel, "The Posse Comitatus and the Office of the Sheriff: Armed Citizens Summoned to the Aid of Law Enforcement," *Journal of Criminal Law and Criminology* 104, no. 4 (2014): 172.

62. Kyle Coplen quoted in Shaula Clark, "Armed Citizen Project Aims to Distribute Free Guns in Tucson," *Nonprofit Quarterly*, April 3, 2013.

63. Pueblo Gardens, Arizona, is one such community the ACP has worked with. See Christina Silva, "Armed Citizen Project: Arizona Gun Proponents Launch Free Gun Program," *Huffington Post*, March 29, 2013.

64. Tom Tancredo, "Organize State, Local Militias to Defend Against Radical Islamist Assaults," *Breitbart News Network*, December 4, 2015. Quoted in Schewitz, "Colorado Republican Proposes Welfare Solution."

65. Roberts, "House Panel OKs Welfare for Arizona Gun Owners."

66. Montenegro quoted in Howard Fischer, "Bill Gives Arizona's Concealed Carriers Tax Credit," *Arizona Daily Star*, January 19, 2016.

67. Tancredo quoted in Schewitz, "Colorado Republican Proposes Welfare Solution."

68. NRA, *Freedom's Safest Place/My Freedom*, YouTube, www.youtube.com/watch?v=n2Aj1WnNkYI, accessed April 24, 2016.

69. David A. Graham, "The Second Amendment's Second-Class Citizens," *Atlantic*, July 7, 2016.

70. Russell-Brown, "Go Ahead and Shoot," 136.

CONCLUSION

Epigraph source: Karla Holloway, *Legal Fictions: Constituting Race, Composing Literature* (Durham, NC: Duke University Press, 2014), 13.

1. Nadia Prupis, "Race, Domestic Abuse and a Warning Shot: Marissa Alexander Released from Prison, But Still Not Free," CommonDreams.org, January 28, 2015.

2. Angela Corey, quoted in Trymaine Lee, "Marissa Alexander, Mom Facing Twenty Years, Shot at Abusive Husband in Anger, Prosecutor Says," *Huffington Post*, May 10, 2012.

3. For details of the case, see Jeannine Amber, "In Her Own Words: Marissa Alexander Tells Her Story," *Essence*, March 4, 2015.

4. See, for example, the "Free Marissa Now Mobilization Campaign," http://www.freemarissanow.org; "The Monument Quilt," https://themonumentquilt.org; and Melissa Harris-Perry, "A Second Chance to Right a Wrong," MSNBC, November 30, 2013.

5. Statement by Congresswoman Corrine Brown, "No Mercy, No Justice," press release, May 14, 2012, https://corrinebrown.house.gov/.

6. Rita Smith, quoted in Kirsten Powers, "Prosecuted for Standing Her Ground," *The Daily Beast*, July 19, 2013.

7. Brown, "No Mercy, No Justice."

8. Larry Hannan, "Stand Your Ground Denied to Jacksonville Woman Who Killed Husband," *Jacksonville News*, June 13, 2014.

9. Lisa Weismann, "Woman Denied Bond After Boyfriend's Death," *Live 5 News*, November 2, 2012.

10. Amanda Marcotte, "South Carolina Says 'Stand Your Ground' Law Doesn't Apply to Abused Women," *Slate*, October 15, 2014.

11. Andrew Knapp, "Charleston Prosecutors Challenge Use of 'Stand Your Ground' Law in Domestic Disputes at Home," *Post and Courier*, October 12, 2014.

12. See Sen. Don Gaetz and Rep. Matt Gaetz, "Standing Up for 'Stand Your Ground,'" *SPB*, May 2, 2012, http://www.saintpetersblog.com.

13. Kidd, quoted in Knapp, "Charleston Prosecutors Challenge."

14. Wallace, *Black Macho and the Myth of the Black Superwoman*. See also Sen. Daniel Patrick Moynihan's 1965 report, *The Negro Family: The Case for National Action*, which characterized Black women as emasculating and as the root of Black familial "dysfunction."

15. Beth Richie, quoted in Melissa Jeltsen, "Jury Begins Deliberations in Trial of Woman Accused of Killing Her Alleged Abuser," *Huffington Post*, March 29, 2016.

16. Quoted in Melissa Jeltsen, "Cop Faces Charges of Serial Rape, Yet His 13 Black Accusers Are on Trial," *Huffington Post*, December 4, 2015.

17. Ibid.; Jason Johnson, "The Holtzclaw Trial: Where Rape Culture Meets #BlackLivesMatter," *NBC News*, November 13, 2015.

18. For details of the case, see Andy Mannix, "The Edge of Doubt," *City Pages*, May 9, 2012; Nicole Pasulka, "The Case of CeCe McDonald: Murder—or Self-Defense Against Hate Crime?," *Mother Jones*, May 22, 2015.

19. Freeman, quoted in Mannix, "Edge of Doubt."

20. Parker Marie Molloy, "CeCe McDonald: Rebuilding Her Life After 19 Months in Prison," *Advocate*, March 3, 2014. Since obtaining her freedom, McDonald has become an outspoken advocate for prison reform.

21. Burgess quoted in Mannix, "Edge of Doubt."

22. The Georgia Bureau of Investigation would later discover Chavez's blood alcohol level to be .165. The following account of this incident draws on Mitch Kellaway and Sunnivie Brydum, "This Black Trans Man Is in Jail for Killing His Rapist," *Advocate*, April 8, 2015.

23. See, for instance, the case of the "New Jersey 7," a group of Black lesbians who fought back against a violent man who threatened to "fuck them straight" on the streets of New York in 2006. Andrea J. Ritchie, Joey L. Mogul, and Kay Whitlock, *Queer (in)Justice: The Criminalization of LBGT People in the United States* (Boston: Beacon Press, 2011), 42–43.

24. *Lesbian, Gay, Bisexual, Transgender, Queer and HIV-Affected Hate Violence* (New York: National Coalition of Anti-Violence Programs, 2013).

25. Carlson, *Citizen-Protectors*, 143.

26. McNelly Torres and Willard Shepard, "Family Outraged After North Miami Beach Police Use Mug Shots as Shooting Targets," NBCMiami.com, January 15, 2015; Derrick Clifton, "The Disturbing Viral Trend of Using Photos of Black Men for Target Practice," *Daily Dot*, July 15, 2015.

27. Jelani Cobb, "Tamir Rice and America's Tragedy," *New Yorker*, December 29, 2015.
28. See "The Counted: People Killed by Police in 2015," *Guardian* database, http://www.theguardian.com/us-news/ng-interactive/2015/jun/01/the-counted-police-killings-us-database.
29. Kimberly Kindy, Marc Fisher, Julie Tate, and Jennifer Jenkins, "A Year of Reckoning: Police Fatally Shoot Nearly 1000," *Washington Post*, December 28, 2015.
30. Ibid. See also Cobb, "Tamir Rice and America's Tragedy." Cobb's statistics conflict with those gathered by the *Washington Post*. Cobb says that 216 unarmed civilians, 72 of them Black, were killed by police in 2015.
31. Prior to the *Washington Post* study, the FBI had been solely responsible for keeping track of police shootings, but they have depended on local police departments to report their data accurately. According to the data collected by the *Washington Post* through analysis of local news feeds, interviews, and police reports, the FBI's data reflected a gross underreporting, by approximately half, of the deaths by police shooting. See Kindy et al., "A Year of Reckoning."
32. Ibid.
33. See Oathkeepers.org, http://oathkeepers.org/oktester/new-leadership-in-missouri-and-march-update, accessed August 31, 2015.
34. Cassandra Vinograd, "Heavily Armed 'Oath Keepers' Patrol Ferguson Protests," MSNBC, August 11, 2015.
35. Missouri Bill of Rights, Section 12, states, "The right of every citizen to keep and bear arms in defense of his home, person and property, or when lawfully summoned in aid of the civil power, shall not be questioned; but this shall not justify the wearing of concealed weapons."
36. Jason Van Tatenhove, "New Leadership in Missouri," Oathkeepers.org, August 31, 2015, https://www.oathkeepers.org/new-leadership-in-missouri-and-march-update, accessed March 30, 2016.
37. Krista Brunson and Corky Siemaszko, "Jamie Gilt, Florida Mom, Accidentally Shot by 4-Year-Old Son," *NBC News*, March 9, 2016.
38. "Witnesses Tell of 'Bloodbath' at Paris Rock Concert," *Yahoo News*, November 14, 2015.
39. Quoted in "Liberty University to Allow Concealed Handguns in Dorms," CBSnews.com April 27, 2016.
40. Lepore, "Battleground America."
41. Mike Moffitt, "More Than 1,000 Mass Shootings Killing 1,300 People Since Sandy Hook," SFGate.com, December 2, 2015.
42. *Small Arms Survey 2007: Guns and the City* (Geneva, Switzerland), http://www.smallarmssurvey.org/
43. Holloway, *Legal Fictions*, 13.
44. Lani Guinier and Gerald Torres, *The Miner's Canary: Enlisting Race, Resisting Power, Transforming Democracy* (Cambridge, MA: Harvard University Press, 2002), 11.

Index

abolitionist movement, 31–33, 59–60
Allen, Alexander, 70–85, 98
Allen v. United States, 70–85
American Legislative Executive Committee (ALEC), 161–162
Anderson, Tanisha, 16
Anti-Lynching Crusaders, 104
Armed Citizen (column in *American Rifleman*), 158

Baker, Lena, 111
Birth of a Nation, The (1915 film), 91, 104
Black Armed Guard, 14, 108–109, 116–120, 128–129
Black codes, 49–50, 58
Black Lives Matter movement, 16, 166, 184–187
Black Nationalism, 14, 122, 124–125
Black Panther Party (BPP), 4, 109, 120–123, 126–131, 168
Black Reconstruction (Du Bois), 87
Blackstone, Sir William, 19–23, 27
Bland, Sandra, 16
Blight, David, 39–40, 57, 69
Brown, Michael, 8, 16, 185
Brown v. Board of Education, 113
Burr, Aaron, 28

Carey, Miriam, 16
Castile, Philando, 8–9, 174
castle doctrine, 12, 20–28, 37–38, 40, 57–62, 78, 99, 133–134, 145, 153, 155–162, 168, 173–175, 179–180, 187
citizenship: armed citizenship, 3, 9, 16–17, 127–128, 131–132, 150, 153–154, 164–165, 167–171, 174–176, 186–187;

Black struggles for, 40–52, 71–73, 86–87, 108–109, 113, 117; Black women's struggles for, 92; citizen protectors, 3, 184; DIY-security citizenship, 2–11, 15–17, 126, 131, 153, 156–157, 168, 170, 172, 174, 176, 182–188; *jus sanguinis* and *jus soli*, 45; for Mexicans and nonwhite peoples in western territories, 65–66; and white masculine ideal, 31, 34, 38
Civil War, US, 39–40, 49, 53, 62, 64, 71, 87–91, 117
Coates, Ta-Nehisi, 1, 10
COINTELPRO, 122
Coke, Sir Edward, 18, 20
Colfax Massacre of 1873, 50–51, 92
Compromise of 1877, 55, 60–61, 71
Confederacy, 13, 42–43, 61; myths about, 87–89, 129–130; resistance to Reconstruction, 39–40, 48–49, 56; resistance to women's suffrage, 46
Congress of Racial Equality (CORE), 109, 119
Constitution, US, 11, 88, 121, 150–152, 185; Fifteenth Amendment, 45–46, 54; Fourteenth Amendment, 42, 44–45, 50, 109; Nineteenth Amendment, 110; Reconstruction ("civil rights") amendments, 41, 43, 59, 71, 130; Second Amendment, 7, 15, 51, 127, 129, 150, 167, 174; Thirteenth Amendment, 42
convict leasing, 108, 110–111
Cooper, Anna Julia, 134
Corey, Angela, 177, 180

Counter Intelligence Program
(COINTELPRO), 122
coverture, 13, 19–24, 31–32, 38, 134, 141;
married women's property laws, 12,
21, 32–34, 40

Davenport v. United States, 69–72, 81–83
Davis, Angela, 111, 138–139
Deacons of Defense, 4, 108, 119–120
death penalty, 82, 92, 100, 106
debt peonage, 108, 110
District of Columbia v. Heller, 6–7
divorce, 21, 33, 135
Dixon, Thomas, 86, 90, 159
domestic violence, 10, 15, 133–139, 143,
145–149, 152–154, 176–180; battered
woman syndrome (BWS), 146–
148; mandatory arrest, 138–141;
"no-drop" rules; warrantless
arrest, 138, 141
Douglass, Frederick, 33, 38, 45, 96
Dred Scott v. Sandford, 44
Du Bois, W. E. B., 87–88, 100, 122
duty to retreat, 11–13, 16–17, 19–20, 30, 38,
39–40, 55–70, 73, 77–78, 83–84, 157,
161, 176, 181, 187
Dyer Anti-Lynching Bill, 104–105

English common law, 11, 13, 18–19. *See
also* duty to retreat
Equal Justice Initiative (EJI), 86–87, 89,
106
equal protection, 13, 16, 42, 44–45, 51, 59,
87–88, 92, 109, 115, 118, 131, 138, 166,
180, 183. *See also* Constitution, US
Erwin v. State of Ohio, 12, 57–67, 78, 159

FBI (Federal Bureau of Investigation),
117, 122–123, 151
feminism, 133–134, 136-140, 149, 154;
anti-domestic violence activism, 132,
136–142; anti-rape activism, 113, 134,
138; and self-defense, 139-140. *See
also* self-defense training for women
feminist organizations: Chicana Service
Action Center, 138; Combahee River
Collective, 137; Mending the Sacred

Hoop, 138; Third World Women's
Alliance, 137; Women of Color Task
Force, 137
firearm carry, 50, 118, 150, 163, 167, 187;
concealed carry, 2, 6, 15, 36, 151,
163–164, 169–171, 173, 185–186; Mulford Act of 1967, 123; open carry, 7,
35–36, 116, 118, 120, 123–124; Students
for Concealed Carry, 170
Franks, Mary Ann, 10, 161–162
Freedmen's Bureau, 42, 44, 52, 92

Garner, Eric, 16
Garza, Alicia, 166
Genovese, Kitty, 127
Gourko v. United States, 63, 79–84
Grant, Ulysses S., 68
Gray, Freddie, 16
Great Migration, 61, 112, 120
Great Society, 124
Griffith, D. W., 90
gun carry. *See* firearm carry

Hale, Matthew, 23, 58, 141
Hamilton, Alexander, 28
Hammer, Marion, 159–162, 170
Harris, Cheryl, 11, 16
Hobbes, Thomas, 19, 28, 35
Holtzclaw, Daniel, 180–181
homicide, 9, 12–13, 22, 36, 69–70, 72, 74,
79, 97–98, 144, 149, 157, 159, 162–163,
183; excusable, 26–27, 85; justifiable,
13, 23, 26–27, 30, 61, 64, 78, 80, 145,
163, 179
honor, 26, 28, 30, 60, 89, 167; and Black
femininity, 102; and dueling, 29; and
white femininity, 90, 96; and white
masculinity, 19, 31, 34–38, 57, 59, 61

immigration, 11, 64
Indian Removal Act of 1830, 71
Indian Territory, 13, 68, 70–71, 79

Jacobs, Harriet, 32–33
Jews for the Preservation of Firearms
Ownership (JPFO), 4, 6, 129
Jim Crow, 14, 16, 91, 110, 112–113;

disenfranchisement, 14, 56–57, 71, 88; grandfather clauses, 50, 57; literacy tests, 50, 57, 71, 108; poll taxes, 50, 57, 71, 108, 110; vagrancy laws, 49, 71; white primaries, 110. *See also* lynching; race riots
Johnson, Andrew, 43–44, 48

Kelley, Robin D. G., 9, 11, 155
King, Martin Luther, Jr., 109, 115–116, 130, 174
Ku Klux Klan, 50, 90–91, 108

LaPierre, Wayne, 6, 133
Lincoln, Abraham, 39, 46, 48
Locke, John, 18–19, 35
lynching, 1, 14, 54, 61–62, 65, 74, 79, 86–87, 94–101, 110; anti-lynching legislation, 14, 103–107; Thomas Moss, 94–95; Laura Nelson, 100; rape/lynch narrative, 14, 91–93, 95, 97, 103, 112, 115–116, 125; Marie Scott, 101–103, 117; and white masculine honor, 86–87, 97. *See also* Till, Emmett; Wells, Ida B.

manifest destiny, 1, 66
Martin, Trayvon, 8, 10, 16, 155, 165–166, 177
mass incarceration. *See* prison industrial complex
mass shootings, 5–6; at Charleston's Emanuel African Methodist Episcopal Church, 5; at Orlando's Pulse Nightclub, 5; at Sandy Hook Elementary School, 5, 187; at Virginia Tech, 170
McDonald, CeCe, 181–182
Mexican-American War, 65
miscegenation, 47, 65
Model Mugging, 139–140. *See also* self-defense training for women
Montgomery Bus Boycott of 1955, 113
Montgomery Improvement Association, 114

National African American Gun Association (NAAGA), 4–6
National Association for the Advancement of Colored People (NAACP), 91, 100, 104, 115
National Association of Colored Women (NACW), 104
National Coalition Against Domestic Violence, 177
National Firearms Act, 119
National Rifle Association (NRA), xi, xiv, 6, 15, 118–119, 123–124, 127–131, 149–155, 157–159, 161–162, 168–171, 173–174; Institute for Legislative Action, 150; NRA Women website, 152; Women in the NRA, 149
"Negro rule," 40, 43, 46, 48, 54, 90
Neighborhood Watch, 126, 165
New Orleans Riot of 1866, 43, 92
Newton, Huey, 120–121, 130
nonviolence, 14, 109, 113–117, 119–120, 130; civil disobedience, 109, 127

Obama, Barack, 3–4, 167–168; "Obama effect," 3, 166
Operation Hero Guard, 166–168

Parker, Isaac C., 13, 28, 30, 57, 68–84, 97–99, 106, 117
Parks, Rosa, 113-114, 130, 134, 137
Pink Pistols, 6
Plessy v. Ferguson, 84, 113
police violence, 6, 8–9, 16, 43, 49, 52, 55, 94, 119–121, 124–126, 137, 174, 180–181, 183–186
prison industrial complex, 111, 156; racial criminalization, 49, 154, 180, 183
privacy, 134–137, 139–141, 148, 156, 179

race riots: as Black response to structural violence, 15, 124–126, 128, 185; as white resistance to Black economic and political power, 55, 112. *See also* Ku Klux Klan; lynching
rape, 14, 22–25, 30, 37, 48, 62, 90–91,

92–93, 95–96, 100, 102–103, 105, 111, 114, 126, 132, 141, 151, 160, 171, 180, 182–183; anti-rape activism, 113, 134, 136–139, 149; campus sexual assault, 171; marital rape, 23–24, 141

Reagan, Ronald, 123–124, 130

reasonableness, concept of, 132–134, 142–148, 155, 157, 160–162, 166, 177–178, 180, 183

Reconstruction, 12, 39–40, 43, 46, 52, 55–56, 59, 61–62, 71, 87–88, 127; Enforcement Acts, 50–51

Rice, Tamir, 8, 16

Roosevelt, Franklin D., 106

Roosevelt, Theodore, 64, 103

Runyan v. State of Indiana, 12, 57–63, 66, 78, 159

Scalia, Antonin, 7

Scott, Walter, 16

Seale, Bobby, 121

self-defense training for women, 139–141, 149–152, 170

Selfridge, Thomas, 12, 18, 21, 23, 25–31, 35–36, 57–58

Semayne's case, 20

Seneca Falls Convention, 33

settler colonialism, 1, 11–12, 23, 187

Sickles, Daniel, 36–38, 57, 147. *See also* temporary insanity

slavery, 9, 11–12, 16, 23–25, 31–32, 35, 38, 40–43, 47, 60–62, 87–90, 110–11, 125; *partus sequitur ventrem*, 24; slave trade, 24, 31

Southern Christian Leadership Conference (SCLC), 109

Southern Horrors (Wells), 96

Southern Strategy, 130

Stallard, Nicki, 6

stand-your-ground (SYG) laws, 7–11, 15, 131, 156, 160–163, 170, 176–179, 181–184, 187–188

Stanton, Elizabeth Cady, 32–33, 45

Sterling, Alton, 174

Stowe, Harriet Beecher, 32

Student Nonviolent Coordinating Committee (SNCC), 109, 119

Talbert, Mary, 104, 107

temporary insanity, 37, 57, 146–147

terrorism, 2, 6, 167, 186–187; Islamic State of Iraq and the Levant (ISIL), 156; as justification for DIY-security citizenship, 6, 187; September 11, 2001, 2–3, 156

Texas Penal Code, 61, 66

Till, Emmett, 112–114

Till-Mobley, Mamie, 112

transgender and gender non-conforming individuals, 15, 143, 181–184

Trump, Donald, 5

Truth, Sojourner, 32

United Daughters of the Confederacy (UDC), 88–89

United League, 108, 126–127

United States v. Cruikshank, 51

vagrancy laws, 49, 71, 110

"war on drugs," 128, 139

War on Poverty, 125

Wells, Ida B., 86, 93–97, 99, 107, 134

White Citizens' Councils, 108

Williams, Mabel Robinson, 128, 130, 132

Williams, Robert F., 128, 130, 132

Wilson, Darren, 185

women's suffrage, 45–46, 59, 93–94

Workman, James, 156–159

Workman, Kathy, 156–159

Zimmerman, George, 165–166, 178